INSIDERS' GUIDE®

P9-DGQ-020

OFF THE BEATEN PATH® SERIES

Off the · Beaten Path®

NINTH EDITION

new york

A GUIDE TO UNIQUE PLACES

WILLIAM G.

AND

KAY SCHELLER

Revised and Updated by
LILLIAN AFRICANO AND NINA AFRICANO

INSIDERS' GUIDE®

GUILFORD, CONNECTICUT
AN IMPRINT OF THE GLOBE PEQUOT PRESS

The prices, rates, and hours listed in this guidebook
were confirmed at press time. We recommend,
however, that you call establishments to obtain
current information before traveling.

To buy books in quantity for corporate use
or incentives, call **(800) 962–0973**
or e-mail **premiums@GlobePequot.com.**

INSIDERS' GUIDE®

Text design by Linda R. Loiewski
Maps by Equator Graphics © Morris Book Publishing, LLC
New York City map by M.A. Dubé © Morris Book Publishing, LLC
Illustrations by Carole Drong, except for drawing on p. 107, courtesy of Dr. Konstantin
Frank Wine Cellars
Spot photography throughout © David South / Alamy

ISSN 1540-9201
ISBN 978-0-7627-4425-1

Manufactured in the United States of America
Ninth Edition/First Printing

To the FDNY and the NYPD, who dedicate their lives
to the people of New York, on 9/11 and every day.

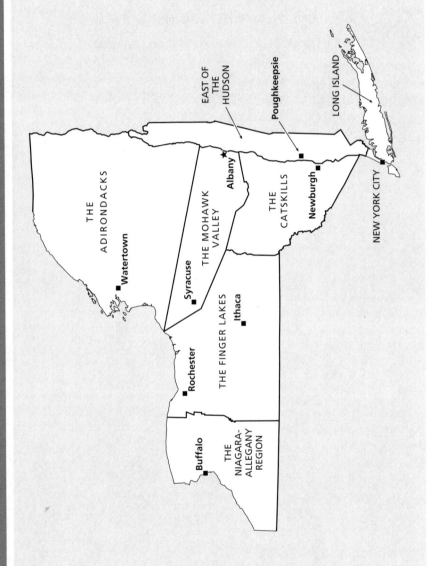

THE ADIRONDACKS

Watertown

THE MOHAWK VALLEY

Syracuse

Albany

EAST OF THE HUDSON

Poughkeepsie

THE CATSKILLS

Newburgh

Ithaca

THE FINGER LAKES

Rochester

Buffalo

THE NIAGARA-ALLEGANY REGION

LONG ISLAND

NEW YORK CITY

Contents

Introduction

In 1784 George Washington referred to New York as the "Seat of the Empire," and centuries later we call it "the Empire State." Yet up until the 1780s, most of New York was practically frontier country, with the exception of the Dutch settlements at New Amsterdam and in the Hudson Valley. Most of the state was settled not just by new arrivals from Europe, but also by migrating New Englanders, setting the pattern for the next hundred years of westward expansion—and making New York a transitional place between "old" coastal America and the horizons of the West.

More than that, New York became a staging area for the people, ideas, and physical changes that would transform the United States in the nineteenth century. Its geographic position between the harbors of the Atlantic Coast and the Great Lakes ensured an early leadership position in the development of canals and, later, of railroads. New York's vast resources made it an industrial power, while its size and the fertility of its soil guaranteed its importance as an agricultural state.

As growth came early in New York, westward expansion created an infrastructure of small towns connected by back roads, rivers, and canals. The coming of the railroads in the nineteenth century gave rise to great cities.

Fast Facts

With an area of 54,471 square miles, New York ranks twenty-seventh in size among the fifty states.

With over nineteen million residents, it ranks third in population.

The state has four mountain ranges: Adirondack, Catskill, Shawangunk, and Taconic.

New York has 70,000 miles of rivers and streams, 127 miles of Atlantic Ocean coastline, and, including lake, bay, and oceanfront, 9,767 miles of shoreline.

The state flower is the rose.

The state bird is the eastern bluebird.

The state freshwater fish is the brook trout; the saltwater fish is the striped bass.

The state tree is the sugar maple.

The state motto is "Excelsior," and the state song is, of course, "I Love New York."

The intellectual and spiritual atmosphere of New York was equally responsive to change. The Empire State is where the Quakers played out much of their experiment in simple living, where Washington Irving proclaimed an indigenous American literature, where the artists of the Hudson River School painted nature in America as it had never been painted before, and where Elbert Hubbard helped introduce the Arts and Crafts movement to the United States.

This book is about the tangible associations that all this history and creativity have left behind. New York is rich, as are few other states, with the homes, libraries, and workshops of distinguished people; with the remnants of historic canals; with museums chronicling pursuits as divergent as horse racing, gunsmithing, and winemaking. In a place where people have done just about everything, here are reminders of just about everything they've done. And since this isn't merely a history book, it will introduce you to New Yorkers who are still enriching their state with creative accomplishments.

It will illustrate the diversity that made New York—and America—great and that continues to flourish today.

East of the Hudson

Named for the English navigator who first explored its waters in 1609, the Hudson River has been the lifeline of New York from its earliest days as a royal colony to its emergence as a world center of commerce and culture.

These days, of course, railroads and highways handle the bulk of commercial traffic, and the river is less of a thoroughfare and more of an escape for pleasure boaters, a way to savor the enduring beauty of the Hudson Valley. It's not hard to see how this majestic landscape inspired the artists of the Hudson River School of painting, who portrayed a vision of the pristine American landscape as the new garden of Eden. In addition to artists like Jasper Cropsey and Fredric Church, the area east of the Hudson has plenty of famous names to drop—Roosevelt, Vanderbilt, and Rockefeller among them.

Over the years, many of the writers, artists, inventors, political leaders, and business tycoons who shaped this state—and the nation—have called this area home. The grand and historic country estates they left behind make a drive along the scenic Taconic Parkway a weekender's delight.

This chapter starts in the crowded bedroom communities of Westchester County. From there, like Friday-night weekenders, we'll travel north.

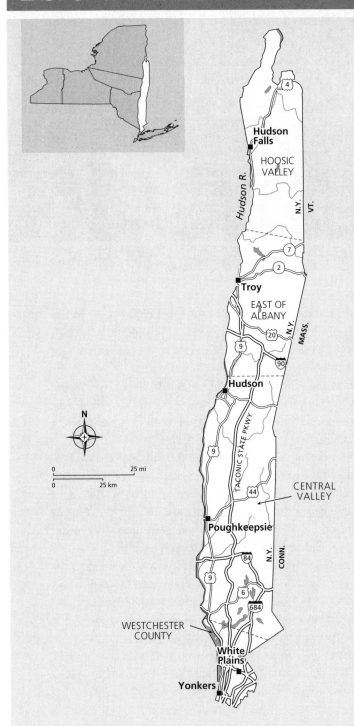

Hudson Falls

HOOSIC VALLEY

Hudson R.

N.Y. VT.

Troy

EAST OF ALBANY

N.Y. MASS.

Hudson

TACONIC STATE PKWY

CENTRAL VALLEY

Poughkeepsie

N.Y. CONN.

WESTCHESTER COUNTY

White Plains

Yonkers

N

0   25 mi
0   25 km

Westchester County

Just beyond the New York City limits, in Yonkers, the ***Hudson River Museum*** occupies the magnificent 1876 Glenview Mansion. As the preeminent cultural institution of Westchester County and the lower Hudson Valley, the museum's resources reflect the natural, social, and artistic history of the area.

A visit to the Hudson River Museum includes a walk through the four meticulously restored rooms on the first floor of the mansion itself. You'll hardly find a better introduction to the short-lived but influential phase of Victorian taste known as the Eastlake style, marked by precise geometric carving and ornamentation—the traceries in the Persian carpets almost seem to be echoed in the furniture and ceiling details.

Aside from the furnishings and personal objects that relate to the period when the Trevor family lived in the mansion, the museum's collections have grown to include impressive holdings of Hudson River landscape paintings, including works by Jasper Cropsey and Albert Bierstadt.

In contrast to the period settings and historical emphases of the older parts of the museum, the state-of-the-art Andrus Planetarium features the Zeiss M1015 star projector, the only one of its kind in the Northeast. A contemporary orientation is also furthered by as many as thirty special art, science, and history exhibitions each year, centered on the work of American artists of the nineteenth and twentieth centuries. There are concerts in summer and a Victorian Holiday celebration each December.

The Hudson River Museum, 511 Warburton Avenue, ***Yonkers*** (914–963–4550; www.hrm.org), is open Wednesday through Sunday noon to 5:00 P.M., Friday until 8:00 P.M. Admission to the museum galleries is $5.00 for adults, $3.00 for senior citizens and children under 12. Admission to the planetarium is $4.00 for adults, $1.50 for senior citizens and children under 12. There is a

AUTHORS' FAVORITES EAST OF THE HUDSON

American Museum of Firefighting	Old Drovers Inn
Chuang Yen Monastery	Old Rhinebeck Aerodrome
Donald M. Kendall Sculpture Gardens	Rodgers Book Barn
Locust Grove	Sunnyside
Olana	Wing's Castle

The Real "FDR Drive"

The Taconic Parkway offers motorists the most scenic of several routes along the east side of the Hudson River. Begun in 1927, the road was planned as an offshoot of the Bronx Parkway, but a major extension was under consideration even before ground was broken. In 1924 the Taconic State Park Commission was formed, and its commissioner, Franklin D. Roosevelt, was eager to push the parkway north as far as Albany. It didn't get quite that far—in 1963 the Taconic eventually reached its northernmost point at the intersection with Interstate 90 in Chatham. It was FDR, however, who insisted on the road's scenic path through some of the most majestic portions of his beloved Hudson Valley. He even prescribed the rustic, thickly mortared stone bridges that help make the Taconic such a handsome rural thoroughfare.

free planetarium star show Friday at 7:00 P.M. Other planetarium shows are held Saturday and Sunday at 12:30, 2:30, and 3:30 P.M. Admission for both museum and star show is $7.00 for adults and $3.00 for seniors and children under 12.

Hundreds of years before Glenview Mansion was built, the Philipse family assembled a Westchester estate that makes Glenview's twenty-seven acres seem puny by comparison. Frederick Philipse I came to what was then New Amsterdam in the 1650s and began using his sharp trader's instincts. By the 1690s his lands had grown into a huge estate, including a 52,500-acre tract that encompassed one-third of what is now Westchester County.

In 1716 Philipse's grandson Frederick Philipse II assumed the title of Lord of the Manor of Philipsborough, greatly enlarged the cottage built by his grandfather, and used *Philipse Manor Hall* as a summer residence. Col. Frederick Philipse (III) rebuilt and further enlarged the Georgian manor house, planted elaborate gardens, and imported the finest furnishings for the hall. His tenure as Lord of the Manor ended when he decided to side with the Tory cause at the beginning of the American Revolution.

Confiscated along with the rest of its owner's properties after the war, Philipse Manor Hall was auctioned by the State of New York and passed through the hands of a succession of owners until 1908, when the state bought the property back. The state has since maintained the mansion as a museum of history, art, and architecture. Home to the finest papier-mâché rococo ceiling in the United States, inside and out it remains one of the most perfectly preserved examples of Georgian style in the Northeast.

Philipse Manor Hall State Historic Site, 29 Warburton Avenue (P.O. Box 496, Yonkers 10701; 914–965–4027; www.philipsemanorfriends.org), is open

April through October, Tuesday through Friday noon to 5:00 P.M., Saturday and Sunday 11:00 A.M. to 4:00 P.M. Admission is free. Group tours are available by appointment.

Fans of the nineteenth-century New York–born Hudson River School painter and architect *Jasper F. Cropsey* will want to make appointments to visit Ever Rest, his Gothic *home and studio,* and the *Newington Cropsey Foundation Gallery of Art* (www.newingtoncropsey.com). Ever Rest is preserved as it appeared when the artist lived here and exhibits his paintings, watercolors, and sketches. The handsome Gallery of Art, with its octagonal gallery built to resemble "Aladdin," Cropsey's studio in Hastings-on-Hudson, New York, houses the world's largest collection of the artist's works.

They're both in *Hastings-on-Hudson:* His home and studio, 49 Washington Avenue (914–478–1372), is open by appointment only. The gallery, 25 Cropsey Lane (914–478–7990), offers forty-five-minute tours by appointment only (at least a week in advance) from February through July and September through December weekdays from 1:00 to 5:00 P.M. Visitors are welcome to tour the grounds weekdays from 1:00 to 5:00 P.M. without an appointment.

Donald M. Kendall, former chairman of the board and chief executive officer of PepsiCo, Inc., had a dream that extended far beyond soft drinks. He wanted to create a garden whose atmosphere of stability, creativity, and experimentation would reflect his vision of the company. In 1965 he began collecting sculptures; today more than forty works by major twentieth-century artists are displayed on 168 acres of magnificent gardens—many created by internationally renowned designers Russell Page and François Goffinet, who picked up where Mr. Page left off.

Alexander Calder, Jean Dubuffet, Marino Marini, Alberto Giacometti, Auguste Rodin, Henry Moore, and Louise Nevelson are just a few of the artists whose works are displayed in the *Donald M. Kendall Sculpture Gardens.* Mr. Kendall's artistic vision has truly been realized.

Happy Holidays East of the Hudson

The holiday season is a perfect time to explore the great houses of the region, which are decked out in festive finery throughout the month of December. Sunnyside, Philipsburg, Lyndhurst, Boscobel, Van Cortlandt Manor, and others offer such events as candlelight tours, bonfires, carols, storytelling, and dancing. Check www.hudsonvalley.org/calendar and the individual Web sites of the manor houses for information on specific events.

ANNUAL EVENTS EAST OF THE HUDSON

JANUARY

Ice Festival
Hillsdale
(518) 325–3200
www.catamountski.com

FEBRUARY

Black History Month Events
Poughkeepsie
(845) 454–1702
www.pokchamb.org

MARCH

Annual HVP String Competition
Vassar College
Poughkeepsie
(845) 473–5288
www.bardavon.org

Annual Maple Weekend
Remsburger Maple Farm and Apiary
Pleasant Valley
(845) 635–9168
www.remsburgermaple.com

APRIL

Great Poughkeepsie Easter Egg Hunt
Waryas Park
Poughkeepsie
(845) 471–7565

Annual Movable Feast
Hudson Opera House
Hudson
(518) 822–1438
www.hudsonoperahouse.org

MAY

Rhinebeck Antiques Fair
Duchess County Fairgrounds
Rhinebeck
(845) 876–4001
www.rhinebeckantiquesfair.com

JUNE

Clearwater Festival
Croton Point
(800) 677–5667
www.clearwater.org

Caramoor International Music Festival
Katonah
(914) 232–1252
www.caramoor.org

Riverfront Arts Festival
Troy
(518) 273–0552

Crafts at Rhinebeck
Duchess County Fairgrounds
(845) 876–4001

The Donald M. Kendall Sculpture Gardens, PepsiCo World Headquarters, 700 Anderson Hill Road, **Purchase** (914–253–2000), is open daily year-round from 9:00 A.M. to dusk. There is no admission fee.

In 1838 the great Gothic Revival architect **Alexander Jackson Davis** designed **Lyndhurst** for former New York City mayor William Paulding. Overlooking the broad expanse of the Tappan Zee from the east, this beautiful stone mansion and its landscaped grounds represented the full American flowering of the neo-Gothic aesthetic that had been sweeping England since the closing years of the eighteenth century.

Hudson Valley Shakespeare Festival
(through August)
Boscobel Restoration
(845) 265–7858 or (845) 265–9575 (for tickets)
www.hvshakespeare.org

JULY

Falcon Ridge Folk Festival
Hillsdale
(860) 364–0366
www.falconridgefolk.com

AUGUST

Bard Music Festival
Annandale-on-Hudson
(845) 758–7410
www.bard.edu/bmf

SEPTEMBER

Battle of Saratoga Encampment
Stillwater
(518) 664–9821, ext. 224
www.stillwaterny.org

OCTOBER

Legend Weekend
Sunnyside and Philipsburg Manor
(914) 631–8200
www.sleepyhollowhalloween.com

NOVEMBER

Thanksgiving Weekend
Sunnyside and Philipsburg Manor
(914) 631–8200
www.hudsonvalley.org/calendar

DECEMBER

Great Estates Candlelight Tours
Hudson River Valley
(914) 631–8200
www.hudsonvalley.org

Lyndhurst remained in the Paulding family until 1864, when it was purchased by wealthy New York merchant George Merritt. Merritt had Davis enlarge the house and add its landmark stone tower, a large greenhouse, and several outbuildings. He also laid out the romantic English-style gardens to complement the Gothic architecture of the main house.

One of the most notorious of America's railroad barons, *Jay Gould,* acquired Lyndhurst in 1880 and maintained it as a country estate. Upon his death in 1892, Lyndhurst became the property of his oldest daughter, Helen, who left it in turn to her younger sister Anna, duchess of Talleyrand-Périgord,

Lyndhurst

in 1938. The duchess died in 1961, leaving instructions that the estate become the property of the National Trust for Historic Preservation.

Lyndhurst, 635 South Broadway (Route 9 just south of the Tappan Zee Bridge), *Tarrytown* (914–631–4481; www.lyndhurst.org), is open mid-April through October, Tuesday through Sunday 10:00 A.M. to 5:00 P.M., and November through mid-April, Saturday and Sunday 10:00 A.M. to 4:00 P.M. Open on Monday holidays. Closed Thanksgiving, Christmas, and New Year's. Guided tours and self-guided audio tours are available. Lunch is served in the historic Carriage House from April through October. Admission is $10.00 for adults, $9.00 for senior citizens, and $4.00 for children 12 to 17, under 12 free with paying adult.

If a visit to Lyndhurst leaves you wanting to live like a robber baron, book yourself some luxurious lodgings at the *Castle at Tarrytown* at 400 Benedict Avenue, Tarrytown (914–631–1980; www.castleonthehudson.com). Built between 1900 and 1910, this Norman-style mansion stands imposingly on ten acres overlooking the Hudson River. Surrounded by a stone wall and a magnificent arboretum, the castle features a 40-foot Grand Room with a vaulted ceiling, stained-glass windows, and a musicians' balcony. One of the dining rooms has paneling taken from a house outside Paris that had been given to the exiled King James II of England by Louis XIV of France. Breakfast, lunch, dinner, and Sunday brunch are served in the elegant Equus Restaurant. High tea is served daily from 2:30 to 5:00 P.M.

One of Tarrytown's best-known residents was *Washington Irving,* author of *Rip Van Winkle, The Legend of Sleepy Hollow,* and *Diedrich Knickerbocker's History of New York.* Irving described his home, *Sunnyside,* as "a little old-fashioned stone mansion, all made up of gable ends, and as full of angles and corners as an old cocked hat."

Irving lived at Sunnyside from 1836 to 1843 and again from 1846 until his death in 1859. Here he entertained such distinguished visitors as Oliver Wendell Holmes, William Makepeace Thackeray, and Louis Napoleon III. On view here

They Trod Shod

In the summer of 1938, to celebrate the 250th anniversary of the settling of New Rochelle, a group of children made a pilgrimage to New York City. They were commemorating the long trek the region's first settlers, the Huguenots, had to make to attend church. According to tradition, these early churchgoers made the trek barefooted. But the children put on their shoes after the first block.

is the writing desk where Irving penned *Astoria,* his account of the Pacific Northwest, as well as *The Crayon Miscellany, Wolfert's Roost,* and *The Life of George Washington.* In his leisure hours, Irving laid out Sunnyside's splendid flower gardens, arborways, and orchards, which still flower and bear fruit to this day.

Located at West Sunnyside Lane (1 mile south of the Tappan Zee Bridge on Route 9) in Tarrytown, Sunnyside (914–591–8763; www.hudsonvalley .org/sunnyside) is open daily 10:00 A.M. to 5:00 P.M. except Tuesdays and major holidays, from April through October. In March it is open weekends from 10:00 A.M. to 4:00 P.M.

One of the most popular times to visit Sunnyside is during Legends Weekend in October (914–631–8200; www.sleepyhollowhalloween.com). Dramatic readings of *The Legend of Sleepy Hollow* take place at both Sunnyside and Philipsburg Manor, along with a host of family activities based on Irving's tale— magic shows, ghost stories, woodland walks, ghostly "apparitions," and even an appearance by the headless horseman himself.

The town of North Tarrytown, home to two wonderful old churches, was so closely identified with Irving's tale that it officially changed its name to **Sleepy Hollow.** The **Old Dutch Church of Sleepy Hollow** on Route 9 (845–631–1123), built in 1685, is still heated by a woodstove, and hence opens seasonally; Sunday services are held at 10:15 A.M. from the third week in June through the first week in September. Tours are given: Saturday and Sunday from 2:00 to 4:00 P.M. from Memorial Day through October; Monday, Wednesday, and Thursday from 1:00 to 4:00 P.M. from Memorial Day through Labor Day; or by appointment.

Adjacent to the Old Dutch Church, the creator of the headless horseman rests in peace in the **Burying Ground** (www.olddutchburyingground.org) alongside the likes of Andrew Carnegie and William Rockefeller. Free guided tours are given daily at 2:00 P.M. Memorial Day through October.

The tiny **Union Church of Pocantico Hills** on Route 448 (914–631–8200) has a magnificent collection of stained-glass windows by Henri Matisse and

Marc Chagall, which were commissioned by the Rockefeller family. It's open daily except Tuesday from April through December, weekdays 11:00 A.M. to 5:00 P.M., Saturday 10:00 A.M. to 5:00 P.M., and Sunday 2:00 to 5:00 P.M. Admission is $4.00. Church activities may preempt visiting hours.

The menu at the lovely *Crabtree's Kittle House Restaurant and Country Inn* changes daily, but the food, ambience, and service remain consistently superb. Guests can choose a cold salad or hot appetizer, with offerings such as butternut squash ravioli or grilled West Coast oysters. Entrees might include braised lamb shank; a portobello mushroom, spinach, and red pepper gâteau; or filet mignon. For many, dessert is the high point of a meal in this 1790 mansion, with fanciful confections such as a poached pear under spun sugar or a delicious warm pecan pie. *Wine Spectator* magazine awarded the restaurant its "Grand Award of Excellence" several times for having one of the most outstanding restaurant wine lists in the world—more than 30,000 bottles and 1,300 selections.

Crabtree's Kittle House Restaurant and Country Inn, 11 Kittle Road, Route 117, *Chappaqua* (914–666–8044), has twelve guest rooms with private bath that rent for $147 per night. Lunch is served weekdays, dinner nightly, and brunch on Sunday from noon to 2:30 P.M. Reservations are highly recommended, especially on weekends. There's live jazz in the Tap Room Friday and Saturday evenings.

The hospitality is far less inviting at *Sing Sing Prison* in *Ossining,* the big house that made getting sent "up the river" part of tough-guy talk. Built in 1826 by convict labor, Sing Sing became famous when "Father" Pat O'Brien walked "gangster" Jimmy Cagney "the last mile" to its electric chair in *Angels with Dirty Faces.*

Today a replica of the chair, along with confiscated weapons and other artifacts, is part of an excellent audiovisual exhibit at the *Ossining Heritage Area Park Visitors Center* (the Joseph G. Caputo Community Center) at 95 Broadway, Ossining (914–941–3189; www.nysparks.state.ny.us/heritage). Open every day except Sunday from 10:00 A.M. to 4:00 P.M. Admission is free.

While it's off the beaten path, the Croton Dam is not easily overlooked— it's the second-largest hand-hewn structure in the world. Built in 1892, the dam is 297 feet high and 2,168 feet long; it's estimated that it contains as much stone as Egypt's Great Pyramid. The reservoir behind the dam supplies about 400 million gallons of water to New York City each day. The dam is part of *Croton Point Park* and the trailhead for the 26-mile-long Old Croton Aqueduct Trail, which ends at 173rd Street in Manhattan.

Croton Point Park, Route 129, Croton (914–862–5290; www.westchester gov.com), is open dawn to dusk. There is an $8.00 fee per car from Memorial Day to Labor Day.

Peekskill is home to more than seventy artists who work in a variety of media. Many of them host ***Open Artist Studio Tours*** the third Saturday of each month, and there's a two-hour guided art tour, which leaves from the Paramount Theater at 10:45 A.M. ($10.00; seniors $8.50) from May through October. If you're visiting between mid-June and October, stop at the ***Peekskill Farmer's Market*** on Bank Street. For information contact The Peekskill Business Improvement District at (914) 737–2780.

Another important figure of the early Republic, political rather than literary, made his country home to the northeast at ***Katonah.*** This was ***John Jay,*** whom George Washington appointed to be the first chief justice of the United States and who, with Alexander Hamilton and James Madison, was an author of the *Federalist Papers.* Jay retired to the farmhouse now known as the ***John Jay Homestead*** in 1801, after nearly three decades of public service, and lived here until his death in 1829.

His son William and his grandson John Jay II lived at the old family homestead, as did John II's son Col. William Jay II, a Civil War officer of the Union Army. The last Jay to live at the Katonah estate was Eleanor Jay Iselin, the colonel's daughter. After her death in 1953, the property was purchased by Westchester County and turned over to the State of New York as a state historic site.

Having survived so long in the Jay family, the John Jay Homestead is still well stocked with furnishings and associated items that date back to the days when the great patriot lived here. Sixty acres of John Jay's original 900-acre farm are part of the state historic site.

The John Jay Homestead State Historic Site, 400 Route 22, Katonah (914–232–5651; www.johnjayhomestead.org) is open April through October, with tours on the hour, Tuesday through Saturday 10:00 A.M. to 4:00 P.M. and Sunday at 11:00 A.M. There is a fee of $7.00 for adults and $5.00 for seniors; children under 12 are free. The grounds are open from dawn to dusk year-round.

Caramoor is yet another of New York's great houses. It was built by Walter and Lucie Dodge Rosen, who filled it with treasures and created the place that became home to the International Music Festival. Like the wealthy robber barons of yore, the Rosens purchased entire rooms from Europe's palaces and churches and had them reconstructed in their own Spanish-style villa—resulting in an arts and antiques collection that is, to say the least, eclectic. In 1945 they bequeathed the estate as a center for music and art in memory of their son. During the 1950s the festival was expanded and outdoor concerts were presented in the Spanish courtyard. As the festival's reputation grew, Lucie Rosen constructed a larger space, the Venetian Theater, which opened in 1958.

Almost Better than His Pulitzer

When people talk about the romance of the rails, they seldom have commuter trains in mind. But New York's Metro-North, which hauls thousands of suburbanites in and out of Grand Central Station each day, has taken on a bit more panache ever since it began naming individual cars after prominent people associated with its territory along the Hudson Valley.

None of these cars is more freighted with poignant associations for Westchester commuters than the John Cheever. Cheever, a longtime resident of Ossining, was the great chronicler of postwar suburban life. His heroes and heroines poured into Grand Central from places like Shady Hill and Bullet Park, imaginary in name only, and rode back each night to seek love and redemption among their rhododendrons.

If you're walking along the Hudson at twilight and see the *John Cheever* roll by, raise a phantom glass (very dry, with an olive) to those phantom commuters and to the man who made their longings universal.

Twenty of the house's magnificent rooms are open to the public; docent tours last about an hour. In the opulent music room, there are chamber concerts throughout the year. On Thursday and Friday afternoons at 3:00 P.M., tea is served on the family's original china in the Summer Dining Room.

At Caramoor, 149 Girdle Ridge Road, Katonah (914–232–5035; www .caramoor.org), guided tours are offered May through December, Wednesday through Sunday from 1:00 to 4:00 P.M. Admission is $9.00 for adults, free for children 16 and under.

In 1907 financier J. P. Morgan built a stone-and-brick Tudor mansion on a hillside overlooking the Hudson River Valley for his friend and minister, William S. Rainsford. The mansion was privately owned until 1973, when it was restored and reborn as a French restaurant called *Le Château.* Today, with its dogwood-lined approach, patio and gardens, richly paneled rooms, and elegantly set tables, the restaurant serves classic French food presented in grand style.

Among the house specialties at Le Château are lobster bisque; snails with garlic butter; roasted sea scallops; and Châteaubriand for two. Elegant desserts include a chocolate and Grand Marnier soufflé and crème brûlée. A three-course a la carte dinner averages $47. Sunday brunch ($34) includes a dessert buffet.

Le Château, Route 35 at the junction of Route 123, *South Salem* (914–533–6631; www.lechateauny.com), serves dinner nightly except Monday and a seasonal Sunday brunch. Reservations are a must, and jackets are required.

During a late-night walk in Tallahassee, Florida, in 1991, French pianist Hélène Grimaud had a life-changing moment. She experienced an unforgettable encounter, which she later decided was with a she-wolf, probably part dog and part wolf. In her memoir, *Wild Harmonies: A Life of Music and Wolves*, Mlle. Grimaud described how the animal slid under her outstretched hand of its own volition. The touch made her feel a spark shoot through her body and she became aware of a "primeval force" calling to her.

It was then that Grimaud conceived her mission: to change the image of wolves as villainous creatures and to educate the public that wolves are essential "biodiversity engineers" that preserve the balance among animal and plant species.

In 1999, with her then-companion, J. Henry Fair, Grimaud opened the **Wolf Conservation Center** in South Salem, a twenty-nine-acre facility that houses seventeen wolves. Some of the wolves are "socialized," which means they are on view to the public. Others are protected from human contact so that they can eventually be returned to the wild.

The Wolf Conservation Center, P.O. Box 421, South Salem (914–763–2373; www.nywolf.org), offers visits by appointment, arranged online. Click on the "Calendar" link to see what programs are available and to register.

Muscoot Farms is an agricultural holdout in the rapidly developing Westchester landscape. Dating to the early 1900s, the 777-acre working farm has a twenty-three-room main house, barns and outbuildings, antique equipment, a large demonstration vegetable garden, and lots of animals. Weekends are a busy time; in addition to hayrides, agricultural programs cover topics such as sheepshearing and harvesting. There's also a full roster of seasonal festivals. The farm, on Route 100 in Katonah (914–864–7282), is open daily 10:00 A.M. to 4:00 P.M.

Central Valley

Named for a prominent nineteenth-century family, the town of **Brewster** in southern Putnam County is home to the **Southeast Museum**. The museum is an archive of the diverse enterprises that have taken root here over the years, including mining, railroading, circuses, and even the manufacture of condensed milk.

The first Europeans settlers arrived in Brewster around 1725, and for more than one hundred years, they farmed and set up modest cottage industries. In the mid-nineteenth century, Brewster's economic horizons expanded with the arrival of the Harlem Railroad, which became part of Commodore Vanderbilt's vast New York Central system, as well as the Putnam Line Railroad, a division of the New York and New Haven Line.

In years gone by Brewster was also the winter quarters for a number of small circuses, many of which were later consolidated by **P. T. Barnum,** who hailed from nearby Bridgeport, Connecticut. The colorful array of early American circus memorabilia and other collections is housed in the 1896 **Old Town Hall of Southeast** at 67 Main Street, Brewster (845–279–7500; www.southeast museum.org). Hours are 10:00 A.M. to 4:00 P.M., Tuesday through Saturday, April through December. Donations are requested.

Visitors to the **Chuang Yen Monastery** in **Carmel,** home of the Buddhist Association of the United States, are greeted by 10,000 statues of the Buddha arrayed on the lotus terrace. Enter the cavernous Tang Dynasty-style Great Buddha Hall to view the largest Buddha statue in the Western hemisphere, a 37-foot-high statue designed by Professor C. G. Chen. Chen also painted the 8-foot-high, 104-foot-long murals depicting scenes from the "Pure Land," or Amitabha Buddha, that cover the walls.

The Chuang Yen Monastery, at 2020 Route 301, Carmel (845–225–1819; www.baus.org), welcomes visitors who wish to tour the buildings and grounds or to stay, study, and meditate.

The nonprofit Dia Art Foundation was founded in 1974 by Philippa de Menil and Heinger Friedrich, both collectors of works by important artists of the 1960s and 1970s. Located on 31 acres on the banks of the Hudson River, the museum occupies a historic printing facility that was built in 1929 by the National Biscuit Company (Nabisco). It houses works by such major artists as Andy Warhol, Cy Twombly, Bruce Nauman, Walter de Maria, and Richard Serra.

Dia:Beacon, Riggio Galleries, 3 Beekman Street, **Beacon** (845–440–0100; www.diabeacon.org), is open 11:00 A.M. to 6:00 P.M. Thursday through Monday during the summer and 11:00 A.M. to 4:00 P.M. Friday through Monday in winter. Guided tours are given every Saturday at 1:00 p.m. The museum is closed on Thanksgiving, Christmas Eve, Christmas, and New Year's Eve. The cafe and bookshop open at 10:30 a.m. year-round. Admission is $10.00 for adults, $7.00 for seniors and students, and children under 12 are free.

Not all of the Hudson Valley landowners were well-to-do. Most were burghers of a far more modest stamp. The legacy of the life led by one such family is preserved in the **Van Wyck Homestead Museum,** a National Historic Site, east of the river in **Fishkill.** The house was begun in 1732 by Cornelius Van Wyck, who had purchased his nearly 1,000 acres of land from an earlier 85,000-acre Dutchess County estate, and was completed in the 1750s with the construction of the West Wing. For all the land its owners possessed, the homestead is nevertheless a modest affair, a typical Dutch country farmhouse.

Like so many other farmhouses, the Van Wyck Homestead might have been forgotten by history had it not played a part in the American Revolution. Located as it was along the strategic route between New York City and the Champlain Valley, the house was requisitioned by the Continental Army to serve as headquarters for General Israel Putnam. Fishkill served as an important supply depot for General Washington's northern forces from 1776 to 1783. Military trials were held at the house; one such event was reputedly the source used by *James Fenimore Cooper* for an incident in his novel *The Spy.*

Another factor leading to the homestead's preservation was its having reverted to the Van Wyck family after the revolution ended. Descendants of its builder lived here for more than 150 years. Today it is operated by the Fishkill Historical Society as a museum of colonial life in the Hudson Valley. The house features a working colonial kitchen fireplace with a beehive oven, which is used during special events. An interesting sidelight is the exhibit of Revolutionary War artifacts unearthed in the vicinity during archaeological digs sponsored by the society.

The Van Wyck Homestead Museum, 504 Route 9, (near the intersection of Routes 9 and 84), Fishkill (845–896–9560; www.hudsonrivervalley.com), is open Memorial Day through October on Saturday and Sunday from 1:00 to 4:00 P.M. and by appointment. There is an admission charge of $2.00. Special events include September and holiday craft fairs, a June midsummer festival, and a St. Nicholas Day holiday tour.

Lewis Country Farms, a sixteen-acre farm with restored 1861 barns (complete with silo, original post-and-beam ceiling supports, and fieldstone walls), is an all-season kids' stop and shopping mecca.

There are live farm animals for petting, a gift and flower shop, a deli, a greenhouse and garden center, and when you get hungry, the folks at Lewis Country Farms will serve up homemade soups and chili and sandwiches.

Lewis Country Farms, Overlook and DeGarmo Roads, *Poughkeepsie* (845–452–7650; www.lewislandscaping.com), is open daily 9:00 A.M. to 5:00 P.M.

As you would expect in a region known for fine seasonal produce as well as wine, the Hudson Valley has many farms and farm markets. Visit www.dutchesstourism.com/farm.asp for a list, along with information on farm-related events and activities.

In 1847 *Samuel F. B. Morse,* inventor of the telegraph and Morse code, purchased one hundred acres of land and a seventeen-year-old Georgian house. With the help of his friend, architect Alexander Jackson Davis, he transformed the original structure into a Tuscan-style villa. Today, *Locust Grove, Samuel Morse Historic Site,* a unique combination of 150 acres of nature preserve, historic gardens, landscaped lawns, vistas, and architecture, is one of the most handsome of the Hudson River estates. In 1963 it became the first in the valley to be designated a National Historic Landmark.

Original family furnishings are exhibited in period room settings and include rare Duncan Phyfe and Chippendale pieces. Paintings include works by Morse himself as well as by artists such as George Inness. There's also a rare bound collection of *Birds of America* by J. J. Audubon. A replica of "the invention of the century" is on exhibit in the Morse Room.

Locust Grove, Samuel Morse Historic Site, 2683 South Road (Route 9), Poughkeepsie (845–454–4500), is open daily May through Thanksgiving, from 10:00 A.M. to 3:00 P.M. Admission is $7.00 for adults, $6.00 for seniors, and $3.00 for those between the ages of 3 and 18. There is no fee to walk the grounds, which are open from 8:00 A.M. to dusk.

You're now in *The Culinary Institute of America* (CIA) country. Founded in 1946 as a trade school to train returning World War II veterans in the culinary arts, it has morphed into one of the most renowned culinary schools in the world. Among its distinguished graduates are *Gourmet* magazine executive chef and TV personality Sara Moulton, chef-restaurateur Charlie Palmer, and *Iron Chef*'s Cat Cora.

Since America launched its love affair with the Food Network, the CIA has become a veritable hub of culinary activity, attracting not only serious students and food professionals, but also enthusiastic "foodies" who sign up for the school's one-day courses and cooking "boot camps." With forty-one state-of-the-art kitchens and bakeshops, the CIA is a food-lover's Eden.

The CIA has also played a major role in making the Hudson Valley a culinary destination, serving as the setting for popular food and wine events and turning out students who have gone on to work in the region's restaurants. In addition, the five student-staffed restaurants on the CIA's 150-acre campus attract tens of thousands of food-lovers each year, all eager to sample the "homework" turned out by the culinary stars of the future.

St. Andrew's Cafe, open Monday through Friday for lunch and dinner, serves a selection of dishes featuring fresh seasonal ingredients with an Asian touch. The *Ristorante Caterina de' Medici,* open Monday through Friday for lunch and dinner, is located in the Colavita Center for Italian Food and Wine and showcases the indigenous foods of Italy's various regions. The casual *Al Forno Room,* located within the Ristorante Caterina de' Medici, serves pizza, salad, and antipasti. The *Escoffier Restaurant,* open Tuesday through Saturday, features classic French cuisine, but with a lighter contemporary touch. The *American Bounty Restaurant,* open Tuesday through Saturday for lunch and dinner, serves regional American dishes as well as a daily special from the Julia Child Rotisserie kitchen. The *Apple Pie Bakery Cafe* offers a selection of sandwiches, pastries, and breads, also available for takeout; it is open Monday through Friday 8:00 A.M. to 6:30 P.M. Reservations are necessary for the formal restaurants but not for the Al Forno Room or the cafe. Call (845) 471–6608 Monday through Friday 8:30 A.M. to 5:00 P.M. for all reservations.

Follow the Food (and Wine)

The annual Taste of the Hudson Wine and Epicurean Arts Festival at the Culinary Institute of America in Hyde Park takes place in November and is one of the major food and wine events in the region. It features dozens of restaurants and food suppliers from the Hudson Valley and celebrates everything culinary. For more information, call (845) 431–8707 or visit www.tastehv.org.

Also in November is the annual Hudson Valley Restaurant Week (actually ten days), a culinary fest featuring bargain-priced prix-fixe lunches and dinners at restaurants throughout the region. For more information, visit www.HudsonValleyRestaurant Week.com.

Foodies and professionals alike may enjoy browsing the CIA's **Conrad N. Hilton Library,** a $7.5-million facility that houses more than 68,000 volumes, a video viewing center, and a video theater. The library is open Monday through Thursday 8:00 A.M. to 11:00 P.M., Friday 8:00 A.M. to 5:00 P.M., Saturday 9:00 A.M. to 5:00 P.M., and Sunday noon to 8:00 P.M.

The Culinary Institute of America is on Route 9, Hyde Park (845–452–9600; www.ciachef.edu).

Whenever Eleanor Roosevelt took time out from the many causes she championed before, during, and after her husband's presidency, she retreated to Val-Kill, a small, fieldstone cottage that F.D.R. had built for her in 1925 by a stream on the grounds of the Roosevelt family estate. The cottage became the permanent home for two dear friends, New York Democratic Committee co-workers Nancy Cook and Marion Dickerman, and whenever Eleanor returned home, she would opt to stay here rather than in the nearby family mansion presided over by Franklin's autocratic mother, Sara Delano Roosevelt.

In 1926 the women, along with Caroline O'Day, built a second, larger building to house Val-Kill Industries, intended to teach farm workers how to manufacture goods, thus keeping them from migrating to large cities in search of work. Until the business closed in 1936—a victim of the Great Depression—the workers manufactured replicas of Early American furniture, weavings, and pewter pieces. At this point, Mrs. Roosevelt converted the building into apartments for herself and her secretary Malvina "Tommy" Thompson, and added several guest rooms. She renamed the building Val-Kill Cottage and wrote to her daughter: "My house seems nicer than ever and I could be happy in it alone! That's the last test of one's surroundings." Among the visitors to Val-Kill were John F. Kennedy, Adlai Stevenson, Nikita Khrushchev, and Jawaharlal Nehru.

After Mrs. Roosevelt died in 1962, several developers tried to take over her home, but they were thwarted when a group of concerned citizens organized to preserve the site. In 1977 President Jimmy Carter signed a bill creating the *Eleanor Roosevelt National Historic Site.* Today visitors can tour the cottages and grounds.

Eleanor Roosevelt National Historic Site, Route 9G, 519 Albany Post Road, Hyde Park, (845–229-9115, (800–337–8474, or 800–967–2283 [reservations only]; www.nps.gov/elro), is open May through October, daily 9:00 A.M. to 5:00 P.M.; and from November through April, Saturday and Sunday 9:00 A.M. to 5:00 P.M. Admission is $8.00 adults, children under 17, free.

Heading north past *Hyde Park,* we're back in mansion territory, but with a difference. Homes such as Philipse Manor Hall were built by men whose fortunes were founded in vast landholdings, but palaces such as *Staatsburg,* formerly Mills Mansion State Historic Site, represent the glory days of industrial and financial captains—the so-called Gilded Age of the late nineteenth century. The idea behind this sort of house building was to live not like a country squire but like a Renaissance doge.

Ogden Mills's neoclassical mansion was finished in 1896, but its story begins more than a hundred years earlier. In 1792 the property on which it stands was purchased by Morgan Lewis, great-grandfather of Mills's wife, Ruth Livingston Mills. Lewis, an officer in the revolution and the third postindependence governor of New York State, built two houses here. The first burned in 1832, at which time it was replaced by an up-to-date Greek Revival structure.

Staatsburg

This was the home that stood on the property when it was inherited by Ruth Livingston Mills in 1890.

But Ogden Mills had something far grander in mind for his wife's legacy. He hired a firm with a solid reputation in mansion building to enlarge the home and embellish its interiors—a popular firm among wealthy clients, one that went by the name of *McKim, Mead, and White.*

The architects added two spacious wings and decked out both the new and the old portions of the exterior with balustrades and pilasters more reminiscent of Blenheim Palace than anything previously seen in the Hudson Valley. The interior was (and is) French, in Louis XV and XVI period styles—lots of carving and gilding on furniture and wall and ceiling surfaces, along with oak paneling and monumental tapestries.

The last of the clan to live here was Ogden L. Mills, at one time U.S. secretary of the treasury, who died in 1937. One of his surviving sisters donated the home to the State of New York, which opened it to the public as a state historic site.

Staatsburg, off Route 9, Staatsburg (845–889–8851; www.hvnet.com/houses), is open from mid-April through October, Wednesday through Saturday 10:00 A.M. to 5:00 P.M. and Sunday 11:00 A.M. to 5:00 P.M. It repopens after Thanksgiving through December. Admission is $5.00 for adults, $4.00 for seniors and students; children under 12 free.

If touring the area's numerous mansions has left you with "mansion envy," reserve a room at **Belvedere Mansion,** a grand Greek Revival hilltop estate overlooking the Hudson River. Guests can choose one of the beautifully appointed "cottage" rooms—each with its own entrance and private bath—in a separate building facing the mansion, or one of the smaller "cozies." A full country breakfast is served fireside in the winter and, in warmer months, alfresco in a pavilion gazebo overlooking a fountain and pond. A candlelit dinner in the elegant restaurant might include delicacies such as an appetizer of gâteau of wild mushrooms and chèvre with a truffle vinaigrette and entrees such as braised lamb shank with saffron risotto, artichokes, and mint.

Belvedere Mansion, 10 Olde Route 9 in *Staatsburg* (845–889–8000; www.belvederemansion.com), is open year-round. Rates range from $75 to $95 for the "cozies" to $275 in the mansion. Rooms in the Carriage House range from $150 to $195; in the Hunt Lodge, there are four suites, including one with a fireplace, for $250 to $450; the Zen Lodge is $140 to $200. Guests have use of the tennis court and outdoor pool.

Troutbeck, on the banks of the trout-filled Webatuck River in Amenia, is an English-style country estate that functions as a corporate conference center during the week and as a country inn on weekends. The 422-acre retreat, with its slate-roofed mansion with leaded windows, is a perfect place for a romantic weekend. There are nine fireplaced bedrooms, many rooms with canopy beds, an oak-paneled library, gardens—even a pool and tennis courts. And, of course, gourmet dining.

The former home of poet-naturalist Myron B. Benton, Troutbeck was a gathering place for celebrities during the early decades of the twentieth century. Ernest Hemingway, Sinclair Lewis, and Teddy Roosevelt are said to have been houseguests of the Springarn family, who owned the house from 1902 to 1978.

The restaurant, open to the public for lunch and dinner Wednesday through Saturday and Sunday brunch, has an excellent kitchen and features dinner entrees such as smoked Maine lobster and oven-braised Black Angus veal shanks. The dessert menu, with "everything that you always wanted to try," includes goodies such as Georgia peach and ginger-cream strudel.

Troutbeck, 515 Leedsville Road, *Amenia* (845–373–9681 or 800–978–7688; www.troutbeck.com), is open year-round. Weekend rates include two nights' lodging and meals, and range from $650 to $1,050 a couple.

The Wetmore family, which owns *Cascade Mountain Winery and Restaurant,* says of its product: "Regional wine is a way of tasting our seasons past. Last summer's sunshine, the snows of winter, rain, and frost; it's all there in a glass." You can sample the Hudson Valley's seasons past at the vineyard, which offers tours and tastings daily year-round from 10:00 A.M. to 5:00 P.M. The excellent restaurant serves lunch Thursday through Sunday and dinner on Saturday.

Cascade Mountain Winery and Restaurant is on Cascade Mountain Road in Amenia (845–373–9021; www.cascademt.com).

Although its location is off the beaten path, the *Old Drovers Inn* is very much on the main track for those who love gourmet dining and superb accommodations. Winner of some of the industry's most prestigious awards, including AAA's Four Diamond Award and an award of excellence for its wine list and cellar from *Wine Spectator,* the inn, a Relais and Chateau property, was also named one of the five Gourmet Retreats of the Year in Andrew Harper's *Hideaway Report.*

Basso Profundo

The year 2003 saw a new New York State record for striped bass caught in freshwater, when a 55-pounder was taken on the Hudson River. The record saltwater striper, taken off Montauk Point on Long Island, tipped the scales at 76 pounds.

Have a Grape Day

As one of the nation's oldest wine-making regions, the Hudson Valley boasts dozens of wineries; a number offer tours and tastings. *The Dutchess Wine Trail* (www .dutchesswinetrail.com), for example, includes not only the Cascade Mountain Winery in Amenia, but also the *Clinton Vineyards in Clinton Corners* (845–266–5372), the *Alison Wines and Vineyards* in Red Hook (845–758–6335), and the *Millbrook Vineyards and Winery* (845–758–6335).

The beautifully restored colonial inn, in continuous use since it was built in 1750, was originally a stop for cattle drovers, who purchased cattle and swine from New England farmers and drove the animals down the post roads to markets in New York City.

The inn's signature dishes, cheddar cheese soup and browned turkey hash, reflect its colonial heritage. Dinner entrees such as grilled magret of duck reflect the kitchen's blending of American and European styles. A tavern menu is also available at lunch and dinner.

Like the food, the four guest suites are elegant. Prices range from $150 midweek for the intimate, antique-filled Rose Room to $475 on weekends and holidays for the Meeting Room, with a unique barrel-shaped ceiling and fireplace. American breakfast and full dinner are included on weekends. Pets are permitted for a fee of $25 per day with advance approval.

Old Drovers Inn, Old Route 22, *Dover Plains* (845–832–9311; www.old droversinn.com), serves lunch Friday, Saturday, and Sunday, and dinner nightly except Wednesday.

When Peter Wing returned from fighting in Vietnam, he was twenty-one years old and wanted to build a place where he could retreat from the world. He and his wife, Toni, worked for the next twenty-five years to create *Wing's Castle,* a fabulously eccentric stone castle overlooking the Hudson Valley. Eighty percent of the structure is made of salvaged materials from antique buildings.

Peter wasn't successful in retreating, however. Visitors from around the world stop in for tours and are surprised to learn that the castle is also the Wings' home. It's furnished with Victorian pieces, more than 2,000 antiques, and mannequins dressed in period clothing. A 7-foot-deep moat that runs under the castle serves as a swimming pool, and 12- and 13-foot hand-hewn rocks that Peter removed from an old building are arranged in a circle to create Stonehenge East.

Wing's Castle, 717 Bangall Road, *Millbrook* (845–677–9085), is open Wednesday through Sunday, Memorial Day weekend through Labor Day, from noon to

4:30 P.M.; Labor Day through Christmas season, weekends only noon to 4:30 P.M. Admission is $8.00 for adults and $6.00 for children ages 4 to 11.

At *Innisfree Garden,* Eastern design concepts combine with American techniques to create a "cup garden," which has origins in Chinese paintings dating back a thousand years.

The cup garden draws attention to something rare or beautiful, segregating it so that it can be enjoyed without distraction. It can be anything—from a single rock covered with lichens and sedums to a meadow. Each forms a three-dimensional picture. Innisfree Garden is a series of cup gardens—streams, waterfalls, plants—each its own picture and each a visual treat.

Innisfree Garden, Tyrrel Road, Millbrook (845–677–8000; www.innisfree garden.org), is open early May to October 20, Wednesday through Friday 10:00 A.M. to 4:00 P.M. and weekends and legal holidays 11:00 A.M. to 5:00 P.M. It is closed Monday and Tuesday except legal holidays. Admission is $4.00 for those 6 years and older on weekdays and $5.00 on weekends and holidays. A picnic area is open to visitors.

"There I was, minding my own business. I was standing by the side of the road, investigating a potential dinner, when some lunatic in a rusty Plymouth knocked me 10 feet into the air."

Thus begins a column by Elizabeth T. Vulture in the *Raptor Report,* news bulletin of the *Hudson Valley Raptor Center.* Luckily for Elizabeth—whose vision was never quite the same—she was rescued and given a home at the center. In addition to caring for injured raptors and returning as many as possible to the wild, the center offers the public a chance to meet and learn about all birds of prey, including bald eagles, red-tailed hawks, peregrine falcons, and great horned owls. It houses more than one hundred raptors of twenty species, many of which are threatened or endangered.

The Hudson Valley Raptor Center, 148 South Road, Stanfordville (845–758–6957; www.hvraptors.com) is open April through October on Saturday and Sunday from 1:00 to 4:00 P.M. Admission is $10.00 for adults, $7.00 for seniors and students, and $3.00 for children ages 12 and under. Check Web site for activities.

The *Old Rhinebeck Aerodrome,* 3 miles upriver from the town of *Rhinebeck,* is more than just a museum—many of the pre-1930s planes exhibited here actually take to the air each weekend.

The three main buildings at the aerodrome house a collection of aircraft, automobiles, and other vehicles from the period 1900–37 and are open throughout the week. On Saturday and Sunday, though, you can combine a tour of the exhibits on the ground with attendance at an air show featuring both original aircraft and accurate reproductions. Saturdays are reserved for flights of planes from the Pioneer (pre–World War I) and Lindbergh eras. On Sundays the show is a period-piece melodrama in which intrepid Allied fliers do battle with the "Black Baron." Where else can you watch a live dogfight?

All that's left at this point is to go up there yourself, and you can do just that. The aerodrome has on hand a 1929 New Standard D-25—which carries four passengers wearing helmets and goggles—for open-cockpit flights of fifteen minutes' duration. The cost is $40 per person, and rides are available on weekends, before and after the show.

Old Rhinebeck Aerodrome, 44 Stone Church Road, Rhinebeck (845–752-3200; www.oldrhinebeck.org), is open daily May 15 through the end of October from 10:00 A.M. to 5:00 P.M. On Saturday and Sunday from mid-June through mid-October, the air show begins at 2:00 P.M. and includes a fashion show, in which ladies from the audience dress up in vintage clothing. Weekday admission is $6.00 for adults, $5.00 for seniors, $2.00 for children ages 6 to 10, and free for children under 6. Admission for weekend air shows is $15.00 for adults, $10.00 for seniors, and $5.00 for children ages 6 to 10. The plane rides cost extra, as mentioned above.

America's oldest continuously operated hotel, the **Beekman Arms,** opened for business as the Traphagen Inn in 1766. A meeting place for American Revolutionary War generals, the Beekman was also the site of Franklin Delano Roosevelt's election eve rallies from the beginning of his career right through his presidency. Visitors can choose from one of fourteen rooms in the inn, the motel, or in the forty-four room **Delamater Inn** (845–786-7080), a block away, built in 1844 and one of the few early examples of American Gothic residences still in existence. The inn's accomodations include seven guest houses, several with fireplaces, clustered around a courtyard.

The Beekman Arms and Delamater Inn, Route 9, Rhinebeck (845–876-7077; www.beekmandelamaterinn.com), is open year-round. Rates range from $120 to $170 in the Arms, $100 to $125 in the contemporary motel, and $95 to $180 in the Delamater House. All rooms have private bath, TV, phone, and a complimentary decanter of sherry. A two-night minimum stay is required weekends from May through October and holiday weekends. Lunch, dinner, and Sunday brunch are served in the restaurant, and there is a cozy tap room.

John and Jan Gilmor create a variety of mouth-blown and hand-pressed stemware, tableware, decorative vessels, and ornaments from glass that John formulates from scratch, working with his wife to develop unique colors and finishes. Their pieces are featured in international and presidential collections. At **Gilmor Glassworks,** at the corner of Routes 22 and 44 in **Millerton** (518–789-6700; www.gilmoreglass.com), visitors are invited to watch the artists while they work at the glass furnaces but are urged to call ahead to find out when the "hot process" can be observed. First-quality and irregular pieces are on sale. Shop hours are Monday through Saturday 10:00 A.M. to 5:00 P.M. and Sunday 11:00 A.M. to 5:00 P.M.

Kaatsbaan is "dedicated to the growth, advancement, and preservation of professional dance." Facilities at the 153-acre site overlooking the Hudson River include a 160-seat performance theater and three dance studios.

Kaatsbaan International Dance Center is located at 120 Broadway, Tivoli. See www.Kaatsbaan.org or call (845) 757–5106 for a list of events.

There was a time when every schoolchild worthy of a gold star knew that the *Clermont* was the first successful steamboat, built by **Robert Fulton** and tested on the Hudson River. Less commonly known, however, is that the boat formally registered by its owners as *The North River Steamboat of Clermont* took its name from the estate of **Robert R. Livingston,** chancellor of New York and a backer of Fulton's experiments. **Clermont,** one of the great family seats of the valley, overlooks the Hudson River near Germantown.

The story of Clermont begins with the royal charter granted to Robert Livingston in 1686, which made the Scottish-born trader Lord of the Manor of Livingston, a 162,000-acre tract that would evolve into the entire southern third of modern-day Columbia County. When Livingston died in 1728, he broke with the English custom of strict adherence to primogeniture by giving 13,000 acres of his land to his third son. This was Clermont, the Lower Manor, on which Robert of Clermont, as he was known, established his home in 1728.

Two more Robert Livingstons figure in the tale after this point: Robert of Clermont's son, a New York judge, and *his* son, a member of the Second Continental Congress who filled the now-obsolete office of state chancellor. It was the chancellor's mother, Margaret Beekman Livingston, who rebuilt the house after it was burned in 1777 by the British (parts of the original walls are incorporated into the present structure).

The Livingston family lived at Clermont until 1962, making various enlargements and modifications to their home over time. In that year the house, its furnishings, and the 500 remaining acres of the Clermont estate became the property of the State of New York.

The mansion at Clermont State Historic Site (also a National Historic Landmark) has been restored to its circa 1930 appearance; however, the collections are primarily half eighteenth- and half nineteenth-century French and early American. Tours of Clermont include the first and second floors. An orientation exhibit and a short film are given at the visitor center. There are formal gardens, woodsy hiking trails, and spacious landscapes (perfect for picnics) on bluffs overlooking the Hudson.

Clermont, 1 Clermont Avenue, off Route 9G, *Germantown* (518–537–4240; www.hudsonrivervalley.com), is open Tuesday through Sunday and on Monday holidays from 11:00 A.M. to 5:00 P.M. (last tour at 4:30). From November through March, hours are 11:00 A.M. to 4:00 P.M. (last tour at 3:30), weekends only. The grounds are open and free daily year-round from 8:30 A.M. to sunset. The Visitor Center is open from April through October, Tuesday through Sunday and Monday holidays 10:30 A.M. to 5:00 P.M. and November through March, weekends 11:00 A.M. to 4:00 P.M. The Heritage Music Festival is held in mid-July. Admission to the mansion is $5.00 for adults, $4.00 for seniors, and children under 12 are free.

Want to paddle a sea kayak around the Statue of Liberty? How about past Sing Sing Prison or up through the northern Hudson Highlands past Bannerman's Castle on Pollepel Island? *Atlantic Kayak Tours,* the largest sea kayaking business in the tri-state area, offers these tours and many more throughout the waters of Connecticut, New Jersey, and the Empire State, and you don't need any experience to join up. They're at 320 West Saugerties Road in Saugerties (845–246–2187). The company also offers kayak tours and lessons on the Lower Hudson River at Annsville Creek Paddlesport Center on the grounds of Hudson Highlands State Park. That facility is open weekends in April; daily from May through August; Saturday, Sunday, and Wednesday through Friday in September and October; and Saturday, Sunday, Thursday, and Friday from October 12 through the end of October. Check out their Web site: www .AtlanticKayakTours.com.

Known for his mammoth landscapes and his theatrical presentations, Hudson River School master *Frederic Edwin Church* built a Persian Gothic castle, *Olana,* commanding a magnificent view of the river south of the town of Hudson.

Olana draws heavily upon Islamic and Byzantine motifs. Persian arches abound, as do Oriental carpets, brasswork, and inlaid furniture. The overall aesthetic is typically Victorian, with no space left empty that could possibly be filled with things. What makes Olana atypical, of course, is the quality of the things.

Although Church employed as a consultant *Calvert Vaux,* who had collaborated with *Frederick Law Olmsted* on the design of New York's Central Park, the artist was the architect of his own house. When scholars describe Olana as a major work of art by Church, they are not speaking figuratively; the paints for the interior were mixed on his own palette.

Olana State Historic Site, Route 9G, Hudson (518–828–0135; www.olana .org), is under renovation and is expected to reopen in summer 2007.

Olana

More than seventy antiques shops fill five historic walking blocks on Warren Street in **Hudson.** Furniture, clocks, porcelains, rugs, ephemera . . . the antiques district is a collector's dream. Most shops are open Thursday through Tuesday. For information call the **Hudson Antique Dealers Association** at (518) 822–9397 or check their Web site: www.hudsonantiques.net. For a complete list of shops, contact Columbia County Tourism Department at (800) 724–1846.

On July 13, 1865, Barnum's American Museum, located at the corner of Ann Street and Broadway in Manhattan and filled with the "wonders of the world," caught fire. Volunteer fire companies, some in newly introduced steam engines, rushed to the rescue and managed to save, among other things, "Old Glory," the flag that was flying from a mast on the roof.

Today Old Glory is one of just 2,500 fire-related articles on display at the **American Museum of Firefighting,** which documents nearly 300 years of firefighting history and houses one of the country's largest collections of fire-fighting apparatuses and memorabilia. Of the sixty-eight firefighting engines on display, the majority are nineteenth-century hand pumpers, ladder trucks, and hose carts, including a 1725 Newsham, the first successful working engine used in New York.

The museum is next door to the Volunteer Firemen's Home, a health care facility for volunteer firefighters who continue to volunteer, this time as museum guides.

The American Museum of Firefighting, 125 Harry Howard Avenue, Hudson (518–828–7695 or 800–479–7695; www.fasnyfiremuseum.com), is open 9:00 A.M. to 4:30 P.M. daily except major holidays. Admission is free.

The road less traveled can sometimes lead us to the nicest places. Route 23 out of *Hillsdale* to Craryville is such a road. It goes—via a right turn off Route 23 onto Craryville Road, and then a left onto West End Road and then right onto Rodman Road (or just follow the signs)—to *Rodgers Book Barn,* a secondhand shop considered by many bibliophiles to be one of the best in the country. The barn—a two-story affair—is packed from floor to ceiling with some 50,000 books. The collection is wonderfully eclectic: There are inexpensive '50s potboilers, tomes on European and American history, gardening books, and rare out-of-print editions in dozens of categories. The shop's owner, Maureen Rodgers, encourages browsing to the point of inviting patrons to bring along a lunch to enjoy in the grape arbor next to the herb garden.

Rodgers Book Barn, Rodgers Road, Hillsdale (518–325–3610), is open November through March, Monday and Friday noon to 5:00 P.M., Saturday 10:00 A.M. to 5:00 P.M., and Sunday 11:00 A.M. to 5:00 P.M.; April through October, Monday, Thursday, and Friday noon to 5:00 P.M.; Saturday 10:00 A.M. to 5:00 P.M.; and Sunday 11:00 A.M. to 5:00 P.M.

The *Crandall Theater* first opened its doors on Christmas Day 1926. Today, Columbia County's oldest and largest movie theater, a Spanish-style building of brick and stucco, remains proudly independent in a world of chain-owned, cookie-cutter megaplexes. Get there early, grab a bag of freshly popped popcorn, and head for the balcony. You'll get a true blast from the past along with a first-run movie for only $4.00 a ticket. The theater is on Main Street in Chatham (518–392–3331).

Donald W. Fisher, Ph.D., knows his rocks and fossils: He's New York's State Paleontologist Emeritus. He's stocked *Fisher's O.K. Rock Shop* (O.K. stands for *Old Kinderhook*) with a wide variety of rock specimens, as well as minerals from around the world (but principally from New York, New England, Ontario, and Quebec) and fossils. Dr. Fisher also sells school kits, mineral and fossil jewelry (including Herkimer "diamonds"), geologic time charts and posters, rockhounding supplies, and a wide variety of related specialty items. And visitors to Fisher's shop can mine him for information on the best mineral and fossil sites in the state.

Fisher's O.K. Rock Shop, 2 Chatham Street (Route 9), Old Kinderhook, (518) 758–7657 (residence, 518–758–9044), is open Sunday, Monday, and Tuesday by appointment only; Wednesday through Friday noon to 5:30 P.M.; and Saturday 10:00 A.M. to 5:30 P.M. Between Thanksgiving and Christmas the shop is open Monday through Saturday 10:00 A.M. to 5:30 P.M., Friday until 8:00 P.M., and Sunday from 12:30 to 4:00 P.M.

East of Albany

The **Shaker Museum and Library** in **Old Chatham** is housed in a collection of buildings located just 12 miles from **Mount Lebanon,** New York, where the Shakers established one of their first U.S. communities.

The Shakers, formally known as the United Society of Believers in Christ's Second Appearing, were a sect founded in Britain and transplanted to America just prior to the revolution. A quietist, monastic order dedicated to equality between the sexes, sharing of community property, temperance in its broad sense, and the practice of celibacy, the sect peaked in the middle nineteenth century with about 6,000 members. Today there are fewer than a dozen Shakers living in a community at Sabbathday Lake, Maine.

Ironically, it is the secular aspects of Shaker life that are most often recalled today. The members of the communities were almost obsessive regarding simplicity and purity of form in the articles they designed and crafted for daily life; "Shaker furniture" has become a generic term for the elegantly uncluttered designs they employed. In their pursuit of the perfect form dictated by function, they even invented now ubiquitous objects such as the flat broom.

The Shaker Museum has amassed a collection of more than 18,000 objects, half of which are on display. The main building contains an orientation gallery that surveys Shaker history and provides highlights of the rest of the collection. The museum's library contains one of the two most extensive collections of Shaker material in the world. The cafe serves snacks and beverages.

The Shaker Museum and Library, 88 Shaker Museum Road (off County Route 13), Old Chatham (518–794–9100; www.shakermuseumandlibrary.org), is open daily except Tuesday late May to late October, from 10:00 A.M. to 5:00 P.M. Admission is $8.00 for adults, $6.00 for senior citizens, $4.00 for children ages 8 to 17, and free for children under 8. Family admission (two adults and two children) is $18.00.

In 1624 Dutchmen sailed up the Hudson River and established a fur-trading station called Fort Orange at present-day Albany. Within twenty-five years it was a thriving community. Across the river is the town of **Rensselaer,** named for

Ring around the Collar

According to local lore Mrs. Hannah Lord Montague of Troy spawned a new industry when, in 1825, she cut the soiled collars off her husband's otherwise clean shirts so she would only have to wash the dirty parts.

Born in the USA

During the War of 1812, Troy brickmaker Samuel Wilson opened a slaughterhouse and sold meat to a government contractor named Elbert Anderson. All of his beef and pork were stamped us-ea, and soldiers made up a story that the us, which stood for United States, actually stood for "Uncle Sam" Wilson, and thus was Uncle Sam born. A monument to his memory stands at the head of 101st Street in Troy.

the family who held the "patroonship," or feudal proprietorship, of the vast area on the east bank. *Crailo*, built in the early eighteenth century by the first Patroon's grandson, recalls a time when the Dutch were still the predominant cultural presence in the area.

Crailo changed with time and tastes. A Georgian-style east wing, added in 1762, reflected the increasing influence of the English in the area; Federal touches were added later in the century. Since 1933 the house has served as a museum of the Dutch in the upper Hudson Valley. Exhibits include seventeenth- and eighteenth-century prints and archaeological artifacts, many from the Fort Orange excavation of 1970–71.

Crailo State Historic Site, 9½ Riverside Avenue, Rensselaer (518–463–8738; www.nysparks.state.ny.us/sites), is open mid-April through late October, Wednesday through Saturday from 10:00 A.M. to 5:00 P.M. Crailo is also open on Tuesday in July and August. From November through March, visits are by appointment Tuesday through Friday 10:00 A.M. to 4:00 P.M. Tours are given on the hour and half-hour; the last tour is at 4:00 P.M. It is also open Memorial Day, Independence Day, and Labor Day. Admission is $3.00 for adults, $1.00 for children ages 5 to 12, and $2.00 per person for tour buses and New York State seniors.

The Children's Museum of Science and Technology (CMOST) is the only science center in the capital area where parents and children can explore and make discoveries together. Recent programs featured birds of prey; an animated adventure exploring the nature of atoms and molecules; experiments on the nature of water; the technology of robots; and an exploration of the nature of color.

The Children's Museum of Science and Technology, 250 Jordan Road (Rensselaer Tech Park), Troy (518–235–2120; www.cmost.com), is open Thursday through Saturday from 10:00 A.M. to 5:00 P.M. and Sunday noon to 5:00 P.M. Admission is $5.00 per person age 2 and up. There is a $1.00 charge for Dome (planetarium) shows.

Hoosic Valley

Most of us know that the Battle of Bunker Hill was not actually fought on Bunker Hill (it took place on Breed's Hill, also in Charlestown, Massachusetts), but how many can identify another military misnomer of the revolution?

We're talking about the 1777 Battle of Bennington, an American victory that laid the groundwork for the defeat and surrender of General Burgoyne at Saratoga that October. The battle, in which American militiamen defended their ammunition and supplies from an attacking party made up of British troops, Tory sympathizers, mercenaries, and Indians, took place not in Bennington, Vermont, but in Walloomsac, New York. True, the stores that the British were after were stashed in the Vermont town, but the actual fighting took place on New York soil.

The State of New York today maintains the site of the battle as an official state historic site. It's on a lovely hilltop in eastern Rensselaer County's Grafton State Park, and is studded with bronze and granite markers that explain the movements of the troops on the American militia's triumphal day. The spot is located on the north side of Route 67 and is open May 1 through Labor Day, daily 10:00 A.M. to 7:00 P.M.; Labor Day to Veterans Day, weekends only 10:00 A.M. to 7:00 P.M. Visitors can check road conditions by calling **Bennington Battlefield State Historic Site** at (518) 279–1902 or get general information at (518) 686–7109 or www.nysparks.state.ny.us/sites. On a clear day you can enjoy fine views of the Green Mountain foothills, prominent among which is Bennington's obelisk monument. Drive over to visit the monument and give the Vermonters their due—but really, doesn't "Battle of Walloomsac" have a nice ring to it?

Will Moses, a great-grandson of the renowned primitive painter Grandma Moses, is a folk artist whose minutely detailed paintings reflect the charm and beauty of the tiny rural community where he lives. Lithographs, printed by master lithographers from original oil paintings done by Will, are exhibited and sold, along with offset prints, at **Mount Nebo Gallery,** 60 Grandma Moses Road, **Eagle Bridge** (518–686–4334 or 800–328–6326; www.willmoses.com). The gallery is open Monday through Friday 9:00 A.M. to 4:00 P.M., Saturday 10:00 A.M. to 5:00 P.M., and Sunday noon to 5:00 P.M.

Our next stop on this ramble up the east shore of the Hudson offers proof that in this part of the world the monastic spirit did not pass into history with the Shakers. **Cambridge** is the home of the **New Skete Communities,** a group of monks, nuns, and laypeople organized around a life of prayer, contemplation, and physical work. Founded in 1966 within the Byzantine Rite of the Roman Catholic Church, the New Skete Communities have been a part of the Orthodox Church in America since 1979.

Visitors to New Skete are welcome at the community's two houses of worship. The small Temple of the Transfiguration of Christ, open at all times, contains a number of icons painted by the monks and nuns, while the larger Church of Christ the Wisdom of God—open to visitors only during services—has, imbedded in its marble floor, original pieces of mosaic that were brought from the A.D. 576 Church of Saint Sophia (Holy Wisdom) in Constantinople. Worship services are usually twice daily.

As in many monastic communities, the monks and the nuns of New Skete help support themselves through a wide variety of pursuits. An important part of their life is the breeding of German shepherds and the boarding and training of all breeds of dogs. The monks have even written two successful books, *How to Be Your Dog's Best Friend* and *The Art of Raising a Puppy*. At their gift shop they sell their own cheeses, smoked meats, fruitcakes, the famous New Skete cheesecakes, dogbeds, religious cards made by the nuns, and original painted icons.

The New Skete Communities are in Cambridge. The convent is accessible from the village of Cambridge via East Main Street on Ash Grove Road, and the monastery is farther out of town on New Skete Lane. For information call the monks at (518) 677–3928 or the nuns at (518) 677–3810. The nuns' bakery is open Tuesday through Friday 9:00 A.M. to 4:00 P.M., and Saturday 10:00 A.M. to 4:00 P.M. Their Web site is www.newskete.com.

At the **Log Village Grist Mill,** built in 1810 by Hezekiah Mann, a 17-foot wooden waterwheel still provides power to three millstones that grind cornmeal, wheat flour, and buckwheat. A museum in the mill barn houses an exhibit of old farm machinery and household items, and the cider mill, built in 1894, still has the original cider press, powered by a seven-horsepower single-cylinder gas engine. Have a picnic, take a tour, and watch as several "obsolete" machines crank and grind their way through the twenty-first century.

The Log Village Grist Mill, County Route 30, **East Hartford** (518–632–5237; www.lloydharwood.com), is open Saturday and some holidays from 10:00 A.M. to 6:00 P.M. and Sunday noon to 6:00 P.M. Memorial Day weekend through mid-October, and by appointment. Allow several hours to visit the mill. Adult admission is $2.50, children, 50 cents.

Places to Stay East of the Hudson

HOPEWELL JUNCTION
Le Chambord
2075 Route 523
(845) 221–1941
www.lechambord.com

HUDSON
Inn at Blue Stores
2323 Route 9
(518) 537–4277
www.innatbluestores.com

HYDE PARK
Journey Inn Bed and Breakfast
One Sherwood Place
(845) 229–8972
www.journeyinn.com

MILLERTON
Simmons' Way Village Inn and Restaurant
33 Main Street (Route 44)
(518) 789–6235
www.simmonsway.com

PEEKSKILL
Peekskill Inn
634 Main Street
(800) 526–9466 and (914) 739–1500
www.peekskillinn.com

POUGHKEEPSIE
Alumnae House, The Inn at Vassar College
161 College Avenue
(845) 437–7100
www.AlumnaeHouse.Vassar.edu

Inn at the Falls
50 Red Oaks Mill Road
(845) 462–5770
www.innatthefalls.com

Sheraton Hotel
40 Civic Center Plaza
(845) 485–5300

RHINEBECK
Bittersweet Bed and Breakfast
470 Wurtemburg Road
(845) 876–7777
www.bittersweetbedandbreakfast.com

Gables at Rhinebeck
6358 Mill Street
(845) 876–7577

The Looking Glass Bed and Breakfast
28–30 Chestnut Street
(845) 876–8986
www.thelookingglassbandb.com

Whistlewood Farm Bed & Breakfast
52 Pells Road
(845) 876–6838
www.whistlewood.com

REGIONAL TOURIST INFORMATION— EAST OF THE HUDSON

Columbia County Tourism
(800) 724–1846 and (518) 828–3375
www.columbiacountyny.org

Dutchess County Tourism
3 Neptune Road
Poughkeepsie
(800) 445–3131
www.dutchesstourism.com

Hudson Valley Tourism
(845) 291–2136
www.travelhudsonvalley.org

Poughkeepsie Area Chamber of Commerce
One Civic Center Plaza
Poughkeepsie
(845) 454–1700
www.pokchamb.org

Putnam County Tourism
(800) 470–4854 and (845) 225–0381
www.visitputnam.org

Rensselaer County Tourism
1600 Seventh Avenue
Troy
(518) 270–2959
www.rensco.com

OTHER ATTRACTIONS WORTH SEEING EAST OF THE HUDSON

Bardavon 1869 Opera House
35 Market Street
Poughkeepsie
(845) 473–5288

Boscobel
1601 Route 9D, Garrison
(845) 265–3638

**FDR's Home and Library
(Springwood)**
4097 Albany-Post Road (Route 9)
Hyde Park
(845) 229–8114 or (800) 337–8474

**Frances Lehman Loeb Art Center
Vassar College**
124 Raymond Avenue
Poughkeepsie
(845) 437–5632

Kykuit (Rockefeller Estate)
Sleepy Hollow
(914) 631–8200

Lebanon Valley Dragway
1746 Route 20
West Lebanon
(518) 794–7130

Madame Brett Homestead
50 Van Nydeck Avenue
Beacon
(845) 831–6533

Mary Flagler Cary Arboretum
Route 44A
Millbrook
(845) 677–5359

Montgomery Place
River Road
Annandale-on-Hudson
(845) 758–5461

Philipsburg Manor
Croton-on-Hudson
(914) 631–8200

Taconic State Park
Route 344 off Route 22
near Copake Falls
(518) 329–3993

Van Cortlandt Manor
Croton-on-Hudson
(914) 631–8200

**Vanderbilt Mansion National
Historic Site**
Route 9
Hyde Park
(845) 229–9115 or (800) 967–2283

Wilderstein
64 Morton Road
Rhinebeck
(845) 876–4818

TARRYTOWN

**Tarrytown House Estate
and Conference Center**
49 East Sunnyside Lane
(914) 591–8200
www.tarrytownhouseestate
.com

TIVOLI

Madalin Hotel
53 Broadway
(845) 757–2100

TROY

Olde Judge Mansion
3300 Sixth Avenue
(518) 274–5698

WHITE PLAINS

**Renaissance Westchester
Hotel**
80 West Red Oak Lane
(800) 359–7234
www.marriott.com

Places to Eat East of the Hudson

AMENIA

Xe Sogni
Route 44
(845) 373–7755

BEACON

Sukhothai Restaurant
516 Main Street
(866) 838–6973

GARRISON

The Bird and Bottle Inn
1123 Old Albany Post Road
(off Route 9D)
(845) 424–2333

Valley Restaurant at the Garrison
2015 Route 9
(845) 424–2339
www.thegarrison.com

HASTINGS-ON-THE-HUDSON

Buffet de la Gare
155 Southside Avenue
(914) 478–1671

KATONAH

Blue Dolphin Ristorante
175 Katonah Avenue
(914) 232–4791

GERMANTOWN

Restaurant
2 Church Avenue
(518) 537–2160

HOPEWELL JUNCTION

Le Chambord
2737 Route 52
(845) 221–1941
www.lechambord.com

OSSINING

Brasserie Swiss
118 Croton Avenue
(914) 931–0319

POCANTICO HILLS

Blue Hill at Stone Barns
630 Bedford Road
(914) 366–9600
www.bluehillstonebarns.com

POUGHKEEPSIE

Cosimo's
120 Delafield Street
(845) 485–7229
www.cosimosrestaurant group.com

RHINEBECK

Sabroso
22 Garden Street
(845) 876–8688
www.sabrosoplatos.com

TARRYTOWN

Equus
The Castle on the Hudson
400 Benedict Avenue
(914) 631–3646
www.castleattarrytown.com

Lago di Como
27 Main Street
(914) 631–7227

Santa Fe Restaurant
5 Main Street
(914) 332–4452

The Adirondacks

To many Manhattanites, upstate New York can mean anything north of Westchester, but to really appreciate the grandeur of the Empire State, city dwellers must motor past Albany and its suburbs to reach the Adirondack Mountains. The Adirondacks count forty-two peaks that soar over 4,000 feet, including Mt. Marcy, near Lake Placid, the state's highest elevation at 5,344 feet above sea level.

Although readily accessible from I–87, much of the Adirondacks remain quite wild, thanks to the Adirondack Park, which encompasses some six million acres of state and private land east of Lake Champlain, including Lake George and northern Saratoga County.

It was certainly the area's incredible natural beauty—rugged mountains, clear lakes and streams, tall pines—that attracted many of the fortunes of the Gilded Age to the Adirondacks. They summered here on great "camps," estates that sprawled over thousands of acres, setting a pattern for generations of children, who bunked in somewhat less luxurious circumstances. But these society swells were not the first to discover the Adirondacks: Visitors will discover museums and sites that document the rich history of the land and its people, from the Indian nations to the settlers who carved towns out of

THE ADIRONDACKS

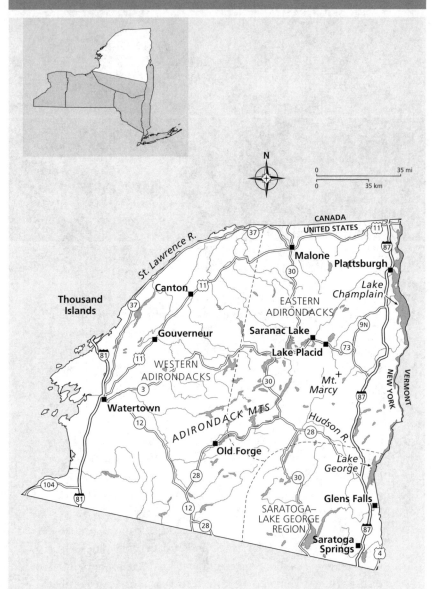

CANADA
UNITED STATES

St. Lawrence R.

Thousand
Islands

Malone

Plattsburgh

Lake
Champlain

Canton

EASTERN
ADIRONDACKS

Gouverneur

Saranac Lake

Lake Placid

WESTERN
ADIRONDACKS

Mt.
Marcy

Watertown

ADIRONDACK MTS

NEW YORK

VERMONT

Old Forge

Hudson R.

Lake
George

Glens Falls

SARATOGA–
LAKE GEORGE
REGION

Saratoga
Springs

N

0   35 mi

0   35 km

the woods, building cabins and boats, and yes, even the comfortable outdoor chairs that take their name from this region.

(*Note:* The overall place-to-place direction followed in this chapter is counterclockwise—south to north to west.)

Saratoga–Lake George Region

To horse-racing fans, Saratoga Springs is simply "The Spa," an annual exodus from New York City, when the August race meeting at Saratoga Racetrack forces touts out into the fresh air. Many hotel rooms are booked from the year before, everywhere from the stately old Adelphi Hotel to the national chains to the many B&Bs housed in lovely old Victorian houses. But there's so much more to Saratoga than racing—there is a rich history to discover as well as the mineral springs, and concerts and shows at the Saratoga Performing Arts Center (www.spac.org), summer home to the Philadelphia Orchestra and the New York City Opera and Ballet.

When puzzling over an exacta gets too taxing, relax and "take the cure" at the **Lincoln Baths** or the **Roosevelt Baths,** both built in the 1930s and modeled after the grand spas of Europe. Both were recently renovated and have added a full menu of facials, massages, and other treatments to complement the traditional effervescent mineral water bath, a uniquely relaxing experience.

The baths are a short stroll from the **Gideon Putnam Resort and Spa,** the grand Georgian Revival–style edifice at the center of the 2,300-acre Saratoga Spa State Park. The resort is a gracious setting for every sort of leisure activity—tennis, golf, swimming, horseback riding, jogging, and, in winter, ice-skating and cross-country skiing. Recently renovated, the Gideon Putnam has returned to its roots, when the flamboyant interior designer Dorothy Draper envisioned

AUTHORS' FAVORITES—ADIRONDACKS

Adirondack Museum	National Museum of Racing and Thoroughbred Hall of Fame
Fort Ticonderoga	
Frederic Remington Art Museum	Sagamore
Hattie's	Stillwater Reservoir
Moose River Recreation Area	Thousand Islands Inn
	Whetstone Gulf State Park

bold colors and patterns for its grand lobby and gracious restaurants. Rates at the Gideon Putnam vary according to season, with rooms running from $114 to $555, with many value-added golf and spa packages offered outside of racing season. Call (800) 732–1560 or go to www.gideonputnam.com for more on the hotel and the baths.

Tradition says the Indians of the Saratoga region visited High Rock Spring as early as 1300 to gain strength from the "Medicine Spring of the Great Spirit." Four hundred seventy years later, in 1771, Sir William Johnson, suffering from a wound received in the Battle of Lake George, was carried on a litter by Mohawk Indians from Johnstown to High Rock Spring. After a short stay his health improved noticeably, and the reputation of the spring quickly grew.

The first person to recognize the commercial value of the mineral waters at Saratoga Springs may well have been *John Arnold*, who in 1774 purchased a crude log cabin built on a bluff overlooking High Rock Spring, improved it, and opened an inn. Thirteen years later, Revolutionary War hero Alexander Bryan purchased the inn, the only Saratoga hotel until 1801, when Gideon Putnam built the Grand Union Hotel. Now *The Olde Bryan Inn*, the inn has been a lodge, tavern, restaurant, and private dwelling. Today you can enjoy prime rib, Gorgonzola New York sirloin, homestyle turkey dinner, or just a pint.

The Olde Bryan Inn, 123 Maple Avenue, Saratoga Springs (518–587–2990), is open Sunday through Thursday 11:00 A.M. until 10:00 P.M., and Friday and Saturday 11:00 A.M. to 11:00 P.M. The tavern is open daily until midnight.

Of course, Lincoln and Roosevelt are not the only tubs in town anymore; *The Crystal Spa* is a day spa at 120 South Broadway, adjacent to the Grand

The Olde Bryan Inn

A Gas Explosion

The discovery of a process to extract carbonic gas (used to make the new carbonated beverages) from Saratoga Springs's waters in 1890 was almost the resort's death knell. Over the next few decades, many of its wells were being pumped dry. In 1910, to protect its natural resources, the state purchased 163 springs and 1,000 acres of land surrounding them, and constructed baths, a research institute, a Hall of Springs, and the Gideon Putnam hotel.

Union Motel, that offers a full array of facials, massages, and body treatments. It also offers mineral baths in water pumped from the Rosemary Spring. Patrons can also drink the spring water from a fountain housed beneath a restored Victorian gazebo. Call (518) 584–2556 or go to www.thecrystalspa.com for reservations and the latest treatments and prices.

Between 1823 and 1889 mineral waters from approximately thirty springs in Saratoga County were bottled and distributed around the world, and an industry was born. The **National Bottle Museum,** housed in a 1901 former hardware store in **Ballston Spa**'s historic district, documents the rise and decline of that industry. Through exhibits of antique bottles and glassmaking tools, videos, and artifacts, it tells the story of a time past, when young men were indentured to the owners of glass factories and apprenticed for fifteen years in order to become glassblowers in the glasshouses that made bottles and jars by hand. It re-creates an industry and a way of life that have vanished from the American scene.

The National Bottle Museum, 76 Milton Avenue, Ballston Spa (518–885–7589), is open daily from June 1 to September 30, 10:00 A.M. to 4:00 P.M.; October 1 to May 31, open Monday through Friday 10:00 A.M. to 4:00 P.M. and closed weekends. Recommended donation is $2.00 for adults. Devotees of glassworks can call ahead to sign up for one of the four-hour, weekend or evening glassblowing courses given by guest artisans in the museum's flameworking shops.

For those born too late to see Secretariat or Seabiscuit in the flesh, the history and traditions of the sport are thoroughly chronicled at the **National Museum of Racing and Thoroughbred Hall of Fame**, directly across from the Saratoga Race Course. Patrons enter the museum through an actual starting gate, complete with life-size representations of a horse, jockey, and starter. Some of the highlights: paintings of outstanding horses, the saddle and boots used by jockey Johnny Loftus on Man o' War, a Hall of Fame, and the actual skeleton of a thoroughbred. *Race America,* filmed at racetracks and stud farms across the country, is shown in the theater. Video booths lining the walls provide films of some of racing's greats.

The National Museum of Racing and Thoroughbred Hall of Fame, 191 Union Avenue, Saratoga Springs (518–584–0400; www.racingmuseum.org), is open year-round. From January 1 through the end of July, hours are Monday through Saturday 10:00 A.M. to 4:00 P.M. and Sunday noon to 4:30 P.M.; during racing season, daily 9:00 A.M. to 5:00 P.M.; and September 1 through December 31, Monday through Saturday 10:00 A.M. to 4:00 P.M. and Sunday noon to 4:00 P.M. Admission is $7.00 for adults and $5.00 for senior citizens, students, and children 6 to 18.

Folks in Saratoga Springs have been flocking to *Hattie's* for Southern fried chicken and biscuits since 1938, and we're assured by the present owner, Jasper Alexander, that Hattie's New Orleans recipes haven't changed. "We've kept her most popular dishes, like fried chicken and pan-fried pork chops, and added some Creole specialties," explains Jasper. Evertyhing—slow-cooked barbecued spare ribs, Hoppin' John (black-eyed peas with chopped onion, salt and pepper, butter, and pork), blackened catfish, Creole jambalaya, gumbo—is authentically prepared and moderately priced.

Hattie's, 45 Phila Street, Saratoga Springs (518–584–4790; www.hatties restaurant.com), is open daily from 8:00 A.M. to 1:00 P.M. and 5:00 to 10:00 P.M.; enjoy courtyard dining in the summer.

The *Petrified Sea Gardens* consists of the exposed remains of a sea reef that thrived here beneath the Cambrian Sea 500 million years ago. Known since 1825 and properly identified in 1883, the "gardens" are the fossilized remains of cabbagelike plants related to modern algae. The reef they formed would have teemed with trilobites, brachiopods, and rudimentary snails, the fossils of some of which are visible among the plant fossils at this site. When the primordial seas receded, the vegetation was exposed, fossilized beneath layers of sediment, and eventually exposed again by the shearing action of the glaciers.

At the Petrified Sea Gardens, visitors can walk among these ancient plants, which can easily be distinguished by the untrained eye. Just look for gray, layered nodules that look as if they might be broken, protruding sections of petrified cabbage. Among the vegetation is the "Iroquois Pine," one of the largest in the Adirondacks and estimated to be 300 years old. There are hands-on activities for children in the nature center.

Petrified Sea Gardens, 42 Petrified Sea Gardens Road (off Route 29), Saratoga Springs (518–584–7102; www.petrifiedgardens.org), is open May (starting Mother's Day weekend) Saturday, Sunday, and Memorial Day 11:00 A.M. to 5:00 P.M.; June, Thursday through Monday 11:00 A.M. to 5:00 P.M.; July and August, daily 11:00 A.M. to 5:00 P.M.; September to mid-October, Thursday

ANNUAL EVENTS IN THE ADIRONDACKS

JANUARY

Lake George Polar Plunge
Lake George
(800) 705–0059

World Cup Freestyle
Lake Placid
(518) 523–1655
www.orda.org

FEBRUARY

Empire State Winter Games
Lake Placid
(518) 523–1655
www.orda.org

Winter Carnival
Saranac Lake
(518) 891–1990
www.saranaclake.com/carny.shtml

APRIL

St. Clement's Saratoga Horse Show
Saratoga Springs
(518) 587–2623

MAY

The Adirondack Paddle Fest
Inlet
(315) 357–6672

Maple Festival
Croghan
(315) 346–6060

JUNE

Americade Motorcycle Rally
Lake George
(518) 798–7888
www.tourexp.com

Lake Placid Film Festival
various locations around Lake Placid
(518) 523–3456
www.lakeplacidfilmfestival.com

LARAC Arts Festival
Glens Falls
(518) 798–1141

JULY

Long Lake Regatta
Long Lake
(518) 624–3077

Hats Off to Saratoga
Saratoga Springs
(518) 584–3255

AUGUST

Travers Festival Week
Saratoga Springs
(518) 584–3255

SEPTEMBER

Adirondack Balloon Festival
Glens Falls
(800) 365–1050
www.adirondackballoonfest.org

OCTOBER

Adirondack Art and Craft Festival
Saratoga Springs
www.craftproducers.com

World's Largest Garage Sale
Warrensburg
(518) 623–2161
www.warrensburggaragesale.com

DECEMBER

First Night
Saranac Lake
(518) 891–2484

A Chip by Any Other Name . . .

One day "Aunt Kate" Weeks, a cook at a hotel on Saratoga Lake, tried to make perfectly crisp french fried potatoes. Instead she created "Saratoga Chips," now known as potato chips.

through Monday 4:00 A.M. to 5:00 P.M.; and late October to early November, weekends 11:00 A.M. to 5:00 P.M. Admission is $3.75 for adults, $2.75 for senior citizens, $3.00 for college students with I.D., and $2.00 for children 6 to 16. Call for group rates.

Not quite so far back in history, *The Battle of Saratoga* was one of the turning points in the American Revolution. One of the first major victories for the colonial forces over the British, it encouraged France to enter the war on the American side. The battle took place in October 1777 on the shores of the Hudson River, near present-day Stillwater, and the battleground is preserved in the 3,200-acre *Saratoga National Historical Park,* where visitors can also tour the colonial Philip Schuyler house on summer weekends. There is a charge of $12 per car to access the park's 10-mile tour road. The Saratoga National Historical Park Visitor Center, 648 Route 32, Stillwater, is open daily except Thanksgiving and Christmas. Call (518) 664–9821 or see www.nps.gov/sara for more.

In June 1885, suffering from throat cancer and longing for fresh air and a healthier climate, President *Ulysses S. Grant* left his home in New York City for Saratoga County. He and his family moved into a summer cottage on top of Mt. McGregor, 8 miles from Saratoga Springs. At the cottage he continued work on his memoirs and, two weeks after completing them, died on July 23, 1885.

The house at *Grant Cottage State Historic Site* is preserved as Grant left it, from the bed where he died to the floral pieces sent from around the country. It is operated by the Friends of the Ulysses S. Grant Cottage, in cooperation with the New York State Office of Parks, Recreation, and Historic Preservation.

Grant Cottage State Historic Site, Mt. McGregor Road, *Wilton* (mailing address: P.O. Box 990, Saratoga Springs 12866) (518–587–8277), is open Memorial Day through Labor Day, Wednesday through Sunday 10:00 A.M. to 4:00 P.M.; through Columbus Day weekend, from 10:00 A.M. to 4:00 P.M. Groups, by advance reservation, are accepted spring and fall only. Admission is $2.50 for adults, $2.00 for senior citizens, and $1.00 for children over 5.

The Hydes of Glens Falls preferred painting to ponies, and spent a fortune amassing the *Hyde Collection.* Charlotte Pruyn, heiress to a local paper fortune, married Louis Fiske Hyde of Boston in 1901. The couple returned to Glens Falls, and in 1912 they began building the Florentine villa that would become their home-as-museum in the mold of Boston tastemaker Isabella Stewart Gardner. With the help of connoisseurs such as Bernard Berenson, the Hydes acquired a collection of American and European art spanning five centuries that included works by Rubens, Botticelli, Rembrandt, Seurat, Degas, Homer, Whistler, Picasso, Cézanne, and Matisse.

No mere check-writers, the Hydes bought with expert eyes, building a collection that is rich with important and expressive works by the world's greatest artists.

The Hyde Collection opened to the public in 1963 after Mrs. Hyde's death at the age of ninety-six, and underwent extensive restoration and renovations in 2004. The Hyde Collection, 161 Warren Street, Glens Falls (518–792–1761; www.hydecollection.org), is open year-round 10:00 A.M. to 5:00 P.M., and Sunday noon to 5:00 P.M.; closed Monday and national holidays. Admission is free, but donations are welcome.

To really get an off-the-beaten-path view of the Adirondacks, get a horse. **Bennett's Riding Stable** conducts guided trail rides—everything from a one-hour ride for $25, to a 2½-hour ride up Beech Mountain for $50, to a half-day ride for $70 or a full day for $125. The 3½-hour sunset ride for $70 includes a steak barbecue. Reservations are advised for longer rides, and families are welcome (helmets are available). The stable is located at 91 Gage Hill Road in **Lake Luzerne,** (518) 696–4444. The stable is open daily in summer; call or go to www.lakegeorgenewyork.com/horses for times the rest of the year.

At the age of nineteen, Marcella (Kochanska) Sembrich made her operatic debut in Athens, Greece, singing in a number of the great opera houses in Europe before joining New York's Metropolitan Opera Company for its first season in 1883. She returned to Europe until 1898 and then rejoined the Metropolitan Opera until 1909, when her farewell was the occasion for the most sumptuous gala in the Met's history. She was founder of the vocal departments of the Juilliard School in New York and the Curtis Institute in Philadelphia and was a preeminent teacher of singing for twenty-five years. She often brought students to a studio near her summer home in **Bolton Landing** on Lake George. The **Marcella Sembrich Opera Museum,** in Mme. Sembrich's converted studio, displays operatic memorabilia she collected from her debut to her death in 1935.

Summer events include studio talks, a lakeside lecture series, a master class in voice, and occasional recitals or chamber concerts.

The Marcella Sembrich Opera Museum, 4800 Lake Shore Drive, Route 9N, Bolton Landing (518–644–9839; www.operamuseum.com), is open daily June

15 through September 15, 10:00 A.M. to 12:30 P.M. and 2:00 to 5:30 P.M. Suggested donation is $2.00 for adults 16 and over.

Drive around Lake George these days and you're sure to see cheesy 1950s Indian-theme motels being razed, yielding their water views to posh developments. Of course, grand lakefront homes have long been part of the culture of this area—just cruise around the lake and it's hard to keep jaws from dropping at the sight of some of the spectacular houses, most of which cannot be seen from the road.

Get a taste of gracious living in Gilded-Age style at **The Sagamore,** a grand old hotel built on a 70-acre private island off Bolton Landing. Two long wings spread out toward the lake, giving many rooms a sparkling view of the water. Time-honored pleasures include formal dining in the Trillium restaurant; sipping afternoon tea (or perhaps a single malt scotch) on the veranda; sailing, swimming, tennis, racquetball, or even golf (the latter on the mainland); and de-stressing in the spa.

Rates at the Sagamore vary seasonally, starting at $185 a night for a garden-view room to $595 a night for a Lake View Suite in the summer season. Still not quite grand enough? Request the ten-room Castle, a nineteenth-century "cottage" close enough to the lake to see if the fish are biting, for $2,000 to $3,600 a night. Call (800) 358–3585 or go to www.thesagamore.com for current rates and specials.

Eastern Adirondacks

Fort Ticonderoga, which stands on a promontory jutting into the southern end of Lake Champlain, was built by the French in 1755 when the colonial administration in Quebec needed a southern defense in its struggle against Great Britain for control of Canada. Called Fort Carillon, it was built of earth and timbers in the classic French fortress design, and later upgraded to stone, with four pointed bastions presenting an interlocking field of fire against attackers.

In 1758 the Marquis de Montcalm repelled a massive attack by the British, but a year later Lord Jeffrey Amherst captured the fort and renamed it "Ticonderoga." Seventeen years later—three weeks after the Battles of Lexington and Concord—Ethan Allen and Benedict Arnold captured "Fort Ti" from the British "in the name of the Great Jehovah and the Continental Congress," giving the Americans their first victory of the revolution.

Last garrisoned in 1777, Fort Ti might be little more than a roadside marker had it not been for the efforts of the Pell family to protect the site since 1820 and the commitment of Stephen and Sarah Pell to restore it beginning in 1908. At today's handsome reconstruction, guides in eighteenth-century clothing and a host of events, such as live artillery demonstrations and fife and drum musters, help bring the fort to life.

Visitors can stride along the ramparts, view the earthworks built during both the French and Indian Wars and the American Revolution, examine the barracks, and visit the museum, which houses North America's largest collection of eighteenth-century artillery as well as paintings, furniture, and military memorabilia. Just outside the fort is the battlefield where, in 1758, Montcalm devastated the 42nd Highland ("Black Watch") Regiment.

Tours of the 600-acre garrison grounds, offered daily, include the "King's Garden," a 1920s-era formal flower garden, and demonstration vegetable gardens including a Native American garden, children's garden, and garrison garden. Throughout the season there are numerous special events, including a Grand Encampment of the French and Indian War in late June, a Memorial Military Tattoo the weekend following the Fourth of July, and a Revolutionary War Encampment in September. Call for information.

Fort Ticonderoga, Route 74, Ticonderoga (518–585–2821; www.fort-ticonderoga.org), is open from early May through late October, daily 9:00 A.M. to 5:00 P.M. Admission is $12.00 for adults, $10.80 for seniors, $6.00 for children ages 7 to 12, and free for children under 7. The Log House is open for breakfast, lunch, and snacks.

As a sidelight to a Fort Ticonderoga visit, drive to the summit of nearby **Mt. Defiance** for a panoramic view of the Champlain Valley. Hop aboard the M/V *Carillon* to visit **Mt. Independence,** site of a Revolutionary War fort, across Lake Champlain in Vermont.

Located west of **Ticonderoga,** deeper in the Adirondacks, **Garnet Hill Lodge,** a remote resort on 600 acres of land, was built by members of the Barton family in 1933 when they came to the area to mine garnet. The architecture of the main lodge is rustic Adirondack-style, but some of the rooms, complete with whirlpool baths and hot tubs, are anything but rustic. The resort offers a host of activities, including tubing, mountain biking, and a special course on fly-fishing. The lodge, at 13th Lake Road in North River (800–497–4207), is open year-round. MAP (Modified American Plan, i.e., breakfast and dinner are included in the rate) rates range from $115 to $250 for a double.

No Barking

Adirondack is an Anglicism of the Iroquois word for the Algonquin Indians, whom they called "Ha-De-Ron-Dah" or "bark-eaters" for their habit of eating certain types of tree bark.

Visitors can tour the **Barton Mines** and look for gemstones in the open pits at Garnet Mine Tours on Barton Mines Road. The mines are open daily from late June through early October, 9:30 A.M. to 5:00 P.M. Monday through Saturday; 11:00 A.M. to 5:00 P.M. Sunday; and on weekends through Columbus Day. A fee is charged for a lecture. Visitors must be escorted in the mines. Call (518) 251–2706 or go to www.garnetminetours.com for information.

At **Jasco Minerals** Jim and Judy Shaw sell minerals and fossils from around the world, and Judy, a gemologist, handcrafts jewelry. The shop, on Route 28 in **North River** (518–251–3196), is open year-round, weather permitting: July and August from 9:00 A.M. to 7:00 P.M. and the rest of the year from 9:00 A.M. to 5:00 P.M. If the shop isn't open, knock on the door or yell.

Brandied French toast with sautéed apples is the breakfast specialty at **Goose Pond Inn** (www.goosepondinn.com), a charming, antiques-filled, turn-of-the-century bed-and-breakfast just a mile from Gore Mountain Ski Center. The inn, open year-round, is on Main Street in **North Creek,** (518) 251–3434. Rates range from $85 to $125 for a mid-week double to $115 to $160 on weekends and holidays.

In North Creek, hop aboard the **Upper Hudson River Railroad** for a two-hour, 17-mile round-trip scenic ride along the Hudson River to Riverside and back. The train leaves from the restored historic **North Creek Railroad Station,** where Vice President Theodore Roosevelt began his journey back to Washington, D.C., after President McKinley was shot. The "stick style" station, built in 1874, was the northernmost terminus of the Adirondack Branch of the D&H Railroad. It now houses a local history and train museum. The train routes change regularly and the ride was more than doubled in 2006, with new runs to the south. Trains run May through October. Call (518) 251–5334 for the schedule; check the Web site at www.uhrr.com for details.

Superb food, an award-winning wine list, and elegant accommodations are hallmarks of **Chestertown's Friends Lake Inn,** built in the 1860s as a boardinghouse to accommodate the tanners who worked in the city's major industry.

The inn has seventeen guest rooms with turn-of-the-twentieth-century furnishings, private baths, and queen-size four-poster beds. Many rooms have panoramic views of the lake.

The dining room serves a New American cuisine featuring homemade pâtés, breads, and international desserts and has the largest wine cellar in northern New York. A full country breakfast, with treats like locally smoked bacon and mango crepes with raspberry *coulis*, is included in the rate.

The inn has a private beach for summer fun, a sauna, and outdoor pool, and in winter its Nordic Ski Center grooms 32 kilometers of cross-country ski trails.

The Friends Lake Inn is on Friends Lake Road, Chestertown (518–494–4751; www.friendslake.com). Rates range from $329 to $429 per couple per night MAP; B&B rates are available, as are ski packages.

For some distance north of Ticonderoga, Lake Champlain remains narrow enough for a single military installation to have commanded both shores and governed the passage of ship traffic in the eighteenth century. This was the purpose of the fortifications that now lie in ruins at *Crown Point State Historic Site* (www.nysparks.state.ny.us/sites).

In the late 1600s the staging area for French raids on English settlements in New England and the Hudson Valley, Crown Point became the location of the French Fort St. Frederic, begun in 1734 and finished in 1737. The fort was designed as a stone citadel within outer walls, defended by fifty cannons and swivel-mounted guns and a garrison of 80 to 120 soldiers.

In 1759 General *Jeffrey Amherst* seized the fort for the British, after it was abandoned by the French, and ordered it enlarged. In 1775 American militiamen captured the fort from the British and used it as headquarters for the navy under Benedict Arnold until 1776.

The survival of the walls, foundations, and partial structures that we see at *Crown Point* today is due to the 1910 conveyance of the property to the state by private owners who wished to see the ruins preserved. In 1975 the area officially became a state historic site. The following year the new visitor center and museum were opened. Highlights of the museum exhibits include artifacts uncovered at the site during extensive archaeological digs.

The visitor center at Crown Point State Historic Site, at the Lake Champlain Bridge, 4 miles east of Routes 9N and 22, Crown Point (518–597–3666), is open May through October, Wednesday through Monday 9:00 A.M. to 5:00 P.M. Grounds are open all year from 9:00 A.M. to dusk. There is a $5.00 admission fee for each car on weekends and holidays; an admission fee is charged for the museum at all times. Group visits by advance reservation.

Tiny *Essex,* in the foothills of the Adirondacks on the shore of Lake Champlain, is one of the state's loveliest villages. Founded in the eighteenth century and one of the earliest European settlements on the lake, it is listed on the National Register of Historic Places and offers visitors a fascinating architectural overview: The streets are lined with homes and public buildings in a multitude of styles including Federal, Greek Revival, Italianate, and French Second Empire. One of the homes, an 1853 Greek Revival twenty-room mansion with 18-inch-thick cut stone walls called *Greystone* (Elm Street, 518–963–8058 or 963–4650), took four years to complete and has been restored by its present owners, who have opened it for tours by appointment.

There are several lodging options in town, including the **Essex Inn** (518–963–8821; www.theessexinn.com), which has been operating almost continuously since it was built in 1810, making it one of the longest lived structures in town. Extensively renovated in 1986, the inn has nine guest rooms (seven with private bath) and rates, ranging from $95 to $160, include a full breakfast. There are several restaurants in town, including one at the inn, which serves meals alfresco when the weather permits.

If you want to take a short boat ride, the **Essex-Charlotte Ferry** (802–864–9804) in town crosses the lake in just twenty minutes to Charlotte, Vermont. If you're on foot, there's not much to see on the other side, but you can hop off and catch a return ferry in a half hour. The ferry does not operate when there is ice on the lake.

For general information contact the Lake Placid/Essex County Convention and Visitors Bureau, Lake Placid, Olympic Center, 2610 Main Street, Lake Placid, (518) 523–2445 or (800) 447–5224 or www.lakeplacid.com.

The **Adirondack Museum** at **Blue Mountain Lake** in the heart of the mountain region chronicles the Adirondack experience throughout the years. Located on a ridge overlooking Blue Mountain Lake, the museum rambles through twenty-two separate exhibit buildings on a thirty-acre compound and has been called the finest regional museum in the United States.

The museum takes as its focus the ways in which people have related to this incomparable setting and made their lives here over the past two centuries. As befits an institution that began in an old hotel, the museum tells the story of how the Adirondacks were discovered by vacationists in the nineteenth century, especially after the 1892 completion of the railroad to nearby Raquette Lake.

Examples of nineteenth-century hotel and cabin rooms are shown, and a restored turn-of-the-century cottage houses a large collection of rustic "Adirondack furniture," currently enjoying a revival among interior designers. Financier August Belmont's private railroad car *Oriental*—a reminder of the days when grand conveyances brought the very wealthy to even grander Adirondack mansions and clubs—is also on exhibit.

The workaday world of the Adirondacks is recalled in mining, logging, and boatbuilding exhibits. The museum possesses an excellent collection of handmade canoes and guideboats, including some of the lightweight masterpieces of nineteenth-century canoe-builder J. H. Rushton. The lovely sloop *Water Witch* hangs in the renovated gatehouse.

Special attention is given to what has been written and painted using Adirondack subjects. The museum's picture galleries display the work of artists from the Hudson River School and later periods.

The Adirondack Museum, Route 28N/30, Blue Mountain Lake (518–352–7311; www.adkmueum.org), is open daily from Memorial Day weekend through Columbus Day, 10:00 A.M. to 5:00 P.M. Admission is $15 for adults; $13 age 62 and over; $8 ages 6 to 12, students and military personnel; under 6 free. Allow three to five hours for your visit.

Of the roughly thirty-five Gilded Age Adirondack "Great Camps" that survive, one of the most spectacular—and least known—is *Camp Santanoni* in Newcomb, part of a 12,900-acre estate within the Adirondack Forest Preserve. Robert and Anna Pruyn of Albany commissioned architect Robert H. Robertson to design their camp, a partly Japanese-inspired, six-building log complex on the shores of Newcomb Lake. The main lodge buildings, completed in 1893, required 1,500 spruce trees for their construction. The buildings' common roof, covering 16,000 square feet and composed of fifty-eight distinct planes, was conceived to resemble a bird in flight.

Saved from demolition and placed on the National Register of Historic Places following their 1972 acquisition by the state, the more than forty-five buildings standing on the estate are under the care of an organization called Adirondack Architectural Heritage, which has undertaken a massive program of stabilization and restoration.

Santanoni is unusual even among remote Great Camps in that its main buildings are inaccessible except by nonmotorized travel. From the rambling gate lodge—itself a mammoth six-bedroom structure incorporating a stone gateway arch—visitors must continue for nearly 5 miles to reach the lake and main lodge. This means hiking, mountain biking, or cross-country skiing to traverse the generally flat terrain. In summer you can rest for the night before beginning the trip back, or go on to Moose Pond, which is even deeper within the preserve. There are eight designated primitive campsites around Newcomb Lake.

Interns posted at the gate lodge and main lodge during the summer months can provide interpretive information on the property, and a program of three guided tours is offered. For tour schedules and general information on Santanoni, contact Adirondack Architectural Heritage, 1790 Main Street, Keeseville 12944 (518–834–9328; www.aarch.org).

Studying a subject in a museum is a great way to learn about it. But experience is often the best teacher—even the best museum in the world can't convey how it *feels* to walk among mountains that are almost one million years old. *Siamese Ponds Wilderness Region* in western Warren County is a wilderness area in the true sense of the word: There are hundreds of miles of state-maintained trails and tote roads winding over hills and mountains, past streams, ponds, and lakes. Rockhounds will love exploring the passageways and valleys through a wide variety of rock formations. They were carved by glaciers of the Ice Age and by erosion caused by aeons of tumbling rocks carried along mountain streams, and hikers have found numerous exposed veins of minerals and semiprecious stones.

Siamese Ponds Wilderness Region has entrance points from Stony Creek, Thurman, Wevertown, Johnsburg, North Creek, and North River. Information is available in the *Guide to Adirondack Trails: Central Region*, published by the Adirondack Mountain Club (518–668–4447; www.adk.org).

Much of the 98-mile-long shoreline of ***Raquette Lake*** is inaccessible by road. But everyone knows the U.S. mail always gets through—this time with the help of the Bird family, who has been providing mail service since 1942. The original delivery boat was a Gar Wood speedboat. Today Bird family members deliver the mail Monday through Saturday and also offer tours of the lake by appointment. The fare is $12.00 for adults and $6.00 for children under 12. The livery also rents canoes, pontoons, motor and pedal boats, and sells bait. ***Bird's Boat Livery*** is on Route 28, Raquette Lake, (315) 354–4441.

With its thirty-one-acre campus, resident naturalists, and live exhibits, the ***Wild Center*** has been described as a base camp for the Adirondacks. Here you can visit theaters showing high-definition films, explore hands-on nature exhibits, and encounter hundreds of live animals that live in the woods and waters: rare native trout, river otters, and even turtles the size of walnuts.

Three trails wind through the Wild Center, leading to boardwalks over Blue Pond, to raised overlooks at the oxbow marsh on the Raquette River.

The museum's Waterside Cafe serves locally produced fare and beverages from 10:00 A.M. to 6:00 P.M. daily. The Wild Center is located at 45 Museum Drive, Tupper Lake (518–359–7800; www.wildcenter.org). From Columbus Day to Memorial Day, the hours are Friday through Monday from 10:00 A.M. to 5:00 P.M. From Memorial Day to Columbus Day, the museum is open daily from 10:00 A.M. to 6:00 P.M. An adult ticket is $14.00; a youth ticket (ages 4–14) is $9.00; a senior ticket is $12.00.

Great Camp Sagamore, on Raquette Lake, is a prototypical Adirondack Great Camp. The National Historic Site with twenty-seven buildings was built in 1897 by William West Durant, who sold it in 1901 to Alfred Vanderbilt as a wilderness retreat. After Vanderbilt died on the *Lusitania* in 1915, his widow continued to entertain family and friends as "the hostess of the gaming crowd" for the next thirty-nine years.

Visitors to Sagamore can take a two-hour guided tour and, with reservations, stay overnight in one of the double-occupancy rooms (twin beds, bathroom down the hall). Buffet meals are served in the dining hall overlooking the lake. There are 20 miles of hiking trails, canoeing, and a semi-outdoor bowling alley! Request a program catalog to learn about special events.

Sagamore, Sagamore Road, P.O. Box 40, Raquette Lake 13436 (315–354–5311), has guided daily tours at 10:00 A.M. and 1:30 P.M. from late June to Labor Day and weekends at 1:30 P.M. in spring and fall. Admission is $12.00 for adults, $6.00 for children 12 and under. Should you wish to stay overnight, the proprietors remind you that "Sagamore is not a hotel, motel, or resort. It is, instead, a complete experience in living a 'bit of history' in an incomparable setting." For further information on acccomodations, check the Web site; www .sagamore.org.

More than 435 species of plants and trees, 18 varieties of orchids, and 28 varieties of ferns thrive in the Adirondacks' largest block of remote public land—the 50,000-acre *Moose River Recreation Area,* which is also home to several rare butterfly species, including the Arctic Skipper and the carnivorous Harvester. There are more than 40 miles of roads and 27 miles of trails to explore, and camping is provided at 140 primitive sites.

Nearby, just off Uncas Road in Inlet, is *Ferd's Bog,* where a 500-foot boardwalk permits visitors to traverse a rare open bog mat. Among the numerous unusual plants growing here are several species of rare orchids, including the white-fringed, rose Patagonia, and grass pink. Also watch for bug-eating pitcher plants.

Both of these areas are administered by New York State's Department of Environmental Conservation. For information call (315) 354–4611.

The Artworks, an artists' cooperative on Main Street in downtown Old Forge, features art and craftwork by Adirondack artists. Media include pottery, stained glass, jewelry, fine arts, basketry, folk art, fabric art, and photography. The shop is open year-round. For hours call (315) 369–2007.

"A Living Museum of Functional and Aesthetic Necessities: Everything from Abacuses to Zoom Binoculars" is how *Old Forge Hardware* describes itself. "The Adirondacks' Most General Store," serving the area since 1900, is fun to poke through anytime, but it's a haven on a rainy day. Old Forge Hardware, Main Street, Old Forge (315–369–6100), is open daily year-round except Easter, Thanksgiving, Christmas, and New Year's. Hours vary with the season, so call ahead.

Stillwater Reservoir, which abuts Pigeon Lake Wilderness, Five Ponds Wilderness, Pepperbox Wilderness, and Independence River Wild Forest, more than qualifies as an off-the-beaten-path destination. Both routes to the reservoir, from either Lowville or the Old Forge–Eagle Bay area, include 10-mile drives along narrow dirt roads through the wilderness. But we certainly can't say it's undiscovered. The site's very remoteness has contributed to its increasing popularity over the years, and the New York Department of Environmental Conservation, which oversees the area, has restricted camping along the shoreline to designated sites, or to at least 150 feet inland from the reservoir's high-water mark.

Camping beyond this perimeter, however, remains relatively unrestricted and affords some of the region's best opportunities for wilderness tenting, as well as fine flat-water canoeing, motorboating (proceed with caution; there are numerous navigational hazards), fishing (splake, bass, perch, and bullheads), snowmobiling, and cross-country skiing.

Campsites at the 6,700-acre reservoir are free of charge and available on a first-come, first-served basis. Permits, however, are required, and can be obtained, along with specific driving instructions, at the Stillwater Forest Ranger Headquarters; call (315) 376-8030 or visit www.stillwaterresevoir.com.

Explore one of the world's largest ice arena complexes at the *Olympic Center Sports Complex* in downtown *Lake Placid.* The venue for the 1932 and 1980 Winter Olympic Games, it's perhaps best remembered as the site of the 1980 "Miracle on Ice," the unlikely victory of the young U.S. hockey squad over the U.S.S.R.'s powerhouse Red Army team. The complex has four indoor rinks, a museum, cafeteria, and gift shop and is open for public skating from late June through early September on weekdays for just $5.00 (skate rental is $3.00). There are ice shows here most Saturday nights throughout the summer months.

If you're looking for a bit more stimulation, how about rocketing down the only dedicated bobsled run in America on a wheeled sled at a speed of more than 45 mph? The sleds at *Verizon Sports Complex* are piloted by professional drivers and brakemen and operate from late June through mid-October, Wednesday through Sunday from 10:00 A.M. to 12:30 P.M. and 1:30 to 4:00 P.M. The fee is $65 for the bobsled and $45 for the luge; the ride is subject to weather and bobsled run conditions. Call (518) 523-4436 for information.

Other activities at the complex include biathlon target shooting (late June through Labor Day), Wednesday through Sunday 10:00 A.M. to 4:00 P.M. with a charge of $5.00 for five rounds; and mountain biking on Mt. Van Hoevenberg (rentals available). From early July through late August, freestyle aerial skiing demonstrations (the skiers end up in the pool) are held on Wednesday at the MacKenzie-Intervale Ski Jumping complex, and, on Saturday, Nordic ski jumping is held at the 90-meter jump.

Visitors can defray costs for all of the above activities as well as take a ride up the chairlift at Whiteface Mountain, visit the Skydeck observation area at the Olympic Jumping Complex, and ride up Whiteface Mt. Veteran's Memorial Highway by purchasing a Kodak Summer Passport for just $19 a person.

For information on all of these activities as well as special events, call the Olympic Center Main Office, Lake Placid, at (518) 523-1655 or (800) 462-6236.

A sauna and a massage are never more welcome than after a day on the wind-chilled ski slopes, and fortunately, Lake Placid is home to the ***Mirror Lake Inn Resort and Spa,*** one of the country's top small hotels. It's perhaps best known for its award-winning kitchen, with both the casual dining and the formal restaurant enjoying flawless service and spectacular views of the lake. Rates for standard rooms range from $220 to $380, suites from $595 to $930. Call (518) 523–2544 or go to www.mirrorlakeinn.com to find out about their special food and wine events.

John Brown's body lies a-moulderin' in the grave, according to the old spiritual, and that grave is in North Elba, near Lake Placid, part of the ***John Brown Farm State Historic Site.*** Brown was a militant abolitionist who led the 1859 raid on the U.S. arsenal at Harper's Ferry, Virginia, in hopes of arming black slaves to revolt against their masters. The plan failed, and Brown was executed and buried here, along with two of his sons and several of his followers, who were killed at Harper's Ferry.

Brown moved to this area in 1849, trying to establish an agricultural community called Timbucto for free blacks. This well-intentioned scheme failed, and Brown joined his sons in Kansas during the volatile 1850s, when the struggle to decide whether the territory would be admitted to the Union as a slave state or a free state earned it the nickname "Bloody Kansas." Brown, of course, made a name for himself in Kansas, taking part in the clash at Osawatomie.

The farmhouse at the John Brown Farm State Historic Site, 2 John Brown Road, Lake Placid (518–523–3900; www.nysparks.state.ny.us/sites), is open from May 1 to October 31, daily (except Tuesday) 10:00 A.M. to 5:00 P.M. The grounds are open all year during daylight hours. Admission for house tours is $2.00 for adults, $1.00 for children and seniors.

At the ***Adirondack Guideboats Woodward Boat Shop,*** Chris Woodward builds Adirondack guide boats using the same techniques that Willard Hanmer, one of the boat's original builders, used back in the 1930s. And he's making them in the same building. The boats—the style is indigenous to the region between Saranac Lake and Old Forge—are used for hunting and guiding. Chris also makes and sells paddles, seats, and oars and sells boat accessories. The shop, at 9 Algonquin Avenue (Route 3), Saranac Lake (518–891–3961), is open weekdays 9:00 A.M. to 5:00 P.M. or by appointment. Call ahead to make sure he'll be there.

In 1887 Robert Louis Stevenson set sail from Bournemouth, England, for a small farmhouse in Saranac Lake, the village he dubbed "the Little Switzerland in the Adirondacks." He lived here with his family, writing *The Master of Ballantrae* and *The Wrong Box,* skating at nearby Moody Pond, and enjoying life in the mountains. He wrote to a friend of his life here: "We are high up in the

Adirondack Mountains living in a guide's cottage in the most primitive fashion. The maid does the cooking (we have little beyond venison and bread to cook) and the boy comes every morning to carry water from a distant spring for drinking purposes. It is already very cold but we have calked the doors and windows as one calks a boat, and have laid in a store of extraordinary garments made by the Canadian Indians."

Today the cottage, preserved in its original state, holds the country's largest collection of Stevenson's personal mementos, including his Scottish smoking jacket, with a sprig of heather in the breast pocket, original letters, and his yachting cap. There's a plaque here by sculptor Gutzon Borglum, donated by the artist who regarded the writer as "the great sculptor of words."

The **Robert Louis Stevenson Memorial Cottage,** Stevenson Lane, Saranac Lake (518–891–1462 or 800–347–1992), is open July through Columbus Day, Tuesday to Sunday 9:30 A.M. to noon and 1:00 to 4:30 P.M. The rest of the year it is opened by appointment. Admission is $5.00 for adults; children under 12, free. Group rates are available.

It's difficult to suggest that a forest preserve encompassing almost six million acres—roughly the size of the state of New Hampshire—is off the beaten path. But **Adirondack State Park** includes some of the state's finest out-of-

Elves Wanted

Many places call themselves **Santa's Workshop,** but how many are actually located in the North Pole? North Pole, NY, that is. This forerunner of modern theme parks opened in 1949, the brainchild of Lake Placid businessman Julian Reiss and designer/artist Arto Monaco. The result of this collaboration was a fantasy village populated by storybook characters, where children can ride the Candy Cane Express or the Christmas Carousel; visit with Santa and Mrs. Claus; mail out cards postmarked "North Pole, NY" and "Santa's Workshop"—and generally make merry.

Santa's Workshop is in the High Peaks area of Adirondacks Park on the Whiteface Mountain Memorial Highway (Route 431), 1½ miles northwest of the intersection with Route 86 in the town of Wilmington (800–806–0215 or 518–946–2211; www.northpoleny.com). General admission is $18.95 for adults, $16.95 for children 2 to 16, and $15.95 for seniors. The park is open from early September through late December, generally on Saturday and Sunday. Hours vary; in early December, the park is open Sunday evenings; as the holidays approach, it's open Monday through Friday evenings as well. Call ahead or check the Web site to avoid disappointment.

From mid-November through mid-December, two-night family packages are offered; they include lodging (at various nearby properties), breakfasts and dinners, entertainment, and admission to Santa's Workshop.

Robert Louis Stevenson Memorial Cottage

the-way attractions and offers some of its best opportunities to leave civilization behind. The park is a unique mixture of public and private lands. Approximately 130,000 year-round residents live in 105 towns and villages, but 43 percent of the total acreage is state owned, constitutionally protected "forever wild" land.

To best get a sense of the park, stop at one of the two **Visitor Interpretive Centers:** Paul Smiths VIC, Route 30, **Paul Smiths** (518–327–3000); or Newcomb VIC, Route 28N, **Newcomb** (518–582–2000; www.apa.state.ny .us/vic). Both are open daily year-round from 9:00 A.M. to 5:00 P.M. except Thanksgiving and Christmas. Admission is free. If you're interested in camping at one of the 500 campsites spread over forty-eight islands on three of the Adirondack's most scenic lakes, request the brochure "Camping in the New York State Forest Preserve."

The Adirondacks and, in fact, much of New York State were once the territory of the **Iroquois Confederacy.** Perhaps the most politically sophisticated of all the tribal groupings of North American Indians, the Iroquois actually comprised five distinct tribes—the Mohawks, Senecas,

howit'sdone

Park administrators from throughout the world have come to New York State to study the management of Adirondack State Park.

Onondagas, Oneidas, and Cayugas—who were later joined by the Tuscaroras to form the "six nations" of the confederation. The history and contemporary circumstances of the Iroquois are documented in the **Six Nations Indian**

Museum, a "living museum" that presents its material from a Native American point of view.

The museum, opened in 1954, was built by the Faddens, members of the Mohawk Nation, and is still operated and staffed by members of that family. The museum's design reflects the architecture of the traditional Haudenosaunee (Six Iroquois National Confederacy) bark house. The longhouse is a metaphor for the Confederacy, symbolically stretching from east to west across ancestral territory.

A visit to the museum—jam-packed with artifacts—is a reminder that for centuries before Europeans arrived, the Iroquois were building a society. Throughout the season Native Americans visit to talk about their histories, cultures, and their people's contributions to contemporary society.

The Six Nations Indian Museum, Roakdale Road (County Route 30), *Onchiota* (518–891–2299), is open daily except Monday from July 1 through Labor Day, 10:00 A.M. to 5:00 P.M. and by appointment in June and September. Admission is $2.00 for adults and $1.00 for children.

Once a part of the corridor used by trading and war parties in the days of the French and Indian Wars, the area around *Plattsburgh,* on Lake Champlain, had settled into a peaceful mercantile existence by the end of the eighteenth century. It was in Plattsburgh that the *Kent-Delord House* was built in 1797 by William Bailey. Following several changes of ownership, the house was purchased in 1810 by Henry Delord, a refugee from the French Revolution who had prospered as a merchant and served as a justice of the peace in Peru, New York, before moving to Plattsburgh. Delord remodeled the house in the fashionable Federal style of the era and in 1811 moved in, thus beginning more than a century of his family's residence here.

Just three years after the Delords moved into their new home, the War of 1812 came to Plattsburgh in the form of a southward thrust by British forces along Lake Champlain. But the enemy was repelled later that month by the Delords' friend Commodore Thomas Macdonough in the Battle of Plattsburgh.

But What about Bridesmaids?

In earlier times, the mothers of Iroquois maidens arranged the marriages of their daughters. A girl would acknowledge her mother's choice by putting a basket of bread at the prospective bridegroom's door. If he and his mother accepted, they would send a basket of food back to the girl and her family. If the offer was turned down, the girl's offering would remain untouched.

Aside from the wartime seizure of the house, the story of the Kent-Delord House might be that of any home of a provincial bourgeois family during the nineteenth century. The difference, of course, is that this house has survived remarkably intact. It offers a fine opportunity to see how an upper-middle-class family lived from the days just after the revolution through the Victorian age and, not incidentally, houses a distinguished collection of American portrait art, including the work of John Singleton Copley, George Freeman, and Henry Inman.

The Kent-Delord House Museum, 17 Cumberland Avenue, Plattsburgh (518–561–1035; www.kentdelordhouse.org), is open March and April by appointment; May through December, Tuesday through Saturday from noon to 4:00 P.M.; the last tour begins at 3:15 P.M. Admission is $5.00 for adults, $3.00 for students, and $2.00 for children under 12.

Dean and DeLuca have nothing on Zaidee and Trevor Laughlin, proprietors of Plattsburgh's *The Grand Onion.* The little shop, tucked onto a side street and jammed to the rafters with gourmet comestibles, is a godsend to every educated palate in the North Country. Here you'll find fresh artisan breads, imported and domestic deli meats, including pungent Italian salamis, cheeses from around the world (and around the Lake Champlain region), and homemade salads. Choices for a carryout dinner might be smoked salmon cakes, chicken piccata, or duck confit with leeks.

The Grand Onion, located at 373 Route 3 (Upper Cornelia Street), is open Monday through Friday 10:00 A.M. to 7:00 P.M., Saturday 10:00 A.M. to 5:00 P.M.; 11:00 A.M. to 3:00 P.M. on Sunday. Subscribe to their e-newsletter to keep up on new products, many of which can be mail ordered (518–56–ONION; www.grandonion.com).

Yarborough Square carries the works of about 200 artists and craftspeople from the United States and Canada. A large collection of pottery, including stoneware, porcelain, and raku, is on display, as are metal sculptures and hand-crafted jewelry—everything from recycled glass to wrought-iron pieces, and candles. The gallery, which also represents several painters and numerous crafts people, is truly a North Country find. It's at 672 Bear Swamp Road, *Peru,* (518) 643–7057 and is open daily from 10:00 A.M. to 6:00 P.M.

The *Alice T. Miner Museum* was created in 1824 by Mrs. Miner, a pioneer in the colonial revival movement and wife of railroad industrialist and philanthropist William H. Miner. She worked for the next twenty-six years, until her death, to assemble the collection in the fifteen-room museum. Included in the exhibit are period furniture; miniature furniture once toted about by traveling salesmen; a large collection of china, porcelain, and glass; early samplers; War of 1812 muskets; and other objects of early Americana.

The Alice T. Miner Museum, 9618 Main Street, Route 9, *Chazy* (518–846–7336; www.minermuseum.org), is open Tuesday through Saturday 10:00 A.M. to 4:00 P.M., with guided tours at 10:00 and 11: 30 A.M. and 1:00 and 2:30 P.M.; closed December 23 through January 31 and holidays. Admission is $3.00 for adults, $2.00 for seniors, and $1.00 for students. School groups are free.

Western Adirondacks, Saint Lawrence Valley, and Thousand Islands

The *Akwesasne Cultural Center* is dedicated to preserving the past, present, and future of the Akwesasne Mohawk people, whose history in the area dates back thousands of years. The museum houses more than 3,000 artifacts and an extensive collection of black-ash splint basketry; it also offers classes in such traditional art forms as basketry, quillwork, and water drums. The library houses one of the largest Native American collections in northern New York and includes information on indigenous people throughout North America.

Akwesasne Cultural Center, Route 37, *Hogansburg* (518–358–2240; www.nc3r.org/akwelibr), is open daily year-round except Sunday and major holidays. In July and August it is open Monday through Friday 8:30 A.M. to 4:30 P.M.; from September to June, Monday 12:30 to 5:30 P.M.; Tuesday through Thursday 8:30 A.M. to 8:30 P.M.; Friday 8:30 A.M. to 4:30 P.M.; and Saturday 11:00 A.M. to 3:00 P.M. Suggested museum contribution is $2.00 for adults and $1.00 for children ages 5 to 16.

Horace Greeley famously said, "Go west, young man," and that's just what young Frederic Remington did. Born in 1861 in Ogdensburg, on the St. Lawrence Seaway, Remington quit Yale at the age of nineteen and headed for the wide open spaces. He spent five years traveling, taking in the vistas and the cowboys and the horses that would inspire his paintings and sculpture. By 1885 he was already making his name as an illustrator and artist. When Remington died after an operation in 1909, he was at the peak of his popularity. His widow returned to Ogdensburg and bequeathed the artist's collection of paintings and sculpture to the Ogdensburg Public Library; the collection now forms the *Frederic Remington Art Museum,* housed in the 1810 house where Mrs. Remington lived until her death.

The collection includes bronzes, oil paintings, and hundreds of pen-and-ink sketches by Remington, as well as pictures he collected by his contemporaries, including Charles Dana Gibson and Childe Hassam.

The Frederic Remington Art Museum, 303 Washington Street, Ogdensburg (315–393–2425; www.fredericremington.org), is open from May 1 through Octo-

Lock and Load?

Fifty years ago, the village of Mannsville, 21 miles south of Watertown, was the site of an unusual orphan asylum. The Klan Haven Home occupied a big frame house set on 300 acres, where boys could train in agriculture and the girls learned what was then called "domestic science." The curriculum probably also included a brand of social studies, because the home was run by the Ku Klux Klan for some thirty orphaned children of Klan members. It has long since ceased to operate.

ber 31, Monday through Saturday 10:00 A.M. to 5:00 P.M. and Sunday 1:00 to 5:00 P.M.; from November 1 to April 30, hours are Wednesday through Saturday 11:00 A.M. to 5:00 P.M. and Sunday 1:00 to 5:00 P.M. Closed legal holidays. Admission is $8.00 for adults, $7.00 for students and senior citizens, and free for children 5 and under.

Around the turn of the century, when Frederic Remington looked west for artistic inspiration, hotel magnate George C. Boldt turned instead to his native Germany. Boldt's creativity wasn't a matter of putting paint to canvas or molding bronze, however. He was out to build the 120-room *Boldt Castle,* Rhineland-style, on one of the Thousand Islands in the St. Lawrence River.

Boldt, who owned the Waldorf-Astoria in New York and the Bellevue-Stratford Hotel in Philadelphia, bought his island at the turn of the century from a man named Hart, but that isn't why it is named Heart Island. The name derives from the fact that the hotelier had the island physically reshaped into the configuration of a heart, as a token of devotion to his wife, Louise, for whom the entire project was to be a monumental expression of his love.

Construction of the six-story castle and its numerous outbuildings began in 1900. Boldt hired masons, woodcarvers, landscapers, and other craftspeople from all over the world to execute details ranging from terra-cotta wall inlays and roof tiles to a huge, opalescent glass dome. He planned and built a smaller castle as a temporary residence and eventual playhouse, and he built an underground tunnel for bringing supplies from the docks to the main house. There were bowling alleys, a sauna, an indoor swimming pool—in short, it was to be the sort of place that would take years to finish and decades to enjoy.

But there weren't enough years left. Louise Boldt died suddenly in 1904, and George Boldt, heartbroken, wired his construction supervisors to stop all work. The walls and roof of the castle were by this time essentially finished, but crated fixtures such as mantels and statuary were left where they stood, and the bustling island fell silent. Boldt never again set foot in his empty castle, on which he had spent $2.5 million.

Boldt died in 1916, and two years later the island and its structures were purchased by Edward J. Noble, the inventor of Life Savers candy. Noble and his heirs ran the deteriorating castle as a tourist attraction until 1977, when it was given to the Thousand Islands Bridge Authority, which has invested millions of dollars in rehabilitation efforts to preserve the historic structure.

Boldt Castle, Heart Island, Alexandria Bay (315–482–2520 or 800–8–ISLAND; www.boldtcastle.com), is accessible via water taxi from the upper and lower docks on James Street in *Alexandria Bay,* as well as to tour-boat patrons departing from both the American and the Canadian shores. The castle is open from Mother's Day to Columbus Day, Saturday and Sunday 10:00 A.M. to 7:30 P.M.; July and August, daily 10:00 A.M. to 6:30 P.M. For information call ahead, or write 1000 Islands International Council, P.O. Box 400, Alexandria Bay 13607. Admission is $5.75 for adults and $3.50 for children ages 6 to 12. Groups of twenty or more, senior citizens, and military personnel receive a discount.

When Boldt bought Heart Island it already had a house on it—if you can call an eighty-room "cottage" a house. It had been built in the late 1800s by Elizur Kirke Hart, who spared no expense in its construction. Boldt and his family summered here for several years before he decided the cottage didn't suit him. When he began construction of Boldt Castle, he had the cottage dismantled and skidded across the frozen St. Lawrence River to nearby *Wellesley Island,* where fifty of the original rooms were reconstructed. The Boldts used the renamed Wellesley House as their headquarters while the castle was being built, but in the 1950s the river cottage was torn down.

what'sinthewater?

The St. Lawrence River is renowned for game fishing. Among the most common: large- and smallmouth bass, Northern pike, yellow perch, and walleye.

The remaining thirty rooms of Hart's original home were also erected on Wellesley Island and became the Thousand Islands Country Club, a place for ladies to sit over afternoon tea while the menfolk played a round of golf. In later years a newer clubhouse was built across the street, and the Hart House was renamed the Golf Course House.

In 1994 Rev. Dudley Danielson and his wife, Kathy, bought the now run-down thirty-room club house and have painstakingly converted it into the elegant *Hart House Inn.* Many of the dwelling's original features have been retained and renovated, including a massive pink granite fireplace in the lobby entrance. Each of the five beautifully decorated guest suites has a canopied bed, Italian ceramic tile whirlpool bath, views of the St. Lawrence, and fireplaces. Three rooms and suites in the older wing (open May through October) have private baths; the classic two-room Sunset Suite is perfect for a family of five, with library fireplace, two bedrooms, and deck with a great river view. A multi-course candlelit breakfast is served on the wraparound porch overlooking the golf course (in the winter, it's served in the fireplaced dining room).

Kathy is the granddaughter of a Hungarian innkeeper and takes great pride in her cooking. Reverend Danielson officiates at many weddings in his Grace Chapel; it also serves as a retreat for quiet contemplation.

The Hart House, P.O. Box 70, Wellesley Island 13640 (315–482–LOVE or 888–481–LOVE; www.harthouseinn.com), is open year-round. Rates range from $135 for a classic room midweek to $315 for the stunning Kashmir Garden suite on a weekend. In winter, two-night packages feature an elegant fireside dinner. The chapel is available from May through November.

If you find the most appealing aspect of George Boldt's heyday to be the sleek mahogany runabouts and graceful skiffs that plied the waters of the Thousand Islands and other Gilded Age resorts, make sure you find your way to the *Antique Boat Museum* in *Clayton.* The museum is a freshwater boat-lover's dream, housing slender, mirror-finished launches; antique canoes; distinctive St. Lawrence River skiffs; handmade guideboats—about 200 historic small craft in all.

The Antique Boat Museum takes no sides in the eternal conflict between sailing purists and "stinkpotters," being broad enough in its philosophy to house a fine collection of antique outboard and inboard engines, including the oldest outboard known to exist. The one distinction rigidly adhered to pertains to construction material: All of the boats exhibited here are made of wood.

The Antique Boat Museum, 750 Mary Street, Clayton 13624 (315–686–4104), is open from early May through mid-October, daily from 9:00 A.M. to 5:00 P.M. Admission is $12.00 for adults, $11.00 for seniors, AAA, and military personnel; $6.00 for students ages 6 to 17; under 6 free.

When the *Thousand Islands Inn* opened in 1897, it was one of more than two dozen hotels serving visitors to the region. Today it is the last of the great hostelries that still offers guests all the amenities of a full-service establishment.

In addition to its distinction as a survivor, the inn has yet another claim to fame: Thousand Island salad dressing was first served to the dining public here in the early 1900s. The dressing was created by Sophia LaLonde for her husband, a guide, to serve to fishing parties as part of their shore dinners. One of his clients, a New York City stage actress named May Irwin, loved the dressing and gave it the name Thousand Island. She also gave the recipe to George C. Boldt, owner of Boldt Castle and New York's Waldorf-Astoria Hotel. He ordered his maître d', Oscar Tschirky, to put it on the hotel menu. But the Thousand Islands

The Secret Recipe

Allen and Susan Benas, owners of the Thousand Islands Inn, sell their Thousand Island dressing, so they are naturally reluctant to give out the recipe. When we called to ask them about the one James Beard gives in his book, *American Cookery,* Allen said, "He's remotely on the right track, especially with the chili sauce—most people use catsup; but ours has several other ingredients." It's the closest we can come, so give it a try.

James Beard's recipe for Thousand Island dressing:

Blend ½ cup chili sauce, I finely chopped pimiento, I tablespoon grated onion, and 2 tablespoons finely chopped green pepper with 1 cup mayonnaise.

Inn had already made it into the record book: LaLonde had also given the recipe to Ella Bertrand, whose family owned the inn, then called the Herald Hotel.

Most of the rooms have a view of the St. Lawrence River and have been restored to re-create the flavor of the late 1800s, but with all modern conveniences. The inn's restaurant is a recipient of the Golden Fork Award of the Gourmet Diners Society of North America. It serves three meals daily.

The Thousand Islands Inn is at 335 Riverside Drive, Clayton (315–686–3030 or 800–544–4241; www.1000islands.com/inn). Room rates range from $75 to $135. The inn is open from mid-May until mid-September.

Are you yearning to sail to a foreign land? ***Horne's Ferry,*** the only international auto/passenger ferry on the St. Lawrence River, crosses over to Wolfe Island, Ontario, Canada, in just ten minutes. The ferry makes hourly crossings from 8:00 A.M. to 7:30 P.M. daily from early May through late October. Rates are $12.00 each way for a car and driver, and $2.00 for additional passengers or pedestrians. For information write to P.O. Box 116, ***Cape Vincent*** 13618 or call (315) 783–0638.

The only place in the northeastern United States to see prairie smoke, a flower whose feathery plumes expand as it goes to seed, is in ***Chaumont Barrens,*** a unique "alvar" landscape characterized by a mosaic of austere, windswept vegetation.

Alvar sites lie scattered along an arc from here, through Ontario, to northern Michigan. Scientists hypothesize that the landscapes, distinguished by a linear pattern of vegetation, were formed during the retreat of the last glacier approximately 10,000 years ago, when a huge ice dam burst and a torrent swept away all surface debris and dissolved limestone bedrock along cracks and fissures.

The rare combination of extreme conditions at ***Chaumont*** have created a 2-mile landscape of exposed outcrops, fissures, moss gardens, patches of woods, shrub savannas, and open grasslands.

Chaumont Barrens, on Van Alstyne Road, Chaumont, is a property of the Nature Conservancy and is open daily from a half hour before sunrise until a half hour before sunset. For information call (585) 546–8030 or (315) 387–3600.

The international cooperation exemplified by the St. Lawrence Seaway and the peaceful coexistence that allows pleasurecraft to sail unimpeded along the boundary waters of the St. Lawrence River and Lake Ontario are things we take for granted today, but this state of affairs has hardly existed since time immemorial. Barely more than a century ago, the U.S. Navy kept an active installation at ***Sackets Harbor Battlefield,*** on Lake Ontario's Black River Bay, against the possibility of war with Canada. And during the War of 1812, this small lakeport actually did see combat between American and British forces.

At the time the war began, ***Sackets Harbor*** was not yet a flourishing American naval port and the site of a busy shipyard and supply depot. It was from here, in April 1813, that the Americans launched their attack upon Toronto; a month later the tables were turned when the depleted American garrison at the harbor was beleaguered by a British attack upon the shipyard. The defenders repulsed the attack but lost most of their supplies to fire in the course of the struggle.

Today's visitor to Sackets Harbor can still see many of the facilities of the old naval base, including officers' homes and sites associated with the 1813 battle.

Sackets Harbor Battlefield State Historic Site, 504 West Main Street, Sackets Harbor (315–646–3634; www.sacketsharborbattlefield.org), is open from Memorial Day to Columbus Day and the first two weekends in December. Admission is $3.00 for adults, $2.00 for seniors and students, free for children under 12.

Ski NY

When powder falls, so many skiers think about heading for the Green Mountains of Vermont; but there are more than thirty fantastic ski resorts here in New York, including the 4,867-foot Whiteface Mountain, site of two Olympic downhills. This peak in the heart of the Adirondack State Park boasts the greatest vertical drop in the East as well as a thirteen-acre terrain park and a 450-foot super half-pipe. Get weather updates and other information on New York ski stations at www.skiandrideny.com.

If you're going to set out on the 454-mile Seaway Trail—the state's only National Scenic Byway—plan to stop first at the *Seaway Trail Discovery Center,* housed in a three-story, 1817 limestone, Federal-style former hotel overlooking the lake. The New York State Office of Parks, Recreation and Preservation opened the facility to provide a "windshield" overview of the trail and its unique characteristics. Nine rooms of exhibits highlight the area's natural history, recreation, agriculture, people, architecture, and maritime history.

The Seaway Trail Discovery Center, P.O. Box 660, Ray and West Main Streets, Sackets Harbor (800–SEAWAY–T; www.seawaytrail.com), is open year-round: daily May through October from 10:00 A.M. to 5:00 P.M.; November through April, Tuesday through Saturday from 10:00 A.M. to 5:00 P.M. Admission is $4.00 for adults, $2.00 for children.

The *American Maple Museum and Hall of Fame,* dedicated to preserving the history and evolution of the North American maple syrup industry, houses three floors of antique sugaring equipment, logging tools, and artifacts. There are replicas of a sugarhouse and a lumber camp kitchen, and a Hall of Fame. The museum hosts three all-you-can-eat pancake breakfasts a year—in February, May, and September—to raise funds. There is also an ice cream social around July 1, with entertainment and maple treats; a Maple Weekend in mid-March; and, in December, "Christmas in *Croghan,*" with hot chocolate and maple cream on crackers. Call for dates.

The American Maple Museum and Hall of Fame, Main Street, Route 812, Croghan (315–346–1107; www.lcida.org/maplemuseum), is open Friday, Saturday, and Monday, 11:00 A.M. to 4:00 P.M. from Memorial Day to June 30; daily except Sunday, 11:00 A.M. to 4:00 P.M. from July 1 to early September. Admission is $4.00 for adults; $1.00 for children 5 to 14; $10 per family (two adults with two or more children).

The *North American Fiddler's Hall of Fame & Museum,* dedicated to "each and every fiddler who ever made hearts light and happy with his lilting music," preserves, perpetuates, and promotes the art of fiddling and the dances pertaining to the art. It displays artifacts and collects tapes of fiddlers, and since its inception in 1976, has inducted a new member (or members) into its Hall of Fame each year. The museum, across from Cedar Pines Restaurant, Motel, and Campground in Osceola, is open Sunday from 2:00 to 5:00 P.M. from Memorial Day through the first Sunday in October (except for the third weekend in September), during major events, and by appointment. Every Sunday afternoon from Memorial Day to the first Sunday in October there's also a free concert (donations are welcome). For information call (315) 599–7009.

In the latter part of the nineteenth century, Joseph and John Moser emigrated from Alsace-Lorraine to Kirschnerville. They cleared a plot of land, built a dwelling, purchased farm animals, and then brought the rest of their family from overseas. The Mosers were Mennonites, and three generations lived and worshiped here until the 1980s, when the farm was purchased by a group who wanted it to be preserved as a living history of the life and faith of the area's settlers.

Today the **Mennonite Heritage Farm,** under the auspices of the Adirondack Mennonite Heritage Association, tells of the life of the early Amish-Mennonite settlers. In addition to exhibits in the farmhouse, there is a Worship Room with the original benches (meetings were held in homes on a rotational basis until 1912, when the Croghan Mennonite Church was built). There are also a number of outbuildings, including a granary with a display of early tools and equipment.

On the first Saturday of July, the farm holds a special, day-long Zwanzig-stein Fest, which features traditional Mennonite foods and crafts, a petting zoo, bread and butter and ice-cream making demonstrations, and horse-pulled wagon rides. The highlight of the day is the mini-auction of quilts, "comforts," and antiques.

The Mennonite Heritage Farm, Erie Canal Road, Croghan (315–346–1122; off-season, 315–853–6879 or 376–8502; www.midyork.org), is open varying hours during July and August, or by appointment. Admission is charged only for the fest, but donations are gratefully accepted at any time.

The 2,100-acre **Whetstone Gulf State Park,** built in and around a 3-mile-long gorge cut in the eastern edge of the Tug Hill plateau, provides one of the most spectacular scenic vistas east of the Rocky Mountains. Mostly undeveloped, the park has sixty-two campsites, six of which are streamfront, a picnic area along Whetstone Creek, a man-made swimming area, and several hiking and cross-country ski trails (one circles the gorge). A 500-acre reservoir above the gorge provides canoeing and fishing (it's stocked with tiger muskies and largemouth bass).

Whetstone Gulf State Park, Route 26, **Lowville** (315–376–6630 or 482–2593; www.nysparks.state.ny.us/parks), is open year-round, with admission charged during the summer months. Limited facilities are available in winter but the heated Beach Building has restrooms and is open from the second week in December until the first week of March. To reserve a campsite call the New York State Campsite and Cabin Reservation Program at (800) 456–CAMP. Admission is charged from two weeks before Memorial Day until two weeks after Labor Day.

The man who built **Constable Hall** was presented with a rather generous birthright: four million acres of Adirondack wilderness. His father, William Constable Sr., purchased the property with two other New York City capitalist real-estate speculators and ultimately became the principal owner and chief developer. He sold large tracts to European and American land companies and families from New England, launching the settlement of the north country. In 1819 William Constable Jr. built a Georgian mansion patterned on a family-owned estate in Ireland, and five generations of the Constable family lived there until 1947, when the house became a museum. The original deed is just one of the family mementos displayed at the home, which still has many of its original furnishings.

Constable Hall, *Constableville* (315–397–2323), is open daily except Monday from June to October 15. Hours are Tuesday through Saturday 10:00 A.M. to 4:00 P.M., and Sunday 1:00 to 4:00 P.M. Admission is $3.00 for adults and $1.50 for children.

There are barely a dozen lighthouses in North America in which visitors can stay overnight. One is *Selkirk Lighthouse,* built in 1838, on Lake Ontario at the mouth of the Salmon River. Listed on the National Register of Historic Places, the lighthouse is heated, has four bedrooms (two single and four double beds), a kitchen, living room, and bathroom, and color cable TV with HBO. The lighthouse can be rented from April through early December and sleeps up to ten people. The lighthouse is part of a five-acre compound that includes a charter fishing fleet, cabins, boat rentals, and a launch ramp. For information contact Lighthouse Marina, Lake Road, P.O. Box 228, *Pulaski* 13142 (315–298–6688), or check out their Web site: www.salmon-river.com.

Just north of Utica, in the foothills of the Adirondacks, you'll find *Steuben Memorial State Historic Site.* Frederick von Steuben was a Prussian officer who, at the age of forty-seven, emigrated to the United States in 1777 to help drill the soldiers of the Continental Army. His first assignment was a challenging one. He was sent to the American winter encampment at Valley Forge, where morale was flagging and discipline, in the face of elemental hardship such as hunger and bitter cold, was virtually nonexistent.

As might be expected of a good Prussian officer, von Steuben rose to the occasion. Washington's troops at Valley Forge might not have had boots, but they learned how to march in file, as well as proceed through the other elements of classic military drill and perform effectively with the eighteenth-century frontline weapon of choice, the bayonet. The German émigré even found time to write a masterful treatise on military training, *Regulations for the Order and Discipline of the Troops of the United States.*

Having served as inspector general of the Continental Army until the end of the war, von Steuben was richly rewarded by the nation of which he had lately become a citizen. Among his other rewards was a New York State grant of 16,000 acres of land. Allowed to pick his own site, he chose the area par-

Steuben Memorial State Historic Site

tially occupied today by the Steuben Memorial State Historic Site and built a simple two-room log house.

In 1936 the state erected a replica of von Steuben's house on a site located within the fifty acres it had recently purchased as his memorial (the drillmaster is buried beneath an imposing monument not far from here, despite his wish that he lie in an unmarked grave). The cabin is open to visitors. Historical interpretations reflecting the military life of the Revolutionary War soldier are held at the memorial, and staff members are available to discuss the baron's life.

The Steuben Memorial State Historic Site, Starr Hill Road, **Remsen** (315–768–7224), is open from Memorial Day to Labor Day, Wednesday through Saturday 10:00 A.M. to 5:00 P.M., Sunday and Monday holidays 1:00 to 5:00 P.M. Guided tours are available; call ahead. Admission is free.

Places to Stay in the Adirondacks

ALEXANDRIA BAY

The Edgewood Resort
22467 Edgewood Road
888–EDGEWOOD
(334–3966)
www.1000islands.com/
edgewood

GLENS FALLS

Glens Falls Inn
25 Sherman Avenue
(646) 824–8379
www.glensfallsinn.com

KEENE

Bark Eater Inn
Alstead Hill Road
(518) 576–2221
www.barkoater.com

LAKE LUZERNE

The Lamplight Inn
231 Lake Avenue
(800) 262–4668
www.lamplightinn.com

LAKE PLACID

**Best Western Golden
Arrow Hotel**
150 Main Street
(800) 582–5540
or (518) 523–3353
www.golden-arrow.com

REGIONAL TOURIST INFORMATION— THE ADIRONDACKS

Adirondacks Regional Information
(800) 487–6867 or (518) 846–8016
www.adk.com

Lake George Regional Chamber of Commerce
P.O. Box 272
Lake George
(518) 668–5755 or (800) 705–0059
www.lakegeorgechamber.com

Lake Placid/Essex County Visitors Center
2610 Main Street
Suite 2
Lake Placid
(518) 523–2445
www.lakeplacid.com

The 1,000 Islands Welcome Center
43373 Collins Landing
Alexandria Bay
(800) 847–5263 or (315) 482–2520
www.visit1000islands.com

Plattsburgh–North Country–Lake Champlain Regional Visitors Center
7061 Route 9
Plattsburgh
(518) 563–1000
www.northcountrychamber.com

Saranac Lake Chamber of Commerce
39 Main Street
Saranac Lake
(800) 347–1992
www.saranaclake.com

Saratoga Convention and Tourism Bureau
60 Railroad Place
Saratoga Springs
(518) 584–1531
www.discoversaratoga.com

Saratoga County Chamber of Commerce
28 Clinton Street
Saratoga Springs
(518) 584–3255
www.saratoga.org

Town of Webb Visitor Center
P.O. Box 68
Old Forge 13420
(315) 369–6983
www.oldforgeny.com

Urban Heritage Area Visitors Center
297 Broadway
Saratoga Springs
(518) 587–3241
www.saratoga.org

Warren County Tourism Municipal Center
1340 State Route 9
Lake George
(800) 365–1050 or (518) 761–6366
www.visitlakegeorge.com

Whiteface Mountain Regional Visitors Bureau
P.O. Box 277
Whiteface Mountain 12997
(518) 946–2255 or (888) WHITEFACE
www.whitefaceregion.com

Hilton Lake Placid Resort
1 Mirror Lake Drive
Lake Placid
(800) 755–5598 or (518)
523–4411
www.lphilton.com

NORTH CREEK

Copperfield Inn
224 Main Street
(518) 251–2500
www.copperfieldinn.com

ROCK CITY FALLS

The Mansion
801 Route 29
(888) 996–9977
www.themansionsaratoga
.com

SARANAC LAKE

**Hotel Saranac of Paul
Smiths College**
100 Main Street
(800) 937–0211 or (518)
891–2000
www.hotelsaranac.com

SARATOGA SPRINGS

Adelphi Hotel
355 Broadway
(518) 587–4688
www.adelphihotel.com

Batcheller Mansion Inn
20 Circular Street
(800) 616–7012 or (518)
584–7012
www.batchellermansion.com

TUPPER LAKE

The Wawbeek
Panther Mountain Road
Route 30
(800) 953–2656 or (518)
359–2656
www.wawbeek.com

WARRENSBURG

Merrill Magee House
3 Hudson Street
(518) 623–2449
www.merrillmageehouse.com

**Seasons Bed and
Breakfast**
3822 Main Street
Warrensburg
(518) 623–3832
www.Seasons-bandb.com

WELLESLEY ISLAND

**Hart House Inn Bed and
Breakfast**
21979 Club Road
Wellesley Island
(888) 481–LOVE (5683)
www.harthouseinn.com

Places to Eat
in the Adirondacks

ALEXANDRIA BAY

Captain Thomson's
45 James Street
(315) 482–9961
www.captthomsons.com

LAKE LUZERNE

Waterhouse Restaurant
Route 9N
(518) 696–3115

LAKE PLACID

**Averil Conwell Dining
Room**
5 Mirror Lake Drive
(518) 523–2544

**Great Adirondack Steak
and Seafood Company**
34 Main Street
(518) 523–1629
www.greateradirondack
steakandseafoodcompany
.com

MAYFIELD

Lanzi's on the Lake
Route 30
(518) 661–7711

SARATOGA SPRINGS

Chez Sophie Bistro
534 Broadway
Saratoga Hotel
(518) 583–3538
www.chezsophie.com

Olde Bryan Inn
123 Maple Avenue
(518) 587–2990
www.oldebryaninn.com

TUPPER LAKE

The Wawbeek
553 Panther Mountain Road
Route 30
(800) 953–2656

WHITEHALL

Finch and Chubb
82 North Williams Street
Whitehall
(518) 499–2049
www.visitwhitehall.com

OTHER ATTRACTIONS WORTH SEEING IN THE ADIRONDACKS

Akwesasne Mohawk Casino
Route 37
Hogansburg
(518) 358–2222 or (888) 622–1155
www.mohawkcasino.com

Almanzo Wilder Farm
Stacy Road
Burke
(518) 483–1207
www.almanzowilderfarm.com

Ausable Chasm
Route 9
Ausable Chasm
(800) 537–1211
www.ausablechasm.com

Enchanted Forest/Water Safari
3183 Route 38
Old Forge
(315) 369–6145
www.watersafari.com

Gore Mountain
Peaceful Valley Road
North Creek
(518) 251–2411 or (800) 342–1234
www.goremountain.com

High Falls Gorge
Route 86, Wilmington Notch
Wilmington
(518) 946–2278
www.highfallsgorge.com

Natural Stone Bridge and Caves
555 Stone Bridge Road
Pottersville
(518) 494–2283
www.stonebridgeandcaves.com

Plattsburgh State Art Museum
SUNY, 101 Broad Street
Plattsburgh
(518) 563–7709
http://clubs.plattsburgh.edu/museum

The Mohawk Valley

Drums along the Mohawk . . . Leatherstocking . . . "I got a mule and her name is Sal/Fifteen miles on the Erie Canal"—the lore of the Mohawk Valley has long been a part of the national consciousness. The reasons are plain: The valley has long been an important highway between the East Coast and the Great Lakes, and countless Americans have passed through here via Indian trails, the ***Erie Canal,*** Commodore Vanderbilt's "Water Level Route" of the New York Central railroad, and today's New York State Thruway. Here Jesuit missionaries met their end at the hands of the Iroquois, ***James Fenimore Cooper***'s Deerslayer stalked, and homesteaders struck out for the Midwest along a water-filled ditch, in barges pulled by draft animals. Surely, this is one of the most storied corridors of the republic.

Along the way, people settled towns and made things—guns in Ilion, pots and pans in Rome, gloves in Gloversville. But much of this gently rolling country is still left to cows and crops.

This chapter begins in ***Albany*** and heads west to Syracuse, loosely following the route of the Mohawk River as well as the New York State Thruway.

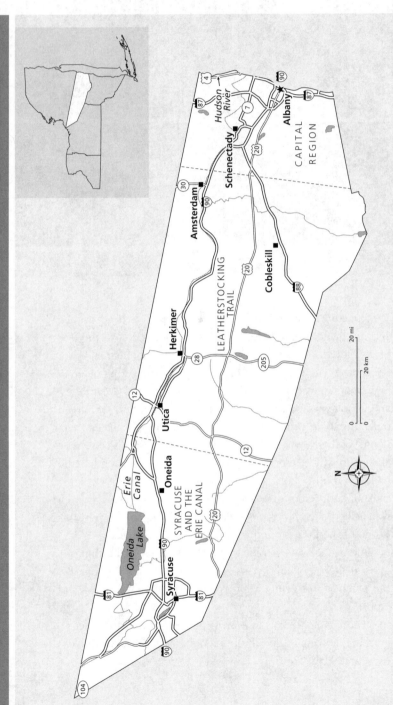

THE MOHAWK VALLEY

Capital Region

The capital of the Empire State, Albany today has all the trappings of a government seat—posh homes and restaurants, traffic, and massive "official" architecture—namely the beautiful and ornate State Capitol building, partly designed by H. H. Richardson, and the four monolithic, marble-clad state office towers so closely associated with the grandiose visions of the late governor Nelson Rockefeller. But visit the *Albany Institute of History and Art* to discover the art, history, and culture of Albany and the upper Hudson River Valley from the seventeenth century to the present.

The Hudson River School is well represented here with works by painters such as Cole, Durand, and Cropsey. But the institute possesses fine examples of an even older regional genre, portraits of the seventeenth- and eighteenth-century Dutch settlers of the Hudson Valley. These pictures echo the Dutch genre paintings that left us a detailed record of the comforts of burgher life in the Netherlands. Here it's easy to imagine the people in the portraits surrounded by the institute's wonderful collection of early Hudson Valley furniture and silver.

The Albany Institute of History and Art, 125 Washington Avenue, Albany (518–463–4478; www.nysparks.state.ny.us/sites), is open Wednesday through Saturday 10:00 A.M. to 5:00 P.M. and Sunday noon to 5:00 P.M. Admission is $7.00 for adults, $5.00 for senior citizens and students, and $3.00 for children ages 6 to 12.

The Schuylers were among the earliest of the Dutch settlers of the upper Hudson Valley and were involved throughout the colonial period in trading, agriculture, land development, and local politics. The most renowned member of the family was *Philip Schuyler* (1733–1804), whose manorial home is today preserved as the *Schuyler Mansion State Historic Site.*

Philip Schuyler designed the elegant mansion himself in the Georgian style, with rose-colored brick walls, graceful fenestration, and double-hipped roof (the awkward hexagonal brick entry vestibule is an 1818 addition). He furnished

AUTHORS' FAVORITES—MOHAWK VALLEY

Children's Museum

Fort Klock Historic Restoration

Iroquois Indian Museum

Mid-Lakes Navigation Company, Ltd.

The Petrified Creatures Museum of Natural History

Remington Arms Museum

Schoharie Crossing State Historic Site

Walter Elwood Museum

it largely with purchases he made during a 1761–62 trip to England and today it houses an excellent collection of colonial and Federal period furnishings.

After Schuyler died in 1804, this architectural gem was sold and used as an orphanage before being acquired by the state in 1912.

The Schuyler Mansion State Historic Site, 32 Catherine Street, Albany (518–434–0834; www.nysparks.state.ny.us/sites), is open mid-April through October, Wednesday through Sunday 11:00 A.M. to 5:00 P.M.; June 1 through September 6, Tuesday through Sunday 11:00 a.m. to 5:00 P.M.; November through mid-April by appointment. Also open on Memorial Day, Independence Day, and Labor Day. Admission is $4.00 for adults, $1.00 for children 5 to 12, and $3.00 for senior citizens and students.

In 1774 Mother Ann Lee, founder of the **Shakers,** left England with a small band of followers and came to New York City. A few years later the group established the country's first **Shaker settlement** in a town named Watervliet (now part of the town of **Colonie**).

Today the **Shaker Heritage Society** maintains a memorial to this historic settlement. Among the points of interest are a garden with some one hundred varieties of herbs (herbs were one of the early Shakers' major trade crops), the Ann Lee Pond nature preserve, and the Shaker Cemetery, where Lee and many of her followers are buried. The museum and gift shop are in the 1848 Shaker Meeting House, on the grounds of the Ann Lee Home.

The Shaker Heritage Society, Albany Shaker Road, Albany (518–456–7890; www.shakerheritage.org), is open February to October Tuesday through Saturday 9:30 A.M. to 4:00 P.M.; November and December Monday through Saturday 10:00 A.M. to 4:00 P.M. A self-guided Walking Tour brochure is available for $1.00. Admission is $3.00 per person donation.

One of Philip Schuyler's interests during his later years was the development of a canal and lock system in New York State. It was in the three decades after his death that canal building really hit its stride in the United States, turning formerly sleepy villages into canal boomtowns involved in the lucrative trade between New York City and points west. One such town is **Waterford,** located near Cohoes just upriver from Albany.

Founded by the Dutch as Halfmoon Point in the early 1620s at the confluence of the Mohawk and Hudson rivers, Waterford was incorporated under its present name in 1794 and is today the oldest incorporated village in the United States. In 1799 it became the head of sloop navigation on the Hudson, but its glory days of commerce came later, in the 1820s, when the new Champlain and Erie canals made the town an important waystation on a statewide transportation system.

It wasn't long before the railroads superseded the canal system, but Waterford prospered as a small manufacturing center during the nineteenth century.

FEBRUARY

Annual Colonial Dinner
Schenectady
(518) 374–0263
www.schist.org

APRIL

Proctor's Annual Laughter Arts Festival
Schenectady
(518) 382–3884
www.proctors.org

MAY

Tulip Festival
Albany
(518) 434–2032
www.albanyevents.org/tulip_festival

JUNE

Old Songs Festival of Traditional Music
Altamont
(518) 765–2815
www.oldsongs.org

Annual Hall of Fame Game
Cooperstown
(888) HALL–OF–FAME
www.baseballhalloffame.org

A Taste of Syracuse
Downtown Syracuse
www.downtownsyracuse.com

JULY

Baseball Hall of Fame Induction
Cooperstown
(888) HALL–OF–FAME
www.baseballhalloffame.org

Glimmerglass Opera
Cooperstown
(607) 547–2255
www.glimmerglass.org

Empire State Games
Albany
(518) 474–8889

New York State Rhythm and Blues Festival
Syracuse
(315) 473–0826
www.nysbluesfest.com

Syracuse Arts and Crafts Festival
Syracuse
(315) 422–8284

AUGUST

The Great New York State Fair
Syracuse
(800) 234–4797 or (315) 487–7711
www.nysfair.com

OCTOBER

Halloween at Howe Caverns
Howes Cave
(518) 296–8900
www.howecaverns.com

Lafayette Apple Festival
Cicero
(315) 677–3644

NOVEMBER

Christmas Parade
Schenectady
(518) 372–5656

DECEMBER

First Night
Albany
(518) 434–2032

Holiday Festival of Trees
Syracuse
(315) 474 6064

The legacy of this era is the village's lovely residential architecture, much of it in the regionally significant "Waterford" style characterized by Federal details and Dutch-inspired single-step gables. Such architectural distinctions have earned the village center inclusion on the National Register of Historic Places. The historic district is the subject of tours given during "Canalfest" the second Saturday of May each year. It features boat rides, hayrides, a boat show, a craft fair, food, and entertainment.

shortandsteamy

The country's first railroad, with an 11-mile track, ran between Albany and Schenectady.

From April through October in the village center at Erie Canal Lock 2, a series of outdoor exhibits details the history of the 1823 canal and the present-day barge canal.

Waterford attractions outside the village center include the **Champlain Canal,** this section of which was dug in 1823 and is still filled with water; the **Waterford Flight,** a series of five locks on the still-operating New York State Barge Canal, whose 169-foot total rise is the highest in the world; a state park at **Lock 6;** and **Peebles Island State Park. Waterford Historical Museum and Cultural Center,** 2 Museum Lane (off Saratoga Avenue), Waterford (518–238–0809; www.waterfordmuseum .com), is open from May 15 through October 1, Wednesday through Friday from 11:00 A.M. to 2:00 P.M., and Saturday and Sunday from 2:00 to 4:00 P.M.; October 2 through October 24, Saturday and Sunday 2:00 to 4:00 P.M.; closed holiday weekends. Admission is free.

Leatherstocking Trail

The **Walter Elwood Museum,** in a former school, offers a wonderful overview of the area's history as well as an eclectic collection of historical and natural objects. Among its 20,000 artifacts, are the fossilized footprint of a Tyrannosaurus rex, the earliest television set (on permanent loan from the Edison Museum in Menlo Park, New Jersey) and an exhibit depicting life in the Victorian era—a life-size home with four completely furnished rooms.

One of the few museums in the country owned by a public school, it is named for a local teacher who opened a museum and bird sanctuary in 1940 so students could study nature and wildlife.

The Walter Elwood Museum, 300 Guy Park Avenue, **Amsterdam** (518–843–5151), is open Monday through Thursday from 10:00 A.M. to 3:00 P.M. during the school year. Call (518) 843–2027 or see www.walterelwoodmuseum .com for summer hours.

At Least They Don't Run

The leather leggings worn by Yankees who settled in this area gave birth to the region's nickname, the Leatherstocking Trail. James Fenimore Cooper immortalized the name in his *Leatherstocking Tales*, which recounted the adventures of wilderness scout Natty Bumppo. Cooper is buried in the family plot in Cooperstown's Christ Church cemetery.

The Erie Canal and the feats of engineering that its building entailed are the focus of **Schoharie Crossing State Historic Site,** farther up the Mohawk, at Fort Hunter. Seven canal-related structures dating from three periods of the waterway's construction or expansion are preserved here and provided with interpretive displays that explain their use. The visitor center has an exhibit on the **Erie Canal** and information on the site and surrounding area. **Putnam's Canal Store,** at Yankee Hill Lock 28 on Queen Anne's Road (2.2 miles east of the visitor center), was built during the 1850s and served as a store along the enlarged Erie Canal for many years. It now houses an exhibit on Erie Canal stores.

Along the old canal towpath are views of modern-day barge traffic on the Mohawk River, the depth of which in this area allows it to be used as a link in the New York State barge canal system.

Schoharie Crossing State Historic Site, 129 Schoharie Street, Fort Hunter (518–829–7516; www.nysparks.state.ny.us/sites), is open May through October 31 and Memorial Day, Independence Day, and Labor Day, Wednesday through Saturday 10:00 A.M. to 5:00 P.M. and Sunday 1:00 to 5:00 P.M. The grounds are open all year during daylight hours. Admission is free.

Long before there were canals or barges in this part of New York State, the waters of the Mohawk and its tributaries carried the canoes of the Iroquois. The Mohawk Valley was the heart of the empire of the Five Nations, one of which was the Mohawk. In present-day Auriesville stood the palisaded village of Mohawk longhouses called Ossernenon in the seventeenth century; here, in 1642, a raiding party of Indians returned with three French and twenty Huron captives in custody. Among the French were a Jesuit priest, Isaac Jogues, and his lay assistant, René Goupil.

Goupil was tomahawked to death when his attempt to teach a child the sign of the cross was interpreted as the casting of an evil spell. Jogues was rescued by the Dutch during a Mohawk trading foray to Fort Orange, and he returned to Europe and eventually Quebec. But he volunteered to go back to

Ossernenon in May 1646, as part of a group attempting to ratify a peace treaty with the Mohawks, and was captured near the village by a faction of the tribe favoring a continuation of hostilities. Both he and a lay companion, Jean Lalande, were killed by tomahawk-wielding braves in October of that year. Canonized by the Roman Catholic Church in 1930 along with five Jesuit missionaries martyred in Canada, Jogues, Goupil, and Lalande are honored at the **National Shrine of the North American Martyrs** in Auriesville.

The shrine, which occupies the hilltop site of the original Mohawk village of Ossernenon amid 600 verdant acres, is maintained by the New York Province of the Society of Jesus, the same Jesuit order to which Isaac Jogues belonged. Founded in 1885, the shrine accommodates 40,000 to 50,000 visitors each year during a season lasting from the first Sunday in May to the last Sunday in October. Mass is celebrated in the vast "Coliseum," the central altar of which is built to suggest the palisades of a Mohawk village; there are also a Martyrs' Museum, rustic chapels, and a retreat house.

For information on the schedule of observances at the National Shrine of the North American Martyrs, Noeltner Road, **Auriesville,** call (518) 853–3033 or see www.martyrshrine.org. The shrine is open from the first Sunday in May to the last Sunday in October, daily 10:00 A.M. to 4:00 P.M.

The French Catholic missionaries working among the Indians in the seventeenth century were not without their successes. The most famous name among Mohawk converts of that era is **Kateri Tekakwitha,** the "Lily of the Mohawks," born at Ossernenon and baptized at what is now the village of Fonda, where the **Fonda National Shrine of Blessed Kateri Tekakwitha** is located. Maintained by the Conventual Franciscan Order, the shrine commemorates the life of the saintly Indian girl who lived half of her life here, before moving to the community of converted Indians established by the French at Caughnawaga, near Montreal, where she died in 1680 at the age of twenty-four. (In 1980, on the tercentenary of her death, Pope John Paul II announced the beatification of Kateri Tekakwitha, which is the last step before canonization in the Catholic Church.)

Aside from its religious connections, the **Fonda** site of the Tekakwitha shrine is interesting because of its identification by archaeologists as the location of a Mohawk village, also called Caughnawaga. Artifacts dug from the village site are exhibited in the shrine's Native American Exhibit, located on the ground floor of a revolutionary-era Dutch barn that now serves as a chapel. Indian items from elsewhere in New York State and throughout the United States are also part of the exhibit.

The Fonda National Shrine of Blessed Kateri Tekakwitha, off Route 5, Fonda (518–853–3646; www.katerishrine.com), is open daily from 9:00 A.M. to 6:00 P.M. Admission is free.

Fitting Famous Fingers

Daniel Storto is the last of a breed—he's the only custom glove maker left in Gloversville. Settling in the one-time glove capital of America in 2002, Storto set up shop to carry on his business of handcrafting gloves for clients such as Whoopi Goldberg, Diane Keaton, and Madonna.

Just north of Fonda and nearby Johnstown is *Gloversville,* home of the *Fulton County Museum.* Gloversville was originally called Kingsborough, but the townspeople adopted the present name in 1828 in homage to the linchpin of the local economy in those days—tanning and glove making. It is the glove industry that provides the Fulton County Museum with its most interesting exhibits, housed in the Glove and Leather Room. Here is the state's only glove-manufacturing display, a complete small glove factory of the last century, donated to the museum and reassembled in its original working format.

There is also a Weaving Room, where craftspeople demonstrate the technique of turning raw flax into the finished product; an Old Country Kitchen; a nineteenth-century Lady's Room, complete with costumes and cosmetics; a Country Store; an old-time Candy Store; an Early Farm display; and a Country Schoolroom. Be sure not to miss the Indian Artifact exhibit on the first floor.

The Fulton County Museum, 237 Kingsboro Avenue, Gloversville (518–725–2203), is open May, June, and September, Tuesday through Saturday noon to 4:00 P.M. and Sunday 10:00 A.M. to 4:00 P.M.; July and August, Tuesday through Saturday 10:00 A.M. to 4:00 P.M. Admission is free.

Fate plays a capricious hand in deciding which industries a town will be noted for. Gloversville got gloves; *Canajoharie,* our next stop along the Mohawk, got chewing gum—specifically the Beech-Nut Packing Company, of which town native Bartlett Arkell was president in the 1920s. Because of Arkell and his success in business, Canajoharie also came into possession of the finest independent art gallery of any municipality its size in the United States: the *Canajoharie Library and Art Gallery.*

Arkell's beneficence to his hometown began with his donation of a new library in 1924. Two years later he donated the funds to build an art gallery wing on the library, and over the next few years he gave the community the magnificent collection of paintings that forms the bulk of the gallery's present holdings. Subsequent additions were made in 1964 and 1989.

This institution has become not merely an art gallery with a library attached, but an art gallery with a small town attached. The roster of American

If It Isn't Haunted, It Should Be

It isn't often that an individual house is unusual enough to make us stop in our tracks, park the car, and gawk, but that's just what happened one summer afternoon while we were driving through the small town of Palatine Bridge, just across the river from Canajoharie.

There it was, the archetype of the spooky, derelict Victorian mansion. An immense, three-and-a-half-story structure, rambling back from Grand Street for half a block, the house was a bold pastiche of just about every cliché of our own American Baroque, the Second Empire style of the 1870s: mansard roof, elaborately detailed dormers, tall entrance tower, and deep shady porches. It was very nearly in ruins. Great flotillas of bats, we could readily imagine, poured nightly out of gaps in the rotted eaves, completing the Charles Addams effect.

A weather-worn state historic marker told whose house it had been. Webster Wagner, a pioneer in the development of luxury railroad passenger cars, built the place in 1877. Nearly twenty years earlier, when he was depot master of the New York Central station at Palatine Bridge, Wagner had presented his plans for a sleeping car to his boss, Commodore Cornelius Vanderbilt. The Commodore liked the idea and helped bankroll what became the Wagner Palace Car Company. Wagner's firm was eventually taken over by George Pullman, of Pullman car fame.

By then, we knew, Webster Wagner had burned to death in one of his own sleepers, in an 1882 crash just north of New York City. If it were possible to make this once-proud pile on Grand Street even more melancholy, more grotesque, this recollection of its builder's horrible end certainly did the trick.

painters exhibited here is astounding, totally out of scale with what you would expect at a thruway exit between Albany and Utica. The Hudson River School is represented by Albert Bierstadt (*El Capitan*), John Kensett, and Thomas Doughty. There is a Gilbert Stuart portrait of George Washington. The Winslow Homer collection is the third largest in the United States. The eighteenth century is represented by John Singleton Copley; the nineteenth, by such luminaries as Thomas Eakins, George Inness (*Rainbow*), and James McNeill Whistler (*On the Thames*). Among twentieth-century painters are Charles Burchfield, Reginald Marsh, N.C. Wyeth and his son Andrew (*February 2nd*), Edward Hopper, Thomas Hart Benton, and even Grandma Moses. There is also a Frederic Remington bronze, *Bronco Buster*. Add a collection of eighty Korean and Japanese ceramics, the gift of the late Colonel John Fox, and you have all the more reason—as if more were needed—to regard Canajoharie as a destination in itself rather than a stop along the way.

The Canajoharie Library and Art Gallery, 2 Erie Boulevard, Canajoharie (518–673–2314; www.clag.org), is open Monday through Thursday 10:00 A.M. to 7:30 P.M., Friday 10:00 A.M. to 4:45 P.M., Saturday 10:00 A.M. to 1:30 P.M.; closed Sunday. Admission is free, but the gallery will be closed for construction until July 2007.

Life was tough in the Mohawk Valley in 1750, when Johannes Klock built the farmhouse-fortress preserved today as the *Fort Klock Historic Restoration.* Located above the river at *St. Johnsville,* Fort Klock is a reminder that defensible stout-walled outposts were not unique to the "Wild West" of the late 1800s; in 1750 the Mohawk Valley *was* the Wild West.

Like his neighbors scattered along the river, Johannes Klock engaged in fur trading and farming. Canoes and bateaux could be tied up in the cove just below the house, yet the building itself stood on high enough ground and at a sufficient distance from the river to make it easily defensible should the waters of the Mohawk bring foes rather than friendly traders. The stone walls of Fort Klock are almost 2 feet thick and are dotted with "loopholes" that enabled inhabitants to fire muskets from protected positions within.

Now restored and protected as a registered National Historic Landmark, Fort Klock and its outbuildings, including a restored Dutch barn, tell a good part of the story of the Mohawk Valley in the eighteenth century—a time when the hardships of homesteading were made even more difficult by the constant threat of the musket, the tomahawk, and the torch.

Fort Klock Historic Restoration, Route 5, St. Johnsville (518–568–7779; www.fortklock.com), is open from Memorial Day through mid-October, Tuesday through Sunday 9:00 A.M. to 5:00 P.M. Admission is $1.00 for adults, 50 cents for children over 10.

The *Iroquois Indian Museum* details the history of the Iroquois Confederacy, but it also specializes in researching the pre-Revolutionary Schoharie Mohawk who lived here. The museum's discovery of a 9,600-year-old Mohawk site is an important part of its archaeological exhibits.

The museum traces the history of the Mohawk and other nations of the Confederacy. The main building at the museum resembles an Iroquois longhouse, and visitors explore the museum in a counterclockwise direction, in the same way that longhouse dancers move.

Two log homes at the edge of the museum's forty-five-acre nature park were moved from Canada's largest Iroquois community, the Six Nations Reserve. A Children's Iroquois Museum on the ground floor utilizes a hands-on approach to help interpret the adult museum for youngsters.

The Iroquois Indian Museum, 324 Caverns Road, *Howes Cave* (518–296–8949; www.iroquoismuseum.org), is open daily from July 1 through Labor

Day weekend, Monday through Saturday 10:00 A.M. to 6:00 P.M. and Sunday noon to 6:00 P.M.; April, May, June, and Labor Day through December, open Tuesday through Saturday 10:00 A.M. to 5:00 P.M. and Sunday noon to 5:00 P.M. It is closed January through March. Admission is $8.00 for adults, $6.50 for senior citizens and students ages 13 to 17, and $5.00 for children ages 5 to 12.

Anyone who yearns for milk shakes and ice-cream sundaes served up at a real, old-fashioned soda fountain must visit the *Historic Throop Drugstore.* The oldest store in Schoharie County, it dates back to 1800.

The pharmacy is owned by David and Sarah Goodrich. David, a registered pharmacist, is also a history buff. The couple has restored the pharmacy to look much as Throop's did in the 1920s and 1930s, with antique druggists' bottles, old issues of *Life* magazine, and old-time ice-cream parlor chairs, where you can savor freshly baked Danish, homemade soups, or your favorite frozen confection.

Historic Throop Drugstore, Main Street, Schoharie, (518) 295–7300, is open Monday through Friday 8:30 A.M. to 5:30 P.M.; Saturday the pharmacy is open from 9:00 A.M. to noon, and the soda fountain is open to "whenever"; closed Sunday.

Renovating a building takes a lot of effort; restoring an entire section of a town is a herculean undertaking, as visitors to *Sharon Springs* will immediately appreciate. The erstwhile resort community, whose waters were said to equal those of Germany's Baden-Baden in therapeutic value, thrived in the mid- to late-1800s when people came seeking cures for everything from "malarial difficulties" to "biliary derangements."

Don't miss the self-guided Historic Main Street Tour. Twenty plaques lining both sides of the historic district depict the village's golden era with stories, architectural facts, diary excerpts from the 1860s, and hundreds of photos from the nineteenth century.

Several lodgings in the historic district are opening as they are restored. Among them: the circa 1840 Greek Revival *Brimstonia Cottage* (518–284–2839) and Edgefield B&B (518–284–9771), an English-style inn. The restored, Spanish Colonial 1928 Adler Hotel and Spa (518–284–2285) has a pool, dining room, kosher kitchen, and sulphur baths.

The handsomely restored *American Hotel,* an 1847 National Register building, has nine rooms with private baths (rates start at $145 per night, breakfast included), a pub, and a restaurant with a good reputation. It serves dinner nightly in spring and summer, closing Monday and Tuesday in the off-season, and Sunday brunch. The American Hotel is located on Main Street in Sharon Springs (518–284–2105; www.americanhotel.com).

Although in far fewer numbers, people still come to Sharon Springs for the waters. They can drink the sulfurous brew at the octagonal beaux-arts White Sulphur Temple and have a facial splash in Blue Stone Spring, once used extensively as a "lotion for inflammatory conditions of the eye." In July and August, bathers can soak in the original tubs of the Imperial Baths. Each summer, the Sharon Springs Citizens Council of the Arts hosts a free Wednesday evening music and theater series in Chalybeate Park. During the summer, from 2:00 to 4:00 P.M. daily, the Sharon Historical Society opens its museum in a restored 1860 schoolhouse on Main Street. Be sure to sign the guest wall at the fourteen-room Cobbler & Company (518–284–2067) on Main Street, a combination museum/gift shop, which sells everything from English china to penny candy.

For information on Sharon Springs, look the town up at either of its Web sites: www.roseboro.com or www.sharonsprings.com.

Just out of town, *Clausen Farms* (Route 20, P.O. Box 395, Sharon Springs 13459, 518–284–2527; www.reu.com/clausen), an eighty-acre Victorian estate and llama farm, has four guest rooms in the main house, which dates to the late 1700s (open year-round) and seven in the Casino, a Victorian gentleman's guesthouse completed in 1892 (open April through October). The inn has great views of the Mohawk Valley, an 1892 swimming pool with a fountain, a 1911 bowling alley with original pins and balls, and cross-country skiing. Call for current rates.

To sports fans, *Cooperstown* is practically synonymous with baseball. Devotees come from all over the country to visit the National Baseball Hall of Fame and Museum, but many miss the three-story *National Baseball Hall of Fame Library,* located in a separate building connected to the museum. It's a treasure trove of baseball: a collection of more than 2.5 million items including clippings, photographs, books, videos, movies, recordings—practically everything ever said or written about baseball. Established in 1939, the library is used by researchers but is open to visitors, who are invited to browse at their leisure. During your visit be sure to include the fifty-six-seat Bullpen Theater, where visitors can view the best in baseball highlight films and footage of the game's greatest plays.

The National Baseball Hall of Fame Library, 25 Main Street, Cooperstown (607–547–0330 or 607–547–7200; www.baseballhalloffame.org), is open daily 9:00 A.M. to 5:00 P.M., with half-hour tours throughout the day, during summer months. Museum visitors can enter the library at no additional charge over the entry fee of $14.50 for adults and $9.50 for seniors.

But there's so much more to Cooperstown than baseball. It's the quintessence of small-town America, founded in 1786 on the southern shore of Otsego

Lake by William Cooper, father of author James Fenimore Cooper. Stand on the veranda of the historic **Otesaga Resort Hotel** at sunset (perhaps with a beverage), looking out over the eighteenth green to the incredible expanse of clear, blue water reflecting an impressionist's palette of colors. You'll see why Cooper called it "Glimmerglass" in his *Leatherstocking Tales*. Built in 1909 by the Clark family, discreet patriarchs of Cooperstown, the Otesaga is at once a part of and apart from Main Street's small-town charms, just a short walk from its front gates. This landmark Georgian Revival edifice, with its mammoth white-columned entry contrasting with the redbrick structure, offers guests a complete destination. In addition to lodgings they'll get fine dining, a cozy pub, and excellent recreation in the form of a vintage 1909 Emmett Devereux layout, the Leatherstocking Golf Course that has been rated among the top public courses in the East.

At the Otesaga Resort Hotel, 60 Lake Street, Cooperstown (800–348–6222; www.otesaga.com), rates vary seasonally, starting at $380 a night for a standard double room, with suites going up to $570 a night. Ask about the many golf and holiday packages.

Just down the street from the Otesaga, the **Fenimore Art Museum** is a splendid showcase for the New York State Historical Association, featuring changing exhibits of works largely from the eighteenth through early twentieth centuries, with an emphasis on paintings, early photographs, textiles, and other items relating to the American experience. Among the works are Hudson River School paintings by such luminaries as Thomas Cole and Asher B. Durand, folk art, and period furniture and paintings associated with Mr. Cooper.

The museum's $10-million, 18,000-square-foot American Indian Wing exhibits the Eugene and Clare Thaw Collection of American Indian Art, more than 700 masterpieces spanning 2,400 years that highlight the artistry of North America's indigenous peoples. The Great Hall features a selection of large-scale objects from regions throughout North America.

The museum, overlooking the lake, has a formal terrace garden and restaurant with outdoor seating that overlooks the lake.

Right across the street is the twenty-three-acre **Farmers' Museum,** a cluster of historic buildings where the trades, skills, and agricultural practices of nineteenth-century rural New York State come to life. The museum's 1845 Village Crossroads is made up of ten early-nineteenth-century buildings all built within 100 miles of Cooperstown and moved here as life-size working exhibits. Among the buildings are a tavern, blacksmith's shop, one-room schoolhouse, and print shop. All are furnished in period-style, and the museum interpreters perform the tasks appropriate to each building. Penny candy is sold at Todd's General Store. Lippitt Farmstead, a nineteenth-century house, barn, and outbuilding complex, presents farming practices of the day. The Herder's Cottage serves a light menu.

Be sure to include a visit to the fascinating *Seneca Log House,* at one time the home of a traditional Seneca family. At the site the daily life of a Seneca family in the 1840s is replicated as closely as possible. A docent demonstrates crafts of the period, including basketmaking, beadwork, and the making of tourist-related objects, and special seasonal events are held here throughout the year.

Among the special events are an old-time Fourth of July, the September Harvest Festival, and a Candlelight Evening at Christmastime that features sleigh rides and hot wassail.

The Farmers' Museum, Lake Road (607–547–1400; www.farmersmuseum .org) in Cooperstown, is open April, May, October and November, Tuesday through Sunday 10:00 A.M. to 4:00 P.M. June through September it's open daily 10:00 A.M. to 5:00 P.M. The Fenimore Art Museum, Lake Road (607–547–1400; www.fenimoreartmuseum.org), is open April, May, and October through December, Tuesday through Sunday 10:00 A.M. to 4:00 P.M. and June through September, daily 10:00 A.M. to 5:00 P.M.

Of course, many travelers first discover the myriad charms of Cooperstown through baseball—the Hall of Fame events or one of the popular fantasy camps, in which wanted-to-be's rub elbows and play games with retired base-ball stars at Doubleday Field, just off Main Street. Fans of the movie *A League of Their Own* may recognize the wonderfully old-timey diamond enclosed by bleachers.

For players whose spirits are willing, but whose bones may creak, *Essential Elements Day Spa and Boutique* is conveniently located next door to the field. Essential Elements offers a full complement of facials, massages, and therapeutic body treatments as well as a fine selection of organic spa products in the boutique. There is also a wonderful secret garden, where tea and dessert are served. Essential Elements is located at 137 Main Street, Cooperstown; call (800) 437–3265 or go to www.essentialelementsdayspa.com to book an appointment.

"When the building starts shaking, they've started making," says *USA Today* of *Fly Creek Cider Mill and Orchard,* a turn-of-the-century water-powered mill where visitors can watch apple cider being made as well as chow down on a host of cider-related products, including hot spiced cider, cider floats, and cider mill donuts. There's also a duck pond, tractorland kids' area, and gift shop selling everything from bagged cheese curds to home accessories. It's at 288 Gloose Street, Fly Creek (607–547–9692 or 800–505–6455; www.flycreek cidermill.com), and is open from mid-May until mid-December, daily 9:00 A.M. to 6:00 P.M.

Hyde Hall, a New York State Historic Site, is fascinating because it's a work in progress that visitors can tour as it's being restored. Built in the early nineteenth century by one of the state's last great land-owning families, it's considered to be the finest example of a neoclassical country mansion north of the Mason-Dixon line.

The estate's builder, George Clarke, secretary and lieutenant governor of the British Province of New York from 1703 to 1743, wanted to build a home similar to the one he'd left behind in Cheshire, England. He retained Philip Hooker, one of America's foremost early nineteenth-century architects, and kept copious records of the house's construction, furnishing, and decoration, allowing today's restorers to replicate many of the original features as they work. Hyde Hall is a fascinating look into one man's vision, the damage time can render on a once-magnificent dwelling, and the dedication of a small group of people determined to restore the hall to its former glory.

Hyde Hall in *Springfield,* adjacent to Glimmerglass State Park and over-looking Otsego Lake, is open for tours May, June, September, and October, daily 10:00 A.M., noon, and 2:00 P.M., and weekends 10:00 A.M. to 5:00 P.M. (last tour at 4:00 P.M.) In July and August it's closed Wednesday, but tour hours are the same, with an additional daily tour at 4:00 P.M. Closed when there are events on site. Admission is $7.00 for adults, $6.00 for seniors, and $4.00 for ages 5 to 12. For information and events contact Friends of Hyde Hall, Inc., P.O. Box 721, Cooperstown 13326 (607–547–5098), or check their Web site: www.hydehall.org.

Outstanding hospitality and gourmet breakfasts are the hallmarks of the *Landmark Inn,* an elegant 1856 mansion in the heart of Cooperstown. Innkeepers Jennifer and Pete Landers have eleven rooms, all with private bath, cable TV, refrigerators, and air-conditioning at their smoke-free B&B. June through September, rates start at $165 per night. Weekends May through October require a two-night minimum stay, and kids are very welcome. The inn is at 64 Chestnut Street, Cooperstown (607–547–7225 or 866–384–3466; www .landmarkinncooperstown.com).

At one point in the nineteenth century, 80 percent of the hops produced in America came from within a 40-mile radius of Cooperstown. The *Brewery Ommegang,* on a 135-acre former hops farm alongside the Susquehanna River, is carrying on the region's proud tradition, using traditional Belgian brewing techniques, which include utilizing specialty malts, Syrian and Saaz hops, rare spices such as curaçao orange peel and paradise grain, and open fermentation, bottle-conditioning, and warm cellaring. Judge the result for yourself: The brewery is open for free half-hour tours year-round, daily from 11:00 A.M. to 6:00 P.M.

Brewery Ommegang is on County Route 33, paralleling Route 28 and midway between Cooperstown and Milford (800–544–1809 or 607–544–1800; www.ommegang.com).

Central New York's oldest museum, ***The Petrified Creatures Museum of Natural History,*** was established more than fifty years ago on land that the Devonian Sea covered 300 million years in the past. Today visitors are invited to climb on the backs of life-size purple and green dinosaurs, learn about life in prehistoric times, and dig for fossils to take home as free souvenirs (tools are provided by the museum). Don't miss the gift shop!

The Petrified Creatures Museum of Natural History, Route 20, ***Richfield Springs*** (315–858–2868; www.petrifiedcreatures.com), is open Thursday to Monday in May and June and daily July through September from 10:00 A.M. to 6:00 P.M. Admission is $8.00 adults and $4.00 children, under 5 free.

In 1816 ***Eliphalet Remington*** was twenty-four years old and in need of a new rifle. He made a barrel at his father's village forge and then walked into the Mohawk Valley town of Utica to have it rifled (Rifling is the series of twisting grooves inside a gun barrel that give the bullet spin—and therefore accuracy—and distinguish it from the smoothbore muskets of earlier days.) He may not have known it then, but gun making was to be his life's work and his Remington Arms Company would produce the dependable firearms that would power America's westward expansion. You can learn the history of America's oldest gun maker at the ***Remington Arms Museum*** in ***Ilion,*** which houses an impressive collection of rifles, shotguns, and handguns dating back to Eliphalet Remington's earliest flintlocks. Here are examples of the first successful breech-loading rifles, for which Remington held the initial 1864 patents; rare presentation-grade guns; and company firsts including bolt-action and pump rifles, autoloading rifles and shotguns, and the Model 32 over-and-under shotgun of 1932.

Other displays include explanations of how firearms are built today, advertising posters and other firearms ephemera, and even antique Remington typewriters—yes, it was the same company.

The Remington Arms Museum, 14 Hoefler Avenue (off Route 5S), Ilion (315–895–3301 or 800–243–9700; www .remington.com), is open year-round, Monday through Friday from 8:00 A.M. to

Antique Double Derringer, Remington Arms Museum

5:00 P.M. and Saturday from 10:00 A.M. to 4:00 P.M. June, July, and August, tours are given Monday through Friday at 10:00 A.M. and 1:00 P.M. Admission is free. There's also a shop, which sells clothes and accessories.

"Herkimer diamonds," found just north of Ilion at *Middleville*, aren't really diamonds. Nor are they generally very valuable. But they're a load of fun to prospect for, and the *Ace of Diamonds Mine and Campground*—once known as the Tabor Estate, where the diamonds were first dug—can provide you with all the tools to begin your hunt.

The "diamonds" are really clear quartz crystals found in a rock formation called dolomite, buried ages ago. Surface water containing silicon seeped down through the earth and was trapped in pockets in the dolomite. Tremendous heat and pressure caused the crystals to form, and over the years erosion, weathering, and water have exposed the strata. The crystals at the Ace of Diamonds are found in pockets in the rock and in soil surrounding the weathered rock. They're primarily used for mineral specimens, but ones of gem quality are used in arts and jewelry.

Ace of Diamonds Mine and Campground, Route 28, Middleville (315–891–3855 or 891–3896; www.herkimerdiamonds.com), is open April 1 through October 31 daily from 9:00 A.M. to 5:00 P.M. There is a digging fee of $7.50 per adult and $3.00 for children 7 and under.

From Ilion it's just a short hop down the thruway to *Utica* and a pair of worthwhile museums. The *Munson-Williams-Proctor Arts Institute* is a multifaceted operation that places a good deal of emphasis on community accessibility and service, with free group tours, a speakers' bureau, and children's art programs, as well as free admission and a modestly priced performing arts series (some performances take place at the nearby Stanley Performing Arts Center). Their collection of paintings is strong in nineteenth-century genre work and the Hudson River School, as well as such moderns as Calder, Picasso, Kandinsky, and Pollock; they also have comprehensive art and music libraries; a sculpture garden; and even a children's room where patrons can leave their kids for supervised play while they enjoy the museum. Also on the grounds of the institute is *Fountain Elms,* a beautifully restored 1850 home in the Italianate Victorian style, which was once the home of the philanthropic Williams family. Four period rooms on the ground floor exemplify Victorian tastes. At Christmastime the house is resplendent with Victorian ornamentation.

The Munson-Williams-Proctor Arts Institute, 310 Genesee Street, Utica (315–797–0000; www.mwpai.org), is open Tuesday through Saturday 10:00 A.M. to 5:00 P.M. and Sunday 1:00 to 5:00 P.M., closed major holidays.

Having retrieved your little ones from the children's room at the institute, take them next to a museum of their own, Utica's *Children's Museum,* founded by the city's Junior League. Since 1980 it has occupied its own five-story, 30,000-square-foot building, which it keeps chock-full of participatory and hands-on exhibits concentrating on natural history, the history of New York State, and technology. Installations designed for children ages two to twelve and their families include a Dino Den; Childspace, for children from infant to twelve; an Iroquois longhouse and artifacts; a natural history center; and bubbles, architecture, and dress-up areas. The museum also offers special exhibitions on a monthly basis and special programs for children and their families on Saturdays beginning at 2:00 P.M., from October through July. Portions of the permanent Railroad Exhibit, which includes a Santa Fe dining car and diesel locomotive, are on display next to the museum.

The Children's Museum, 311 Main Street, Utica (315–724–6129; What's Up Line, 724–6128; www.museum4kids.net), is open year-round, Monday, Tuesday, Thursday, Friday, and Saturday from 9:45 A.M. to 3:45 P.M. The museum is closed on most major holidays but open when school is closed. Admission is $8.00 per person; children under age one are admitted free.

In 1888 German-born F. X. Matt II opened a brewery in West Utica. Today the **Matt Brewing Company** is the second-oldest family-owned brewery—and twelfth largest—in the country. In addition to the Saranac family of beers, it also produces numerous specialty microbrews, including New Amsterdam and Harpoon.

You can tour the brewery and then sample the wares for free in the 1888 Tavern (the brewery makes 1888 Tavern Root Beer for kids and teetotalers). The tour includes a visit to the seven-story brew house, the fermenting and aging cellars, and the packaging plant.

The Matt Brewing Company (now also known as Saranac Brewery), 830 Varick Street, Utica (315–732–0022 or 800–765–6288; www.saranac.com), is open for tours year-round. June 1 through Labor Day, tours are given Monday through Saturday from 1:00 to 4:00 P.M., every hour on the hour. On Sunday tours are given at 1:00 and 3:00 P.M. The rest of the year, tours are given Friday and Saturday at 1:00 and 3:00 P.M. (closed major holidays). Advance reservations are recommended. Admission is $5.00 for adults and free for children under 13. Free parking is available in the Tour Center Concourse at the corner of Court and Varick Streets.

Syracuse and the Erie Canal

Hop aboard a horse-drawn canal boat at **Erie Canal Village,** which opened in Rome in 1973 near the site where the first spadeful of dirt for the Erie Canal was dug on Independence Day in 1817. The short-lived canal era may have been only a prologue to the age of the railroad, but in the 1820s New Yorkers thought the Erie Canal was one of the wonders of the world.

The *Chief Engineer,* which keeps to a regular schedule of thirty-five-minute trips on the restored section of the original canal at the village, was built of Mohawk Valley oak to the same specifications as the passenger-carrying packet boats of the canal's early years. The Harden Carriage Museum displays a varied collection of horse-drawn vehicles used on roads and snow. Other buildings in the village—nearly all more than a hundred years old and moved here from other communities in the area—include a tavern, church, smithy, canal store, settler's house, barn, and the New York State Museum of Cheese. The Erie Canal Museum explains the technological and social importance of the Erie Canal. Fort Bull, dating from the French and Indian Wars, is also on the premises.

The village presents historical craft demonstrations, interpretive programs, and seasonal festivals, with the primary focus on canal and harvest activities.

Erie Canal Village, 5789 New London Road, Routes 49 and 46, **Rome** (315–337–3999 or 888–374–3226; www.eriecanalvillage.com), is open daily from Memorial Day weekend through Labor Day, Wednesday through Saturday from 10:00 A.M. to 5:00 P.M. and Sunday noon to 5:00 P.M. Admission to all attractions is $15.00 for adults, $12.00 for seniors and students, and $10.00 for children 4 to 17.

Back in 1790, the Holland Land Company sent its young agent John Lincklaen to America to scout investment possibilities. Two years later he reached the area around **Cazenovia Lake,** between present-day Rome and Syracuse, and his enthusiasm led his firm to invest in 120,000 acres here. A village, farms, and small businesses soon sprang up, with Lincklaen remaining in a patriarchal and entrepreneurial role that in 1807 allowed him to build himself a magnificent Federal mansion, today preserved at the **Lorenzo State Historic Site**.

The little fiefdom of Lorenzo offers an instructive glimpse into why New York is called the Empire State. Lincklaen and the descendants of his adopted family, who lived here until 1968 (the same year that the house, with its contents, was deeded to the state), were involved with many of the enterprises that led to the state's phenomenal growth during the nineteenth century—road building, canals, railroads, and industrial development.

The mansion, surrounded by twenty acres of lawns and formal gardens, sits on the shores of a 4-mile-long lake. It is rich in Federal-era furnishings and the accumulated possessions of a century and a half of Lincklaens, including a fine selection of Hudson River School artworks. In the latest renovations Zuber & Cie, of Rixheim, France, used their original nineteenth-century printing blocks to reproduce an 1870 paper originally hung in Lorenzo in 1901. These projects

Mansion at Lorenzo

are part of an ongoing process to fully restore the site to its turn-of-the-century beauty.

Lorenzo State Historic Site, 17 Rippleton Road, Cazenovia (315–655–3200; www.lorenzony.org), is open from early May through October 31, Wednesday, Thursday, and Saturday, and Monday holidays 10:00 A.M. to 5:00 P.M., Sunday 1:00 to 5:00 P.M. The grounds are open all year, 8:00 A.M. to dusk. Admission is $3.00 for adults, $2.00 for seniors, and $1.00 for children.

Adding to the already considerable charm of the Mohawk Valley is *Skaná: The Spa at Turning Stone,* which opened in late 2006 at the Turning Stone Resort and Casino, a 17,000-acre resort, gaming, entertainment, and golf complex that is an enterprise of the Oneida Indian Nation.

The 33,000-square-foot state-of-the-art spa, salon, and fitness facility—the name is the Oneida word for "peace"—has twelve treatment rooms, including one private VIP Spa Suite and a Couple's Suite. The 10,000-square-foot Fitness Center has an indoor pool for laps and aquatic classes, cardiovascular training machines, plus an exercise studio with cushioned flooring for daily group and private classes.

One of the unique features at Skaná Spa is its traditional American Indian Sweat Lodge. This facility allows guests to experience a Sweat Lodge ceremony, which features storytelling, drumming, chants, and prayers that have been used for centuries as a way of spiritually cleansing body and soul.

Skaná Spa at Turning Stone Resort and Casino is located at 5218 Patrick Road, Verona (800–771–7711; www.turningstone.com).

Around the turn of the twentieth century, the Arts and Crafts Movement swept America. It was an aesthetic revolution that rejected the superfluous

Calling Don Quixote

The first commercial wind farm east of the Mississippi stands on a 120-acre site along a ridge in Madison County, not far from Cazenovia. Seven 220-foot-high windmills with 100-foot blades each produce 1.65 megawatts of electricity—collectively, enough to power 10,000 homes when operating at full capacity.

ornamentation of Victorian furniture, advocating a return to clean lines, honest craftsmanship, and sturdy construction. Gustav and Leopold Stickley, leaders of the movement, began making Craftsman—also known as Mission—furniture.

Today Mission furniture is all the rage again, and cheap knockoffs can be found at discount stores throughout the country. But to see what the Stickleys had in mind, visit the company that continues to craft the same fine pieces that the brothers did at the turn of the twentieth century.

L. & J. G. Stickley, Inc., Stickley Drive, Manlius (315–682–5500; www .stickley.com), offers free tours Tuesday at 10:00 A.M. Tours take 1½ hours, and children under 13 are not permitted.

Hunt for your own Stickley treasures at the *Madison-Bouckville Outdoor Antiques Show,* the state's largest antiques event, held the third weekend in August in *Bouckville.* More than 1,000 dealers from the United States and Canada sell antiques and collectibles at stalls spread over ninety acres of farmland. A Dixieland band is on hand to provide entertainment, and a shuttle provides transportation to and from the parking lots. For information call (315) 824–2462 or check the Web site: www.bouckvilleantiquesshows.com.

At the beginning of the nineteenth century, a swamp south of Oneida Lake became Syracuse, a city that grew around the salt industry and the Erie Canal. Today, visitors can see the last of the "weighlock" buildings that once dotted the waterway. Built in 1850 in Greek Revival style, this weigh station for canal boats today houses the *Erie Canal Museum.*

Exhibits in the Weighlock Building include a 65-foot replica of a canal boat. The *Frank Buchanan Thomson,* named after a late museum director, offers a look at a typical Erie Canal vessel's crew quarters, immigrant accommodations, and cargo storage. Immigration along the canal is a special focus of the museum's exhibits, particularly with regard to its effects on Syracuse. The museum experience also includes a hands-on display of canal equipment and explanations of the engineering involved in connecting Albany and Buffalo by means of a 363-mile artificial waterway, with eighty-three locks and eighteen aqueducts. The job wasn't easy, but the result was the longest and most successful canal in the world.

The Erie Canal Museum, 318 Erie Boulevard East, Syracuse (315–471–0593; www.eriecanalmuseum.org), is open Tuesday to Saturday from 10:00 A.M. to 5:00 P.M. and Sunday 10:00 A.M. TO 3:00 P.M.; closed major holidays. Admission is free, but donations are appreciated.

From swamp to canal boomtown, Syracuse was a major commercial and industrial center by the end of the nineteenth century, and ready for culture with a capital C. The ***Everson Museum of Art*** was founded by George Fisk Comfort, who had been instrumental in establishing New York City's Metropolitan Museum and who served as founder and dean of the College of Fine Arts at Syracuse University. Comfort established the Syracuse Museum of Fine Arts, which had its the first exhibition in 1900. This initial show featured the work of impressionists such as Monet, Sisley, and Pissarro, as well as older, more recognized masters.

Renamed the Everson Museum in 1959 following a large bequest from Syracuse philanthropist Helen Everson, the museum moved in 1968 into its present quarters, a massive, modernist concrete structure that was architect I. M. Pei's first museum building. Its three exhibition levels contain nine galleries and a 50-foot-square two-story sculpture court.

The Everson Museum has extensive holdings of American art, including colonial portraits (one very famous one of George Washington), the works of nineteenth-century genre and luminist painters, and paintings by twentieth-century artists such as Robert Henri, John Sloan, Grandma Moses, Maxfield Parrish, Reginald Marsh, and Grant Wood. The museum possesses a good graphic-art collection and a small but comprehensive photography section.

onebigoldtree

In Camillus Forest Unique Area, just west of Syracuse, there is a sugar maple tree with a diameter of 42 inches. It is believed to be nearly 300 years old. The sugar maple is New York State's Official Tree.

The museum's Syracuse China Center for the Study of American Ceramics houses the nation's premier collection in this field, with holdings dating from A.D. 1000 to the present. Here are pre-Columbian Native American vessels, colonial and nineteenth-century pieces, and contemporary functional and art pottery, as well as some 1,200 examples of ceramic craftsmanship from cultures outside the Western Hemisphere.

The Everson Museum of Art, 401 Harrison Street, Syracuse (315–474–6064; www.everson.org), is open Tuesday through Friday noon to 5:00 P.M., Saturday 10:00 A.M. to 5:00 P.M., and Sunday noon to 5:00 P.M. Closed holidays. Admission is free, although a suggested donation of $5.00 is welcome.

A Tale of Salt City

Charles Dickens visited Syracuse, once also known as "Salt City," in 1869 to give a reading in the Weiting Opera House. He stayed in the Syracuse Hotel and wrote:

"I am here in a most wonderful out-of-the-world place, which looks as if it had begun to be built yesterday, and were going to be imperfectly knocked together with a nail or two the day after tomorrow. I am in the worst inn that ever was seen, and outside is a thaw that places the whole country under water . . .

"We had an old buffalo for supper and an old pig for breakfast and we are going to have I don't know what for dinner at 6. In the public room downstairs, a number of men (speechless) with their feet against window frames, staring out the window and spitting dolefully at intervals . . . And yet we have taken in considerably over 300 pounds for tomorrow night."

At *Clark's Ale House,* 122 West Jefferson Street (315–479–9859), you may be in a quandary about what to drink: It carries thirty-two draughts from around the world, including the house beer, Armory Ale, from Middle Ages Brewery just up the road. But eating is a breeze: The specialty is hot roast beef on an onion roll. The pub is in the Landmark Theatre building and is open Monday through Wednesday 11:00 to 1:00 A.M., Thursday through Saturday until 2:00 A.M.

If you've always wondered where salt comes from, visit the *Salt Museum* near Syracuse, "The City That Salt Built." At one time the area supplied the entire nation with the "white gold." The museum, constructed of timbers from former salt warehouses, explains the method of turning brine into salt, a process that endured until the 1920s.

The Salt Museum, in Onondaga Lake Park, 106 Lake Drive, Onondaga Lake Parkway, *Liverpool* (315–453–6712; www.onondagacountyparks.com), is open May through mid-October, daily 1:00 to 4:00 P.M. Admission is free.

Bed & Breakfast Wellington, a National Historic Landmark designed by Ward Wellington Ward, is a 1914 brick and stucco Tudor-style home with canvas flooring, an arched foyer, leaded glass windows, and tile insets. Rates for the five guest rooms (including a housekeeping suite) range from $75 to $125, including private bath and breakfast. The B&B is at 707 Danforth Street in Syracuse (315–474–3641 or 800–724–5006; www.bbwellington.com).

If your curiosity about canals has not yet been sated, you might want to sign on for a grand tour—a two-, three-, or four-day journey down the Cayuga-Seneca, the Oswego, the Champlain, and the Erie Canals. *Mid-Lakes Navigation Company, Ltd.,* offers escorted, navigated, and catered cruises, with departures from Buffalo, Syracuse, and Albany. During the day passengers

Lockmaster Hireboat, Mid-Lakes Navigation Company, Ltd.

travel and dine aboard *Emita II,* a reconverted passenger ferry. At night the boat ties up on shore, and passengers check into a local hotel. It's a perfect blending of the nineteenth and twentieth centuries.

The company also runs weeklong bare-boat charters from Syracuse aboard European-style Lockmaster hireboats, as well as daily cruises on the Erie Canal and Skaneateles Lake.

Mid-Lakes Navigation Company, Ltd., is headquartered at 11 Jordan Street, P.O. Box 61, *Skaneateles* 13152 (315–685–8500 or 800–545–4318; www.mid lakesnav.com).

Places to Stay in the Mohawk Valley

ALBANY

Angels Bed and Breakfast
96 Madison Avenue
(518) 426–4104
www.angelsbedandbreakfast
.com

Desmond Hotel
660 Albany-Shaker Road
(518) 869–8100
www.desmondhotelsalbany
.com

ALTAMONT

Appel Inn
590 Route 146
(518) 861–6557
www.appelinn.com

LITTLE FALLS

Gansevoort House Inn and Galleries
42 West Gansevoort Street
(315) 823–3969
www.gansevoorthouse.com

ONEIDA CASTLE

Governor's House B&B
50 Seneca Avenue
(800) 437–8177

ROTTERDAM

Malozzi's Belvedere Hotel
1926 Curry Road
(518) 630–4020
www.malozzis.com

SCHENECTADY

Parker Inn
424 State Street
(518) 688–1001
www.parkerinn.com

SCOTIA

The Glen Sanders Mansion
1 Glen Avenue
(518) 374–7262

SYRACUSE

The Craftsman Inn
7300 Genesee Street
(800) 797–4464
www.craftsmaninn.com

Places to Eat in the Mohawk Valley

ALBANY

Jack's Oyster House
42 State Street
(518) 465–8854
www.jacksoysterhouse.com

Miss Albany Diner
893 Broadway
(518) 465–9148
www.missalbanydiner.com

Nicole's Bistro
351 Broadway
(518) 465–1111
www.nicolesbistro.com

COOPERSTOWN

Hoffman Lane Bistro
2 Hoffman Lane
(607) 547–7055
www.hoffmanlanebistro.com

T.J.'s Place
124 Main Street
(800) 860–5670
www.tjs-place.com

Turncliff Inn Tap Room
34 Pioneer Street
(607) 547–9860
www.turncliffinn.com

SCHENECTADY

Bourbon Street Bar and Grill
2209 Central Avenue
(518) 382–1110

Center Stage Deli at Proctor's
432 State Street
(518) 377–5401

SCOTIA

The Glen Sanders Mansion
1 Glen Avenue
(518) 374–7262

SYRACUSE

Dinosaur Bar-B-Cue
246 Willow Street
(315) 476–4937
www.dinosaurbarbque.com

SYLVAN BEACH

Harpoon Eddie's
611 Park Avenue
(315) 762–5238
www.sylvanbeach.com/harpoons

REGIONAL TOURIST INFORMATION— THE MOHAWK VALLEY

Regional Information
(800) 732–8259
(Capital-Saratoga)
www.capital-saratoga.com

Albany County Convention & Visitors Bureau
25 Quackenbush Square
Albany 12207
(518) 434–1217 or (800) 258–3582
www.albany.org

Fulton County Gateway to the Adirondacks
2 North Main Street
Gloversville 12078
(800) 676–3858
www.fultoncountyny.org

Otsego County Tourism
(800) 843–3394
www.visitcooperstown.com

Schenectady County Chamber of Commerce
306 State Street
Schenectady 12305
(800) 962–8007
www.schenectadychamber.org

Syracuse Convention & Visitors Bureau
572 South Salina Street
Syracuse 13202
(800) 234–4797 or (315) 470–1910
www.visitsyracuse.org

OTHER ATTRACTIONS WORTH SEEING IN THE MOHAWK VALLEY

Historic Cherry Hill
523½ South Pearl Street
Albany
(518) 434–4791
www.historiccherryhill.org

Howe Caverns
Caverns Road
Howes Cave
(518) 296–8990
www.howecaverns.com

New York State Capitol
Albany
(518) 474–2418

New York State Museum
Empire State Plaza
Albany
(518) 474–5877
www.nysm.nysed.gov

Proctor's Theater
432 State Street
Schenectady
(518) 382–3884 or (518) 346–2604
www.proctors.org

Schenectady Stockade Area
Front Street
Schenectady
(518) 372–5656 or (800) 962–8007

Ten Broeck Mansion
9 Ten Broeck Place
Albany
(518) 436–9826

The Finger Lakes

Here, between New York's "northern seaboard" along Lake Ontario and the Pennsylvania border, lies the region that many visitors consider to be the most beautiful part of the state. South of the Lake Ontario plain, the land appears to have been furrowed on a vast scale, with hilly farmland descending toward each of the Finger Lakes only to rise again before the next. The aptly named elongated lakes extend roughly north and south across an 80-mile swath of the state, offering vistas so reminiscent of parts of Switzerland that it's no wonder the city at the northern end of Seneca Lake was named Geneva.

Another distinctly European aspect of the Finger Lakes area is its status as New York State's premier wine-growing region. No longer limited only to the cultivation of native grape varieties, New York's vintners have come a long way, as visits to individual vineyards and the wine museum described in this section will demonstrate.

Scenes of well-tended vines in rows along steep hillsides may put you in mind of Europe, but the Finger Lakes region is rich in Americana. Here are museums of coverlets, Victorian dolls, and horse-drawn carriages. You'll even find Mark Twain's study and a museum devoted to Memorial Day.

THE FINGER LAKES

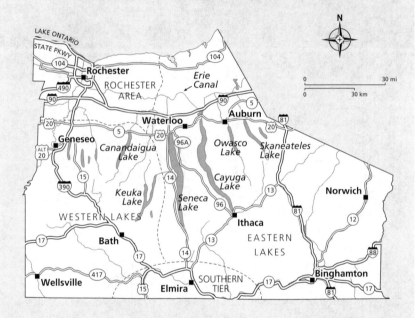

We'll approach this area from the south, beginning near the Pennsylvania border and continuing up toward Rochester, then heading east along the New York State Thruway and the northern Finger Lakes.

The Southern Tier

Mark Twain is revered for his tales of life on the Mississippi, but in fact, he wrote many of the stories here in New York, in a charming little summer house now located on the campus of Elmira College and preserved as the **Mark Twain Study.**

In 1870 Twain married an Elmira woman named Olivia Langdon, and for years the author and his family took leave of their palatial Hartford home to spend many productive summers with Olivia's sister, Mrs. Theodore Crane. Mrs. Crane and her husband lived on a farm outside Elmira, where in 1874 they built Twain a freestanding octagonal study, with windows on all sides and a massive stone fireplace. Here Twain wrote *Tom Sawyer* and completed sections of *Huckleberry Finn, Life on the Mississippi, A Connecticut Yankee in King Arthur's Court*, and other works. It was, he said, "the loveliest study you ever saw."

Difficult to maintain and protect from vandalism, the study was donated to Elmira College by the Langdon family in 1952, whereupon it was removed to its present site.

The Mark Twain Study, on the Elmira College Campus off Main Street, Elmira (607–735–1941), is open from mid-June to Labor Day, Monday through Saturday 9:00 A.M. to 5:00 P.M. and Sunday noon to 5:00 P.M. To arrange off-season visits write The Center for Mark Twain Studies, Quarry Farm, Box 900, Elmira College, Elmira 14901.

Head up Jerusalem Hill Road in Elmira to the **Hill Top Inn Restaurant**'s outdoor terrace for a great view of the Chemung Valley along with satisfying

AUTHORS' FAVORITES—FINGER LAKES

Dr. Konstantin Frank Vinifera Wine Cellars

House of Guitars

Letchworth State Park

Mark Twain Study

National Soaring Museum

Paleontological Research Institution

Pat Mitchell's Homemade Ice Cream

Rockwell Museum of Western Art

Schein-Joseph International Museum of Ceramic Art

Willard Memorial Chapel

Sundae's Cool

While other cities may lay claim to the invention of the sundae, it is Ithaca that has the earliest documentation, dating back to April 5, 1891: a newspaper advertisement announcing the "Cherry Sunday, a New 10 cent Ice Cream Specialty Served only at Platt & Colt's Famous day and night Soda Fountain."

traditional American cuisine. The Sullivan family has been greeting and feeding patrons since 1933. Their menu ranges from American staples such as steak, broiled seafood, and lamb, to Italian dishes including veal Marsala; homemade desserts are a specialty. The Hill Top Inn Restaurant is open for dinner Monday through Saturday beginning at 5:00 P.M., and in June, July, and August from 4:00 to 8:00 P.M. Closed some holidays. Reservations are recommended. Call (607) 732–6728 or (888) 4–HILL–TOP.

The three-story Italianate mansion *Lindenwald Haus,* with its twenty-one renovated Victorian guest rooms, has been a popular place to stay for more than 115 years since it was built to house widows of the Civil War. There are nine rooms with private bath, ten with shared bath. The five-acre grounds are dotted with fruit trees; guests are welcome to walk, bike, or swim.

Lindenwald Haus, 1526 Grand Central Avenue, Elmira (607–733–8753 or 800–440–4287; www.lindenwaldhaus.com), is open year-round. Rates range from $74 to $115 for a deluxe suite and include a full breakfast.

When Mark Twain's study was at its original site on the Quarry Farm belonging to his in-laws, it commanded a lovely view of the undulating hills along the Chemung River Valley. Little did Twain suspect that within a few decades after his death, these same hills would attract recreationists content not merely to walk the trails and pastures but instead to soar quietly far above them. By the 1930s Harris Hill, outside Elmira, had become the "Soaring Capital of America." The science and sport of motorless flight is today kept vigorously alive at the *National Soaring Museum,* which offers visitors earthbound exhibits and the opportunity to go aloft in sailplanes piloted by experienced professionals.

Regardless of whether you agree with the museum's philosophy that soaring is "flying as nature intended," a visit to the facility offers a good introduction to this often overlooked aspect of modern aviation. The museum houses the world's largest exhibit of contemporary and historic sailplanes, along with displays explaining the development of soaring and its relation to the parallel fields of meteorology and aerodynamics. You can even climb into a cockpit simulator, similar to those used to teach soaring, and learn what the experience of controlling a motorless plane is like.

Well, almost. To really understand soaring, you have to get off the ground. This can easily be arranged at the museum or at the Harris Hill Soaring Corp. Visitors' Center, which has a staff of competent pilots licensed by the FAA. Just check in at the Harris Hill Gliderport—the rides are available all summer long and on weekends throughout the year, weather permitting. Even if you don't go up yourself, it's fun to watch the graceful, silent flights and landings of the sleek sailplanes.

The National Soaring Museum, Harris Hill, RD 3, Elmira (607–734–3128 for office or 734–0641 for glider field; www.soaringmuseum.org), is open daily from 10:00 A.M. to 5:00 P.M. (closed some holidays). Admission is $6.50 for adults, $5.50 for seniors, and $4.00 for children ages 5 to 17. Call regarding schedules and cost of sailplane flights.

Upstream along the Chemung River is *Corning,* indelibly associated with the Corning Glass Company, its famous Steuben Glass Factory, and the Corning Glass Center and Museum. A more intimate environment in which magnificent glass pieces are created by traditional glassblowing techniques is *Vitrix Hot Glass Studio* in Corning's historic Market Street district. Since 1959 Vitrix has been turning out some of the country's finest handblown glass pieces.

Vitrix Hot Glass Studio, 77 West Market Street, Corning (607–936–8707), is open Monday through Friday 10:00 A.M. to 6:00 P.M., Saturday 10:00 A.M. to 8:00 P.M., and Sunday noon to 5:00 P.M. Glassblowers are at work on weekends only.

The aptly named *Glass Menagerie* is one of the world's largest dealers in kaleidoscopes. The shop represents more than 100 scope artists, inventories at least 200 examples of their work at all times, and hosts annual summer kaleidoscope shows. But the store has a much broader scope: It also carries leaded glass guardian angels made by Carl Goeller, a huge selection of mouth-blown hand-painted Christopher Radko limited edition Christmas ornaments, and unique paperweights. Also for sale: glass animals, perfume bottles, and glass and ceramic menorahs. One of the owners, Dick Pope, is a professional

As in Life, So in Death

Elmira's Woodlawn Cemetery, burial place of Mark Twain, also contains the graves of Union and Confederate Civil War soldiers. The Confederates are facing south, and the Union graves surround them—exactly as the Union soldiers surrounded their prisoners of war when all died in a nearby railroad accident during the war.

ANNUAL EVENTS IN THE FINGER LAKES

MARCH

Central New York Maple Festival
Marathon
(607) 849-3278
www.maplefest.org

MAY

Lilac Festival
Rochester
(585) 256-4960
www.lilacfestival.com

JUNE

Ithaca Festival
Ithaca
(800) 273-3646
www.ithacafestival.org

Strawberry Festival
Owego
(607) 687-2556
www.strawberryfestival.owego.org

Waterfront Festival and Cardboard Regatta
Watkins Glen
(607) 535-3003
www.watkinsglen.com/festival

JULY

Finger Lakes Grassroots Festival
Trumansburg
(607) 387-5144
www.grassrootsfestival.org/trumansburg

Finger Lakes Wine Festival
Watkins Glen
(866) 461-7223
www.flwinefest.com

Hill Cumorah Pageant
Palmyra
(315) 597-5851
www.hillcumorah.org/Pageant

The Great American Antiquefest
Onondaga Lake Park
Liverpool
(315) 457-6954
www.antiquefest.biz

magician and often gives impromptu performances when he's around. Take time to duck upstairs to *Books of Marvel.* The antiquarian enterprise has one of the world's largest collections of old and rare juvenile series fiction.

The Glass Menagerie, 37 East Market Street, Corning (607–962–6300), is open year-round. During the summer the shop is open daily from 9:30 A.M. to 9:30 P.M. Call for hours the rest of the year.

The ***Rockwell Museum of Western Art*** owes its existence almost entirely to Robert F. Rockwell, an area native and former proprietor of a small department store chain whose interest in western art dates to his youth spent on a Colorado ranch. He began collecting seriously in the late 1950s, acquiring works bymasters of "cowboy" art such as Charles M. Russell and Frederic Remington, as well as by landscapists of the caliber of Albert Bierstadt and Thomas Hill and by animal artists A.F. Tait and Carl Rungius.

AUGUST

Empire Farm Days
Seneca Falls
(585) 526–5356
www.empirefarmdays.com

NASCAR Winston Cup at the Glen
Watkins Glen
(607) 535–2486

Monroe County Fair
Henrietta
(585) 334–4000
www.mcfair.com

SEPTEMBER

Grand Prix Festival
Watkins Glen
(607) 535–3003
www.grandprixfestival.com

Golden Harvest Festival
Baldwinsville
(315) 638–2519

Great Grape Festival
Naples
(585) 374–2240
www.naplesvalleyny.com/grapefestival
.php

OCTOBER

Letchworth Arts and Crafts Show
Mount Morris
(585) 493–3600 or (585) 237–3517

NOVEMBER

Lights on the Lake
Onondaga Lake Park
(through early January)
Liverpool
(315) 437–5627
www.lightsonthelake.com

DECEMBER

Dickens Christmas
Skaneateles
(315) 685–2268
www.skaneateles.com/dickens.html

Rockwell's protean interests went beyond western art and sculpture to include an area dear to him as a Corning resident: the beautiful art glass created by Frederic Carder, cofounder of the Steuben Glass Works, which was later incorporated into Corning Glass Works, now Corning, Inc. Rockwell even collected antique toys.

By the 1980s, Rockwell's collections were too extensive to be casually shown in his department stores and as part of exhibitions lent to other institutions. He needed a museum, and he found a suitable venue in Corning's old city hall, a Romanesque Revival structure built in 1893. The Corning Company acquired the building from the city for $1.00, renovations were undertaken, and in 1982 the Rockwell Museum opened. At present it houses the largest collection of western art on the East Coast, more than 2,000 pieces of Carder Steuben glass, Navajo weavings, antique firearms, Indian artifacts, and the toy collection as well.

The Rockwell Museum of Western Art, 111 Cedar Street at Denison Parkway, Corning (607–937–5386), is open daily 9:00 A.M. to 5:00 P.M. In summer it stays open until 8:00 P.M. The museum is closed Thanksgiving, Christmas Eve, Christmas Day, and New Year's. Admission is $6.50 for adults, $5.50 for senior citizens and students. Youths 17 and under are free.

Western Lakes

The southern Finger Lakes region is a tranquil, easy-paced corner of the world that nevertheless nurtured one of twentieth-century America's great speed demons. At **Hammondsport,** on the southern tip of Keuka Lake, the **Glenn H. Curtiss Museum** chronicles the lifework of this native son, who was also a serious pioneer in motorcycling and aviation.

Glenn Hammond Curtiss started out, as did the Wright brothers, in the bicycle business. He quickly turned to motorcycles, building a V-8–powered bike on which he sped more than 136 miles per hour in 1907. He also built engines that powered lighter-than-air craft, and in that same year he became involved with Dr. Alexander Graham Bell and other enthusiasts in the "Aerial Experiment Association." Curtiss's engineering helped lift the association's airplane *Red Wing* off the ice of Keuka Lake on the first public flight (as opposed to the Wrights' secret 1903 experiment) of a heavier-than-air craft in the United States.

Glenn Curtiss's accomplishments over the next twenty years dominated the adolescence of aeronautics. In 1910 he landed a plane on water for the first time, and in 1911 he became the first American to receive a pilot's license. In 1919 a Curtiss "flying boat" made the first transatlantic crossing by air. Meanwhile he had built his Curtiss Aeroplane and Motor Company into an industrial giant, employing 10,000 men at the peak of production during World War I. Sensing the traveling trends of the motor age, he even manufactured the first successful house trailers. Following a merger, the company became Curtiss-Wright, producer of World War II aircraft such as the Navy Helldiver and the P-40 of "Flying Tigers" fame. The museum, founded in 1960, houses seven historic aircraft and three reproductions; one of the latter is a flyable replica of the inventor's 1908 *June Bug*.

The Glenn H. Curtiss Museum, Route 54, ½ mile south of Hammondsport (607–569–2160), is open from May 1 through October 31, Monday through Saturday 9:00 A.M. to 5:00 P.M. and Sunday 10:00 A.M. to 5:00 P.M.; from November 1 through April 30, it is open Monday through Saturday 10:00 A.M. to 4:00 P.M. and Sunday 10:00 A.M. to 4:00 P.M. Admission is $7.00 for adults, $5.00 for senior citizens, $4.00 for students, and free for children ages 6 and under.

There's hardly anyplace more off-the-beaten-path than **Dr. Konstantin Frank Vinifera Wine Cellars,** on the western banks of Keuka Lake. Yet oenophiles still wend their way through the vineyards to reach the tasting room, eager to sip the Pinot Noirs, the Gewürztraminers, the sparkling wines, and especially the Rieslings. Dr. Frank's wines have won dozens of gold medals and have been ranked among the country's best wines by tastemakers like *Wine Spectator* magazine, finally bringing New York vintages into the national spotlight.

Back in the 1950s, when Dr. Frank arrived from Europe speaking not a word of English, vintners in the Finger Lakes were using indigenous American grapes to make wine that was pretty harsh and unsophisticated. A doctor of viticulture in his native Ukraine, Dr. Frank believed that the *Vitis Vinifera,* the wine grapes of Europe, could be cultivated here, even with the cold winters. He proved it by grafting the varietal vines onto hardy rootstock, and today we can savor the fruits of his labor.

Seek out Dr. Konstantin Frank Vinifera Wine Cellars at 9749 Middle Road, Hammondsport (800–320–0735; www.DrFrankWines.com), or purchase some of Dr. Frank's finest at your local wine merchant.

Dr. Frank's success inspired the neighboring vineyards to follow his lead, sparking a revolution in the New York wine industry. Explore this and a century and a half of winemaking history at the **Taylor Wine Museum** next door to Bully Hill Vineyards.

Dr. Konstantin Frank Vinifera Wine Cellars

The Taylor Wine Museum, G.H. Taylor Memorial Drive, Hammondsport (607–868–3610; www.bullyhill.com), is open from mid-May through October 31, Monday through Saturday 9:00 A.M. to 5:00 P.M., Sunday noon to 5:00 P.M. The visitor center offers wine tastings every half hour and tours every hour. Donations are welcome. A restaurant next door specializes in moderately priced homemade pasta and dishes prepared with wine. The Bully Hill Vineyards can also be visited for tours and tastings; call (607) 868–3610.

Want to spend the night on a train? Check into the *Caboose Motel,* 8620 State Route 415N, *Avoca* (607–566–2216; www.caboosemotel.net). In addition to eighteen standard units, the state's only caboose motel rents five N5 cars equipped with all modern amenities and a speaker that provides train sounds. One unit can accommodate six, the others up to five in upper and lower berths. The cabooses are available spring and summer for $80 a night. There are also fourteen conventional rooms that range from $57 to $71.

Although far less well known than southeastern Pennsylvania for its Amish and Mennonite populations, the Finger Lakes region long ago attracted members of these peaceful and industrious sects because of its rich farmland and relative isolation from modern big-city hubbub. One of the most valued and enduring of Amish and Mennonite traditions is quiltmaking, and at *The Quilt Room* in *Penn Yan,* more than 200 quilts and wall hangings reveal the meticulous artisanship of women from the surrounding area. In addition to the quilts on display—many of them one of a kind—The Quilt Room can engage quilters to create special-order goods based on any of several thousand traditional designs. Repair work is available as well.

The Quilt Room, 1870 Hoyt Road, Penn Yan (315–536–5964 or 877–536–5964; www.quiltroom.org), is open year-round; call for hours.

The Victorian *Finton's Landing Bed & Breakfast* overlooking Keuka Lake—nicknamed "the American Rhine"—was built in the 1860s as a steamboat

Uncork New York

There are about one-hundred wineries large and small in the Finger Lakes. Visitors can either let serendipity be their guide, taking a leisurely drive through the area and stopping when the spirit moves, or they can carefully plan a tasting route with the help of several Web sites: www.fingerlakeswinecountry.com (866–946–3386); www.senecalakewine.com (877–536–2717); www.keukalakewinetrail.com (800–440–4898); www.cayugawinetrail.com (800–684–5217); and www.newyorkwines.org (585–394–3620). You can find listings of wineries as well as places to eat, shop, and stay overnight; download the information you need or request maps and brochures.

landing for loading grapes harvested in the area. Today the carefully restored, secluded inn, with a gazebo and L-shaped dock, has four guest rooms with private baths and queen-size beds, air conditioning, and handmade quilts; and a wraparound porch where a two-course breakfast is served (weather permitting). There's also a private beach.

Finton's Landing Bed & Breakfast, 661 East Lake Road, Penn Yan (315–536–3146; www.home.eznet.net/~tepperd), is open year-round. The rate ranges from $139 to $169 for a double (there is a two-night minimum) and includes breakfast. The inn is smoke-free.

If you're looking for seclusion—and magnificent mountain views—check out the **Vagabond Inn.** The 7,000-square-foot inn stands in splendid isolation on top of a mountain in the **Bristol** range. Popular with honeymooners, the inn has a 60-foot-long Great Room with two massive fieldstone fireplaces, a Japanese garden, and an in-ground pool.

Don't be hasty in choosing a room: Each of the five has its special charms. For example, the Bristol has its own fireplace, a Jacuzzi for two (with views of the mountains), and rents for $225. The Lodge, for $245, has a huge river-stone fireplace and hot-tub chamber. Rates include breakfast.

The Vagabond Inn, 3300 Sliter Road, Naples (585–554–6271; www.thevagabondinn.com), is open all year.

If you're visiting the area in late September, you might be just in time to sample one of the region's most unusual delicacies—Naples Grape Pie. Local bakeries produce more than 10,000 grape pies six weeks of the year, beginning with the start of the Annual **Naples** Grape Festival. If you're there any other time of the year, stop in for a slice at **Arbor Hill.** They serve them up all year, along with their wines and other wine food products, in a restored eighteenth-century building that once served as the local post office. They also serve light barbecue-style lunches featuring wine soup, wine sausage, and—for dessert— hot grape sundaes. In summer and fall, the winery hosts several five-course gourmet dinners and buffets featuring its vintages.

Arbor Hill, 6461 Route 64, **Bristol Springs** (Naples) (800–554–7553 or 585–374–2406), is open daily from May through the first week in January, Monday through Saturday 10:00 A.M. to 5:00 P.M. and Sunday 11:00 A.M. to 5:00 P.M., open weekends only from January through May. For a dinner schedule, check www.thegrapery.com.

At the southeast corner of the **Alfred University** campus is the **Stull Observatory,** considered to be one of the finest teaching observatories in the Northeast. It exists largely through the efforts of John Stull, who built or rebuilt all of the telescopes and many of the buildings. There are five major telescopes at the observatory: a 9-inch refractor dating from 1863, a 16-inch Cassegrain reflector, and 14-, 20-, and 32-inch Newtonian reflectors.

The Stull Observatory at Alfred University, **Alfred** (607–871–2208; www.merlin.alfred.edu/stull), offers public viewings (weather permitting) at the following times: September, October, November, February, March, and April, Friday from 9:00 to 11:00 P.M.; May, June, and July, Thursday from 10:00 P.M. until midnight. Admission is free.

Nearly 8,000 ceramic and glass objects—from pottery shards left behind by ancient civilizations, to works that reflect the cutting edge of ceramic technology—are housed at the **Schein-Joseph International Museum of Ceramic Art.** The museum is a teaching and research arm of the New York State College of Ceramics at Alfred University. Among its permanent collections are tomb sculptures from the Neolithic period through the Yuan dynasty, Chinese funerary jars, and works by artists such as Charles Fergus Binns, Walter Ostrom, Mary Roettger, Rosanjin Kitaoji, and Bernard Leach.

The Schein-Joseph International Museum of Ceramic Art, New York State College of Ceramics, Alfred University, Alfred (607–871–2421), is just off Route 244. It is just across from the Horticulture Building on the second floor of the Ceramics Corridor Innovation Center. The museum is open Wednesday through Friday 10:00 A.M. to 4:00 P.M. Admission is free.

In July 1937 a freight train pulled into Alfred Station carrying thirty-five bells from Antwerp, Belgium. Eighteen of the bells, which weighed a total of 5,153 pounds (one, called the Bourdon, weighs about 3,850 pounds), were made in 1674 by Pieter Hemony, a famous Netherlands bellfounder. They were hung in a wooden tower overlooking the valley and, shortly after, the **Davis Memorial Carillon** rang out over the hills for the first time.

A carillon is a musical instrument consisting of twenty-three or more cast bronze cup-shaped bells, which are precisely tuned so that many bells can be sounded together to produce a harmonious effect (the bells are stationary, only the clappers move). And if you're lucky enough to be in the vicinity on one of the days that the carillonneur is performing, you can hear just how harmonious a sound the carillon (which now has forty-seven bells) can make. Recitals are given Saturday (except over Christmas break and in August) at 4:00 P.M. throughout the year (except January and August) and on Monday, Wednesday, and Friday from 12:30 to 12:45 P.M. during the academic year. In addition the Wingate Memorial Summer Carillon Recital Series brings guest recitalists to perform Tuesday evenings in the month of July.

For information contact the Alfred University Division of Performing Arts, Alfred (607–871–2562; www.alfred.edu/map/carillon). There is no admission fee.

At the 14,350-acre **Letchworth State Park,** nicknamed the "Grand Canyon of the East," the Genesee River cascades down more than twenty waterfalls as it winds its way north through a series of beetling gorges, some almost 600 feet high. Visitors can drive through the park on a road that parallels the gorge or hike one of twenty hiking trails of varying difficulty and length.

Accommodations at the park include a campground, cabins, and the yellow-and-white Victorian *Glen Iris Inn* (585–493–2622; www.glenirisinn.com) overlooking Mid Falls, which offers clean, comfortable rooms starting at $80 and suites from $140 from early April to early November. In winter, houses are available from $185 to $285. The inn, the former home of William Pryor Letchworth, who began construction on the building in 1859 and deeded the building and grounds to the state in 1907, has welcomed guests since 1914. Glen Iris serves three meals a day, and offers a special picnic menu.

Just across from the inn, the *Letchworth Museum* is stuffed with exhibits relating to the park's history. On a hill in back of the museum is the grave of Mary Jemison, the "white woman of the Genesee." A prisoner of the Seneca from the age of fifteen, she eventually married a chief and later became a leader of her adopted people. Under the Big Tree Treaty of 1797, she was granted a large parcel of land along the river and lived there until she moved to Buffalo Creek Reservation. William Letchworth had her remains brought back and interred here in 1910.

Letchworth State Park, Genesee State Park and Recreation Region, 1 Letchworth State Park, Castile (585–493–3600; www.nysparks.state.ny.us/parks), is open year-round. There is an admission fee of $6.00 per day per car on weekends off-season; daily Memorial Day weekend through October. The museum (585–493–2760) is open daily from May through October between 10:00 A.M. and 5:00 P.M. A $1.00 donation is requested.

For those who would rather float over the falls than drive alongside them, *Balloons Over Letchworth* offers flights in the *Gentle Giant*, a seven-story hot-air balloon. The voyages, which last approximately one hour (guests should plan on a total time of 2½ to 3 hours) end with a champagne celebration and cost $189 for one person or $179 each for three or more. There is a $10 surcharge per person during the month of October. The launch area is at the Middle/Upper Falls picnic area, a thousand feet south of the Glen Iris Inn. The office is at 6645 Denton Corners Road, Castile (585–493–3340).

While at the park, tour the $25-million *Mt. Morris Dam,* which, since it began operating in 1952, has prevented flood damages estimated at $1 billion. For information call (585) 658–4220.

Just west of Canandaigua Lake, the little town of Bristol has become renowned for pottery, hand-thrown and hand-decorated by "the Wizard of Clay," master potter Jim Kozlowski, and his assistants at *The Wizard of Clay Pottery.* Jim's production facilities and retail stores are housed in seven geodesic domes he designed himself.

The potter's wheel and eight kilns are in the workshop. All pieces are fired at a temperature of 2,265° F, which makes them extremely hard and durable, then treated with a specially formulated glaze that gives them a richly colored finish. The Wizard's most original pottery is decorated with delicate imprints from real leaves gathered from the Bristol hills.

The Wizard of Clay Pottery, 7851 Route 20A in Bristol, 3 miles east of Honeoye Lake (mailing address: 7851 Route 20A, Bloomfield 14469), (585–229–2980), is open daily from 9:00 A.M. until 5:00 P.M.; closed major holidays.

The town of **Horseheads** got its name in 1789 when settlers coming into the valley came upon the bleached skulls of pack horses left behind by General John Sullivan after his battle against the Six Nations of the Iroquois. The **Horseheads Historical Society Museum,** in the former train depot at the corner of Broad and Curns Streets, exhibits cartoons and paintings by the nationally renowned humorist Eugene Zimmerman, better known as "Zim." He lived in a home he designed at the corner of Pine and West Mill Streets: It is maintained by Historical Tours and open for tours by appointment. Zim also designed the bandstand in Teal Park.

The Horseheads Historical Society Museum is at the Depot, 312 West Broad Street & Curns Street, Horseheads (607–739–3938). Call for hours.

Wings of Eagles, formerly known as the National Warplane Museum, houses an impressive collection of aircraft dating from World War II to the present, as well as exhibits tracing the development of flight, ongoing special events, and a flight simulator in which visitors can experience virtual flight and gain an understanding of what it's like to fly in the cockpit of a warplane.

Wings of Eagles, Elmira-Corning Regional Airport, off Route 17 in Horseheads (607–739–8200; www.warplane.org), is open Monday through Friday 10:00 A.M. to 4:00 P.M., Saturday 9:00 A.M. to 5:00 P.M., and Sunday 11:00 A.M. to 5:00 P.M. Closed some major holidays. Admission is $7.00 for adults, $5.50 for senior citizens, $4.00 for children ages 6 to 17, and free for children under 6. A family admission is available for $18.00.

Rochester Area

"Spend a day in the nineteenth century," reads the invitation of the **Genesee Country Village & Museum,** the state's largest living history museum. It is located in **Mumford** on the southern outskirts of Rochester. The fifty-plus reconstructed buildings represent different periods in the development of upstate New York, from frontier days to late Victorian times.

The rail-fenced pioneer settlement reveals what rural living was like up near Lake Ontario around 1800. Just twenty-five years later prosperity brought

On a Pedestal

In 1899 Theodore Roosevelt, governor of New York, came to Rochester to dedicate the country's first public statue to be erected to honor an African American, Frederick Douglass (1807–95). The escaped slave, abolitionist, and newspaper publisher lived here for seventeen years. His home on Alexander Street was a station on the Underground Railroad. The bronze statue is in Highland Park on Highland Avenue. Douglass is interred in Mt. Hope Cemetery along with other luminaries, including his friend, women's rights champion Susan B. Anthony.

sumptuous Greek Revival homes such as Livingston Manor. Later came the Victorian quirks and fussy comforts of the 1870 Octagon House, with its tidy cupola and broad verandas. Other village buildings include a carriage barn containing a collection of forty horse-drawn vehicles; a Gallery of Sporting Art, showcasing paintings and sculpture inspired by wildlife and the hunt; and the *George Eastman* birthplace, moved here in homage to the man who made nearby Rochester a "film capital" of an entirely different sort than Hollywood, California. The John L. Wehle Gallery of Wildlife and Sporting Art exhibits North America's premier collection of wildlife and sporting art.

The Genesee Country Village & Museum, 1410 Flint Road off Route 36 in Mumford (585–538–6822; www.gcv.org), is open July through Labor Day Tuesday through Sunday 10:00 A.M. to 5:00 P.M.; the rest of the year Tuesday through Friday 10:00 A.M. to 4:00 P.M. and weekends and holidays 10:00 A.M. to 5:00 P.M. Closed Mondays except on holidays. There is a nature center at the village that is open all year, and special programs are held year-round. Admission is $14.95 for adults, $11.00 for seniors and students with ID, and $8.00 for children ages 4 to 16; under 4, free.

Richard Greeve's *Kiowa*, Genesee Country Village & Museum

If you picture a little girl in crinoline playing in the parlor of the Genesee Country Museum's Octagon House, you can well imagine the sort of dolls she might have for companions. Up near Rochester, in **North Chili,** Linda Greenfield has assembled a wonderful collection of these delicate and elaborately dressed playthings in her **Victorian Doll Museum.** The thousands of dolls at the museum not only reflect the tastes of the Victorian era but also show many types of doll construction that have faded from the picture in these days of molded plastic doll faces and bodies.

The Victorian Doll Museum premises are also the home of the **Chili Doll Hospital,** also run by Linda, who is an expert at doll restoration and repair. Antique dolls are appraised by appointment, and a collector's gift shop offers fine modern and period reproduction specimens.

The Victorian Doll Museum and Chili Doll Hospital, 4332 Buffalo Road, North Chili (585–247–0130), are open February through December, Tuesday through Saturday 10:00 A.M. to 4:30 P.M. Admission to the museum is $2.00 for adults and $1.00 for children ages 12 and under.

"Please touch, feel, and explore" is the motto at one of the state's most unusual—and fun—museums. **Strong Museum,** the legacy of buggy-whip heiress Margaret Woodbury Strong, explores American life and tastes since 1820 with a variety of imaginative permanent and changing exhibits. Among the more than 500,000 objects is the world's largest and most historically significant collection of toys and dolls and the country's most comprehensive collection of homecrafts, souvenirs, and advertising materials. The Time Lab, a hands-on learning lab and interactive warehouse, exhibits thousands of items, such as lava lamps and political buttons, from different periods. Visitors can select a tune from their tabletop jukebox while they dine on burgers and fries at the vintage Skyline Diner or enjoy a sundae at Louie's Sweet Shoppe.

nodistractions?

John D. Rockefeller Sr., Jay Gould, F. W. Woolworth, and George Eastman were among a host of nineteenth- and early twentieth-century tycoons who rose from the obscurity of small-town birthplaces in upstate New York.

The Strong Museum, One Manhattan Square, Rochester (585–263–2700; Events Line: 585–263–2702; www.strongmuseum.org), is open Monday through Thursday from 10:00 A.M. to 5:00 P.M., Friday 10:00 A.M. to 8:00 P.M., Saturday 10:00 A.M. to 5:00 P.M., Sunday from noon to 5:00 P.M. Closed Christmas and Thanksgiving. Admission is $9.00 for adults, $8.00 for senior citizens and students with school ID, and $7.00 for children ages 2 to 17.

The music emporium with the acronym HOG, which counts among its customers Metallica, Aerosmith, Motley Crue, Jon Bon Jovi, and Ozzy Osbourne, is actually a rambling complex of five warehouses "jam" packed with an array of "musicana" from guitars to amplifiers to concert T-shirts to a pair of Elvis Presley's leather pants.

The **House of Guitars** was established in 1964 by three brothers named Schaubroeck. Today the musical mecca in **Rochester**'s suburbs calls itself the "World's Largest Music Store" and stocks just about every brand of instrument (if they don't have it, they'll order it), including more than 11,000 guitars ranging in price from $60 to $50,000. Potential customers are invited to test the merchandise in one of several small rooms set aside for that purpose.

Don't be surprised if you stop by and find throngs of people at HOG. Throughout the year the musical brothers Schaubroeck host promotions and in-store appearances, featuring unknown, rising, and well-known performers. The winner of one of their most successful events, the "World's Worst Guitar Player Contest," won a $400 guitar and amp, six free lessons, and a one-way bus ticket to Canada.

The House of Guitars, 645 Titus Avenue, Rochester (585–544–3500), is open Monday through Saturday from 10:00 A.M. to 9:00 P.M. and Sunday 1:00 to 5:00 P.M.

South and east of Rochester is a monument to another important development in the history of American popular culture: the shopping mall. Not the steel-and-glass malls of the 1950s, but a sturdy wooden structure erected in

An Apple a Day

Drive along upstate New York's highways and byways in spring and you're sure to see apple orchards in bloom. The Empire State produces more than 25 million bushels a year, making it number two in the United States (number one is Washington state). The New York State Agricultural Experiment Station (NYSAES) in Geneva, part of Cornell University, has been improving the quality and quantity of apples grown for more than 125 years. In quest of fruit that is drought- and pest-resistant, the NYSAES has developed some of the tastiest hybrids. Among them are the Cortland, Jonagold, Jonamac, Macoun, and the most popular: the Empire apple, a cross between McIntosh and Red Delicious. Look for the more recently perfected Liberty and Fortune apples in stores, too.

Apple facts: Apples are a good source of vitamin C, fiber, boron, and the polyphenols quercitin and chlorogenic acid, powerful antioxidants that can protect against cancer, heart disease, stroke, and other conditions. An apple a day really can keep the doctor away! But be sure to eat the skin—that's where all the good phytochemicals are.

1879, it was built by Levi Valentine as an all-purpose market and community center for the settlement he was developing. Thus it lays claim to being the first multistore "shopping center" in the United States. Today it houses the **Valentown Museum,** a collection of nineteenth-century small-town memorabilia that includes a reconstruction of the first railroad station in the Rochester area and a "Scientific Exhibition," which traveled around the country in a covered wagon from 1825 to 1880.

Valentown Hall, as Valentine called his "mall," had front doors opening into a general store, meat market, cobbler shop, barber shop, bakery, and harness shop. The upstairs contained a Grange lodge, rooms where classes in the arts and trades were held, and a community ballroom. The ambitious scheme lasted only thirty years, since the promised railroad connection never materialized (the restored station interior belonged to an earlier rail operation). The building was saved from demolition and restored in 1940 by J. Sheldon Fisher, a member of the Fisher family that gave its name to the town of **Fishers,** in which the hall is located. Contact the Valentown Museum, at Valentown Square, Fishers (585–924–2645).

"Ganondagan . . . a city or village of bark, situated at the top of a mountain of earth, to which one rises by three terraces. It appeared to us, from a distance, to be crowned with round towers." This is how M. L'Abbé De Belmont described a major town of the Seneca people, one of the five original Indian nations that have inhabited central New York since prehistoric times. A short time later the governor general of New France led an army from Canada against the Seneca in an effort to eliminate them as competitors in the international fur trade.

The story of the Seneca people and the Iroquois (Haudenosaunee) Confederacy to which they belonged is recounted at **Ganondagan State Historic Site,** the state's largest Seneca community in the seventeenth century. The 522-acre National Historic Landmark encompasses the palisaded granary M. L'Abbé De Belmont described, a sacred burial ground, and a system of trails. A twenty-seven-minute video in the visitor center relates the history of Ganondagan. A reconstructed bark longhouse similar to ones lived in by the Seneca people is one of the site's high points.

The Visitors Center at Ganondagan State Historic Site, 1488 Victor-Holcomb Road, **Victor** (585–742–1690; www.ganondagan.org), is open Tuesday through Sunday 9:00 A.M. to 5:00 P.M. May through October. Interpretive trails are open year-round from 8:00 A.M. to sunset, weather permitting. The bark longhouse is open Tuesday through Sunday 10:00 A.M. to noon and 1:00 to 4:00 P.M. The trails are open all year. Admission is $3.00 for adults and $2.00 for children.

The early days of vacuum tubes and crystal radios are chronicled in the Antique Wireless Association's **Electronic Communication Museum** south of the thruway in **East Bloomfield.** The museum's collections, housed in the handsome 1837 quarters of the East Bloomfield Historical Society, have been amassed by AWA members throughout the world. They include nineteenth-century telephones (in working order!), some of Marconi's original wireless apparatus, early shipboard wireless equipment, and the crystal radio sets that brought the first broadcast programs into American living rooms. A special attraction is a fully stocked replica of a circa 1925 radio store; another is wireless station W2AN, an actual broadcast operation staffed by AWA members.

The AWA Electronic Communication Museum, on the Village Green just off Routes 5 and 20, Bloomfield (585–657–6260; www.antiquewireless.org/museum, is open May 1 to October 31, Sunday 2:00 to 5:00 P.M.; also open Saturday 2:00 to 4:00 P.M. during July and August. Closed holidays. Admission is free.

Preserved Americana seems to be the order of the day in this part of upstate New York, and the theme is carried along nicely at the **Granger Homestead and Carriage Museum** in **Canandaigua.** "Homestead" is actually a bit too homespun a term for this grand Federal mansion, which must have been the talk of Canandaigua and all the farms around when it was built in 1816 by Gideon Granger, a lawyer who had served as postmaster general under Jefferson and Madison. Granger came here to live the life of a country squire in his retirement, and his descendants lived here until 1930. Nine restored rooms contain the furniture of the nineteenth century, including Federal, Empire, and Victorian styles. Decorative objects, original artworks, and China Trade porcelain are also displayed.

A distinctive attraction of the Granger Homestead is the Carriage Museum, which exhibits more than fifty horse-drawn vehicles made or used in western New York. The sociological implications of the various conveyances on display are explained in an informative exhibit titled "Sleighs and Surreys and Signs and Symbols." Forty-five-minute horse-drawn antique carriage rides through the town's historic neighborhoods are offered by reservation on Friday at noon, 1:00, 2:00, 3:00 and 4:00 P.M. through late October. Adults are $20; children 4 to 12 are $10; under 3 free. The carriage can hold up to three adults or two adults and three children. The museum also gives horse-drawn antique sleigh rides on Sunday from 1:00 to 3:00 P.M., mid-January to mid-March, weather permitting. Adults are $5.00, ages 4 to 12, $3.00. Call for conditions and availability.

The Granger Homestead and Carriage Museum, 295 North Main Street, Canandaigua (585–394–1472; www.grangerhomestead.org), is open late May through early October. Guided tours are offered on the hour Tuesday and Wednesday 1:00 to 5:00 P.M. and Thursday and Friday 11:00 A.M. to 5:00 P.M. May through October in June, July, and August, it is also open on Saturday and

The Rose Garden, Sonnenberg Gardens

Sunday 1:00 to 5:00 P.M. Admission is $5.00 for adults, $4.00 for seniors, and $1.00 for children.

Sonnenberg Gardens are part of a Gilded Age extravaganza, part Tudor Revival, part Queen Anne, built in 1887 by Frederick Ferris Thompson, who founded the First National Bank of the City of New York. The forty-room mansion is well worth a tour, but even more impressive than the heavily carved Victorian furniture and fine Oriental rugs contained beneath the house's multicolor slate roof are the gardens themselves.

Frederick Thompson died in 1899, and in 1902 his widow, Mary Clark Thompson, began the extensive formal and informal plantings on the estate as a memorial. She worked for the next fourteen years, utilizing just about every major mode of horticultural expression—a Japanese garden, a rock garden, an Italian garden, a sunken parterre display in a Versailles-inspired fleur-de-lis motif, an old-fashioned garden, a garden planted entirely in blue and white flowers, and a rose garden containing more than 2,600 magnificent bushes blossoming in red, white, and pink. After the Roman bath, the thirteen-house greenhouse complex with a domed palm house conservatory, the fountains and statuary everywhere, the mansion itself almost seems like an afterthought.

The Peach House, an informal restaurant in the greenhouse, has indoor and outdoor seating and is open daily in season from noon to 3:30 P.M.

There is no fee to visit the Wine Center (585–394–9016) in Bay House, which sells gourmet foods and wines from the Finger Lakes region. At the tasting room, visitors can sample ten to fifteen different wines and choose from more than one hundred.

Sonnenberg Gardens, 151 Charlotte Street off Route 21, Canandaigua (585–394–4922; www.sonnenberg.org), is open daily mid-May through October, 9:30 A.M. to 4:30 P.M.; in summer, it is open until 5:30 P.M. Walking tours are offered weekdays at 1:00 P.M. and on weekends at 10:00 A.M. and 1:00 P.M. (no tours before Memorial Day or after Labor Day). Admission is $10.00 for adults, $9.00 for senior citizens, and $5.00 for students, children under 12 free. A season pass is available for $20.00 if purchased after the gardens open, $17.00 if purchased before. A free tram provides transportation around the grounds.

The gracious 1810 **Morgan Samuels Inn,** nestled on forty-six acres of land, is an 1810 English-style stone mansion with five elegantly furnished bedrooms with fireplaces and one suite, three balconies, and a tennis court. Guests are served breakfast by candlelight. The Victorian porch is a delightful spot to relax and view the gardens. It's at 2920 Smith Road, Canandaigua (585–394–9232; www.morgansamuelsinn.com). Rates range from $149 to $395 a night, depending on season.

Things made by women are often undervalued, but one lady who appreciated skilled hand work was Mrs. Merle Alling of Rochester. Over thirty years she amassed the country's largest collection of homespun coverlets, which are now displayed at the **Alling Coverlet Museum,** part of **Historic Palmyra.** Heirlooms all, they represent both the simple spreads hand-loomed by farmwives and the somewhat more sophisticated designs woven on multiple-harness looms by professionals during the nineteenth century. The collection also includes a number of handmade nineteenth-century quilts and antique spinning equipment.

The Alling Coverlet Museum (Historic Palmyra, Inc.), 122 William Street, Palmyra (315–597–6737; www.historicpalmyrany.com), is open daily June through mid-September, 1:00 to 4:00 P.M. and by appointment. Admission is free, although donations are welcome.

Another facet of Historic Palmyra is the **William Phelps General Store Museum.** Erected in 1825, this commercial building was purchased by William Phelps in 1867 and remained in his family until 1977. Having remained virtually unchanged over the past 130 years, the store, along with its stock, furnishings, and business records, amounts to a virtual time capsule of Palmyra in the nineteenth and early twentieth centuries. An unusual note: The gaslight fixtures in the store and upstairs residential quarters were used by a Phelps family member until 1976, electricity never having been installed in the building.

The William Phelps General Store Museum, 140 Market Street, Palmyra (315–597–6981), is open June through mid-September, Tuesday through Saturday from 1:00 to 4:00 P.M. Open Saturday only in October.

Historic Palmyra, Inc.'s final holding is the **Palmyra Historical Museum,** which was erected about 1900 as a hotel. It is now a museum housing a unique display of elegant furniture, children's toys and dolls, household items, tools, gowns, and other artifacts of bygone ages.

The Palmyra Historical Museum, 132 Market Street, Palmyra (315–597–6981), is open June through October, Tuesday through Thursday and Saturday from 1:00 to 4:00 P.M. and by appointment. Admission is $5.00 for all three museums.

Eastern Lakes

For a fabulous day of fishing, head for **Sodus Bay** on the shore of Lake Ontario. In season more than twenty-five charter boat companies offer their services in this small fishing paradise. Stop for a bite at **Papa Joe's Restaurant** on **Sodus Point.** The only restaurant open here year-round, it has a children's menu and entertainment on the deck on summer weekends. Lunch and dinner are served from 11:30 A.M. until 10:00 P.M. A two-bedroom apartment overlooking the bay is available for rent on a nightly basis. Call (315) 483–6372.

The lighthouse at **Sodus Bay Lighthouse Museum** (Sodus Point 14555, 315–483–4936) was built in 1871 and remained in use until 1901. Museum displays include ship models, dioramas, shipboard equipment, a lens repair shop, and other maritime exhibits. There's a wonderful view of the lake from the tower. It's open May 1 through October 31, Tuesday through Sunday 10:00 A.M. to 5:00 P.M. Donations are suggested.

The 1870 Victorian **Carriage House Inn** (corner of Ontario and Wickham Boulevard, 315–483–2100; www.carriage-house-inn.com), charges from $120 to $135 for rooms and suites with a private bath, TV, and full breakfast. Rooms are also available in the stone carriage house, which overlooks the lake and lighthouse. Two efficiencies, which sleep up to four, have outdoor decks and picnic tables.

Bonnie Castle Farm Bed & Breakfast, on fifty acres of landscaped grounds overlooking Great Sodus Bay, is a three-story Victorian with private balconies and bilevel decks. Each of the eight rooms has its own bath; the Bonnie Castle Suite has a kitchen. If you need three bedrooms, there's also an 1890 Victorian summer home—the Aldrich Guest House—whose balcony and porch overlook the water. Locust Grove Cottage, overlooking the meadow, can accommodate three to six people.

Bonnie Castle Farm Bed & Breakfast, 6603 Bonnie Castle Road, **Wolcott** (315–587–2273), is open year-round. Rates range from $89 to $169 for rooms to $250 for the guest house and include a full breakfast buffet with such dishes as appleknocker sausages, seafood pasta, and Mexican frittatas. There's also a private beach.

From coverlets to clocks . . . the northern Finger Lakes region seems to be New York State's attic, filled with interesting collections of things we might oth-

No Passengers, Please

If you're planning to put a boat into any of the Finger Lakes, make sure the trailer, hull, and external motor or drive apparatus have been thoroughly cleaned—especially if the vessel has been in the Great Lakes, St. Lawrence River, Lake Champlain, or connected waters. Zebra mussels and the aquatic weed milfoil are invasive, non-native pests whose spread you can help prevent by scrubbing down hulls, motors, and trailers with hot water.

erwise take for granted. In *Newark* the *Hoffman Clock Museum* comprises more than a hundred clocks and watches collected by local jeweler and watch-maker Augustus L. Hoffman. Housed in the Newark Public Library, the collection includes timepieces from Great Britain, Europe, and Japan, although the majority of the clocks and watches are of nineteenth-century American manufacture, with more than a dozen having been made in New York State. Each summer the museum's curator mounts a special exhibit devoted to a particular aspect of the horologist's art.

The Hoffman Clock Museum, Newark Public Library, 121 High Street, Newark (315–331–4370), is open Monday noon to 8:00 P.M., Tuesday through Thursday 9:30 A.M. to 8:00 P.M., Friday 9:30 A.M. to 5:00 P.M., and Saturday 10:00 A.M. to 3:00 P.M.; closed Sunday and holidays. Admission is free.

If your interest in antiques extends beyond timepieces, head south a few miles to *Geneva* for a tour of *Rose Hill Mansion,* the Geneva Historical Society's National Historic landmark property overlooking the east shore of Seneca Lake. Built in 1839, the twenty-six-room mansion is one of the nation's premier examples of the Greek Revival style at its peak of refinement and popularity. Formal, symmetrical, and serene within its boxwood garden, Rose Hill Mansion has been exquisitely restored and furnished with as many pieces original to the house as it has been possible to collect. The twenty-one-room tour highlights the dining room, with its 5-foot-long 1815 Portuguese crystal chandelier; the front parlor, containing a seven-piece Rococo rosewood ensemble; and the Green Bedroom, decorated in the Empire style that paralleled the Greek Revival architectural trend. Rose Hill's formality is offset by its airy, spacious character—all of its front windows open from the floor, making a seamless link between ground-floor rooms and the colonnaded front porch.

Rose Hill Mansion, Route 96A, Geneva (315–789–5151; www.genevahistorical society.com/rose_hill.html), is open May through October, Monday through Saturday 10:00 A.M. to 4:00 P.M.; Sunday 1:00 to 5:00 P.M. Admission is $6.00 for adults; $4.00 for students age 10 to 18 and seniors. Children under 10 are free.

Two of the Finger Lakes' most elegant inn-restaurants overlook its deepest lake, Seneca, in Geneva, the self-proclaimed "Trout Capital of the World."

It took fifty men more than four years to build the turreted red Medina stone **Belhurst Castle,** overlooking Seneca Lake. When it was finally completed in 1889, the cost of construction exceeded $475,000. Today the Richardsonian Romanesque inn, on the National Register of Historic Places, has a reputation as one of the finer places in the region at which to stay and/or dine.

There are fourteen period mansion rooms in the castle (including one with a private balcony and one in the castle turret, with a widow's walk) and several houses on the grounds behind the castle. These include the Carriage House, with a four-poster bed and private patio, and the Ice House, with a loft bedroom; both of these offer more private accommodations. A three-bedroom ranch house adjacent to Belhurst is also available. Rates range from $105 to $300 in season; off-season rates are available.

The restaurant, with six dining rooms, offers dishes such as osso buco, filet mignon, and veal and spinach crepes. Dinner is served on the lakefront veranda, weather permitting. Sunday brunch features chef-carved meats, hot entrees, and omelets made to order. Reservations are recommended for all meals. A lunch buffet is served Monday through Saturday.

White Springs Manor, sister property to Belhurst Castle, was once owned by a wealthy lawyer and land baron. The imposing 1806 Georgian Revival mansion, perched on a hilltop in the middle of eighteen acres, affords guests a panoramic view of Seneca Lake and beyond. Each of the twelve guest rooms and the "playhouse" (a detached house) has a private bath, gas fireplace, and queen- or king-size bed. Belhurst's new Vinifera Inn, opened in summer 2004, offers rooms with lake views, opulent appoimntments, fireplaces, and two-person jacuzzis. Rates are $160 to $295.

Belhurst Castle, 4069 Lochland Road (Route 14S), Geneva (315–781–0201; www.belhurst.com), is open year-round.

"An oasis, a little island of beauty, peace, and friendliness in a busy world" is how **Geneva On The Lake** describes itself. The inn, with its terra-cotta tile roof, Palladian windows, Ionic columns, classical sculptures, and magnificent formal gardens, was built in 1910 by Byron Nester, who was inspired by the summer residences around northern Italy's Lakes Garda and Maggiore. All rooms are suites and range in price, depending on time of year, from $104 to $770 for a night's stay. Rates include wine, fresh fruit and flowers, the *New York Times* delivered to your door, a wine and cheese party on Friday evening, and Continental breakfast, weather permitting, on the terrace overlooking the gardens and lake.

Lunch is served on the terrace daily except Sunday, from mid-June to early September; candlelight dinners with live musical entertainment are served each evening; and an elegant brunch is served Sunday.

Geneva On The Lake, 1001 Lochland Road, Route 14S, Geneva (315–789–7190; www.genevaonthelake.com), is open all year.

"To honor in perpetuity these women, citizens of the United States of America, whose contributions to the arts, athletics, business, education, government, the humanities, philanthropy and science have been the greatest value for the development of their country." Thus were the parameters for entry outlined when the women of **Seneca Falls** created the **National Women's Hall of Fame** in 1969, believing that the contributions of American women deserved a permanent home.

And, indeed, the list of members reads like a "Who's Who": Marian Anderson, Pearl S. Buck, Rachel Carson, Amelia Earhart, Billie Jean King, Sally Ride, Dorothea Dix, and a host of others who have left their mark on American history and the American psyche.

Exhibits, housed in the bank building in the heart of the Historic District II, include a panel celebrating Elizabeth Cady Stanton, who led the way to rights for women, and artifacts and mementos about the members, events, and activities significant to women's history.

The National Women's Hall of Fame, 76 Fall Street, Seneca Falls (315–568–8060; www.greatwomen.org), is open from May through September, Monday through Saturday from 10:00 A.M. to 5:00 P.M. and Sunday noon to 5:00 p.m.; October through April, Wednesday through Saturday 10:00 A.M. to 5:00 P.M. Closed Thanksgiving, Christmas, and the month of January. Admission is $3.00 for adults, $1.50 for senior citizens and students. There is a family rate of $7.00.

Once a stop on the Underground Railroad, the **Hubbell House Bed & Breakfast** overlooking Van Cleef Lake was built in the 1850s as a Gothic

A Snake in the Grass

Just outside the town of Geneva is Bare Hill, sacred to the Seneca. According to legend, it was here the Creator opened up the earth and allowed their ancestors to enter into the world. But a giant serpent lay in wait, eating the newborns as they appeared. Finally, a warrior, acting upon a dream in which the Creator told him to fear not, slew the snake with a magic arrow, and the snake, in its death throes, disgorged all those he'd eaten.

Revival cottage and later enlarged and remodeled in the Second Empire style. The result is a delightfully eccentric building with scrolled bargeboards, wooden pinnacles, windows of all sizes, and a rear mansard roof with diamond-shaped slate tiles. It's furnished with an eclectic mix of antiques, including an 1860s Eastlake dresser, armchair, and rocker, and has four guest rooms (two with private bath). The wrap-around porch overlooks the lake.

Hubbell House Bed & Breakfast, 42 Cayuga Street, Seneca Falls (315–568–9690), is open all year. Rates, which include a full breakfast, range from $125 to $140 a night. Guests can swim and use paddleboats from the inn's private dock. Check out its Web site: www.hubbellhouse.com.

For a small town *Waterloo* is large on preserving history and has two museums well worth a visit. It was in the village of Waterloo, in the summer of 1865, that a patriotic businessman named Henry C. Welles put forward the idea of honoring the soldiers who fell in the Civil War by placing flowers on their graves on a specified day of observance. On May 5 of the following year, thanks to the efforts of Welles and Civil War veteran General John B. Murray, the village was draped in mourning, and a contingent of veterans and townspeople marched to the local cemeteries and, with appropriate ceremonies, decorated their comrades' graves. Thus Memorial Day was born.

In 1966 President Johnson signed a proclamation officially naming Waterloo the birthplace of Memorial Day. On May 29 of that same Memorial Day centennial year, Waterloo's *Memorial Day Museum* opened in a reclaimed mansion in the heart of town. The once-derelict, twenty-room brick structure is itself a local treasure, especially distinguished by the ornate ironwork on its veranda. Although built in the early Italianate Revival era of 1836–50, the house is being restored to its appearance circa 1860–70, the decade of the Civil War and the first Memorial Day observances.

The museum's collections cover the Civil War and the lives and era of the originators of the holiday, as well as memorabilia from all other U.S. wars.

The Memorial Day Museum, 35 East Main Street, Waterloo (315–539–0533; www.waterloony.com/mdaymuseum), is open Memorial Day weekend through mid-September; spring and fall, Friday through Monday noon to 5:00 P.M., Tuesday through Saturday 1:00 to 4:00 P.M. Admission is by donation. Tours are given by appointment.

Just a block from the Memorial Day Museum is the *Waterloo Terwilliger Historical Museum,* where the "antique and elegant" combine with the "long-lasting and functional" to tell the story of Waterloo and surrounding areas. The collection includes everything from Native American artifacts to Roaring Twenties fashions. Authentic full-size vehicles and a replica of a general store offer a slice of life as it used to be; five rooms, decorated down to the last detail, each depict a specific era.

I See London, I See France . . .

Although Amelia Jenks Bloomer didn't invent "bloomers" (they were invented by Elizabeth Smith Miller), she was instrumental in making them the uniform of nineteenth-century suffragists. The *New York Tribune* described Mrs. Bloomer's outfit: " . . . a kilt descended just below the knees, the skirt of which was trimmed with rows of black velvet. The pantaloons were of the same texture and trimmed in the same style. She wore gaiters. Her headdress was cherry and black. Her dress had a large open corsage with bands of velvet over the white chamesette in which was a diamond stud pin. She wore flowing sleeves, tight undersleeves, and black lace mitts. Her whole attire was rich and plain in appearance."

Mrs. Bloomer and her fellow suffragists abandoned their costume when they became objects of ridicule and children would follow them, chanting:

> "Hi Ho,
>
> In sleet and snow,
>
> Mrs. Bloomer's all the go.
>
> Twenty tailors to take the stitches,
>
> Plenty of women to wear the britches."

The Waterloo Terwilliger Historical Museum, 31 East William Street, Waterloo (315–539–0533; www.waterloony.com/library), is open year-round, Tuesday through Friday 1:00 to 4:00 P.M. Admission is by donation. Tours are given by appointment.

Between 1942 and 1946, Sampson Naval Training Station prepared 411,429 sailors and Waves to serve in World War II. The *Sampson WW-2 Navy Museum,* established in the station's original Navy brig facility, is filled with military artifacts donated by members of the Sampson WW-2 Navy Veterans organization and the U.S. Navy Department. The museum, in Sampson State Park, Route 96A, *Romulus* (315–585–6392), is open from May 30 to Labor Day, Friday through Sunday 10:00 A.M. to 4:00 P.M. (last tour at 3:30 P.M.), and from Labor Day until Columbus Day on weekends only. Admission is free, but there is a park entrance fee of $7.00 per vehicle ($6.00 until mid-June) from mid-June through Labor Day.

The *Cayuga Museum* in Auburn is really two museums in one; founded in 1936 in the 1836 Willard-Case Mansion, it tells the rich history of *Auburn,* "the village that touched the world," and surrounding Cayuga County. On display are business timekeeping devices such as the "Thousand Year Clock," manufactured by Auburn's Bundy brothers, whose Binghamton, New York, operation evolved into IBM, as well as an exhibit on the early history of the now-giant corporation. Other notables from Cayuga County who are high-lighted at the museum include President Millard Fillmore; E. S. Martin, founder of the original, pre-Luce *Life* magazine; prison reformer Thomas M. Osborne; and Ely Parker, the Seneca Indian who penned the surrender at Appomattox.

In the Stanton Gallery, which once served as the dining room in the Willard-Case mansion, the Dyckman Collection of period furnishings typifies the decor found in upper-class European and American homes in the mid- to late 1800s.

In 1911 Theodore W. Case proved that recording sound on film was pos-sible, and in late 1922 he made it a reality with the assistance of E. I. Sponable. Restored in 1993 after being forgotten for sixty years, the **Case Research Lab Museum** opened its doors to the public on the second floor of the Cayuga Museum's carriage house. Exhibits include the laboratory building, the sound-stage, and many examples of the early history, inventions, and laboratory equipment developed to commercialize sound on film. The building where Theodore Case developed the first "talkies" now houses an exhibit telling the story of how this medium was developed in the museum's backyard.

The Cayuga Museum and the Case Research Lab Museum, 203 West Gene-see Street, Auburn (315–253–8051), are open February through December, Tuesday through Sunday noon to 5:00 P.M.; closed Thanksgiving, Christmas, and New Year's Day. Admission is free.

The "Woman Called Moses" is remembered at the **Harriet Tubman Home** in Auburn, where she settled after making nineteen trips to the South to rescue more than 300 enslaved persons. A guided tour includes a visit to the Tubman House, the Home for the Aged, the ruins of the John Brown Infirmary, the for-mer Thompson Memorial A.M.E. Zion Church building, and Mrs. Tubman's grave at Fort Hill Cemetery.

The Harriet Tubman Home at 180 South Street (315–252–2081; www.ny history.com/harriettubman), is open Tuesday through Friday 10:00 A.M. to 4:00 P.M. and Saturday by appointment. There are extended hours in February, Black History Month. Admission is $5.00 for adults, $3.00 for seniors, and $2.00 for children.

Experts believe that the **Willard Memorial Chapel**—all that remains of the Auburn Theological Seminary campus, which thrived here from 1818 to 1939—is the only extant example of a complete **Louis Comfort Tiffany** interior. The handsome gray limestone and red sandstone Romanesque Revival building, designed by A. J. Warner of Rochester, has a magnificent interior designed and handcrafted by the Tiffany Glass and Decorating Company. Among the high-lights: a three-paneled stained-glass window of "Christ Sustaining Peter on the Water," nine leaded-glass chandeliers, and fourteen opalescent nave windows.

"The Tiffany Treasure of the Finger Lakes" hosts numerous concerts throughout the year, including the Tiffany Summer Concert Series on Wednesdays at noon in July and August. Admission is by donation. For a complete concert schedule, contact the Community Preservation Committee, Inc., at the number below.

The Willard Memorial Chapel, 17 Nelson Street, Auburn (315–252–0339; www.willardchapel.org), is open Tuesday through Friday 10:00 A.M. to 4:00 P.M., on Saturday from 1:00 to 4:00 P.M. in summer, or by appointment; closed holidays. Admission is $3.00 per person.

"Quando mangiate da Rosalie sembra mangiare in Italia" (When you eat at Rosalie's, it's like eating in Italy), proclaims the menu at **Rosalie's Cucina.** Patrons and critics agree: The food here is superb and authentic. Most of the dishes are northern Italian, and many are family recipes, such as *pesce diavolo* (shrimp, scallops, mussels, and calamari in a spicy red sauce), and *pollo marsala.* House specialties include rotisserie duck ($25) and cioppino ($29). The restaurant is at 841 West Genesee Street, Skaneateles (315–685–2200) and is open for dinner nightly.

Classic cars, historic race cars, and racing memorabilia are all exhibited at the **D.I.R.T. Motorsports Hall of Fame & Classic Car Museum,** along with a "Hall of Fame" of legendary race car drivers.

Among the classic cars on display are a 1926 Duesenberg, the 1929 Dodge Roadster that won first place in a cross-country race in 1993, and a 1969 Dodge Charger Hemi 4-speed. For stock car enthusiasts, there's the Buzzie Reutimann "00" coupe, which won the first two Schaefer 100s, and "Batmobile" #112 driven by Gary Balough in 1980. In the Jack Burgess Memorial Video Room, the "master of the microphone" recounts exciting racing events of the past. The Northeast Classic Motorsports Extravaganza is held each August.

Also here is Cayuga County Fair Speedway, home of Drivers Independent Race Tracks (D.I.R.T.), the second-largest race-sanctioning body in the nation (races every Sunday night May through September).

D.I.R.T. Motorsports Hall of Fame and Classic Car Museum, 1 Speedway Drive, **Weedsport** (315–834–6606), is open May through October, Saturday and Sunday 10:00 A.M. to 5:00 P.M. Admission is $4.00 for adults and $3.00 for children and senior citizens.

In England, Americans Victoria and Richard MacKenzie-Childs worked for a small pottery shop, taught art, and designed and made clothing for stage and street wear. When they returned here, they opened **MacKenzie-Childs, Ltd.,** a multifaceted design studio and factory where more than 150 workers turn out handcrafted, hand-painted giftware including Majolica, glassware, linens, and floorcloths—all done, according to the couple, "within the elegance of a gentlemanly nineteenth-century estate . . . in an atmosphere of ethics, order, and grace."

MacKenzie-Childs, Ltd., 3260 State Route 90, *Aurora* (888–665–1999; www.mackenzie-childs.com), showroom and shop are open year-round, Monday through Sunday 9:30 A.M. to 6:00 P.M.

Beaver Lake Nature Center is an Onondaga County park incorporating several different ecosystems, all connected by 9 miles of well-maintained hiking trails. A 200-acre lake, offering beautiful vistas but no recreational facilities, is a migration-time magnet for up to 30,000 Canada geese. Guided canoe tours of the lake are available during the summer; rental canoes are available for these tours, and you must preregister. The entire center is a great place for birders; more than 180 species have been sighted here over the years. The informative Beaver Lake Visitor Center is the starting point for a regular schedule of hour-long guided tours of the trails, given by professional naturalists each weekend.

Beaver Lake Nature Center, 8477 East Mud Lake Road, *Baldwinsville* (315–638–2519; www.onondagacountyparks.com/parks/beaver), is open all year, daily from 7:30 A.M. to dusk; closed Thanksgiving and Christmas. Admission is $2.00 per car.

Ithaca, home to Cornell University, is also home of the *Paleontological Research Institution* (PRI), whose Museum of the Earth houses more than two million fossils, one of the premier collections in the Western Hemisphere, telling the story of the planet's 4.6-billion-year history, with a focus on the Northeast, through exhibits, hands-on activities, and audiovisual presentations. The institution, located in a former orphanage on the southwest shore of Cayuga Lake, was founded by Gilbert D. Harris, a professor of geology at the university from 1894 to 1934.

Paleontological Research Institution

Among the fossils exhibited are single-celled microfossils, ancient plants, the remains of ancient vertebrates such as dinosaurs, whales, and woolly mammoths, and a magnificent 425-million-year-old trilobite. The Hyde Park Mastodon Fossil skeleton is one of the most complete in the world.

PRI, 1259 Trumansburg Road, Route 96, Ithaca (607–273–6623; www.pri web.org), is open from Labor Day through Memorial Day, Monday and Wednesday through Saturday 10:00 A.M. to 5:00 P.M., Sunday 11:00 A.M. to 5:00 P.M. (closed during school breaks), and after Memorial Day until Labor Day, Monday through Saturday, 10:00 A.M. to 5:00 P.M. and Sunday from 11:00 A.M. to 5:00 P.M. Admission is $8.00 for adults, $5.00 for seniors and students with ID, $3.00 for youths 4 to 17, and free for children 3 and under.

Thanks to a poor boy who grew up to be a wealthy shoe manufacturer and benefactor, six of approximately 170 carved wood *carousels* remaining in this country are located in *Broome County.* Between 1919 and 1934 George F. Johnson donated six carousels manufactured by the Allan Herschell Companies of North Tonawanda to the county. He placed one stipulation on the gift: Remembering his poor childhood, he felt that everyone should be able to ride and insisted that the municipalities never charge a fee.

Today, gorilla chariots, pigs, and horses with lions hidden in saddle blankets transport riders on their backs to magical realms. And at two of the carousels—Recreation and Ross Parks—the animals twirl to the sounds of the original Wurlitzer band organs. Riders who take a spin on all six merry-go-rounds receive a special button.

The carousels are located at C. Fred Johnson Park, Johnson City (607–797–9098); George W. Johnson Park, Endicott (607–757–2427); West Endicott Park, Endicott (607–754–5595); Recreation Park, Binghamton (607–722–9166 or 662–7017); Ross Park, Binghamton (607–724–5461); and Highland Park, Endwell (607–754–5595). They operate from Memorial Day to Labor Day, and riders are asked to donate a piece of litter collected along the way. An exhibit at Ross Park explores the history of carousel making. For general information contact the Broome County Chamber of Commerce at (800) 836–6740.

For more than sixty-five years, Endicott has been home to *Pat Mitchell's Homemade Ice Cream.* Founded in 1920 by Joseph Travis, the store began to thrive in 1948 when Raymond "Pat" Mitchell bought the business and, using a vintage 1920s batch freezer, began making ice cream that has become legendary in these parts. Today's owners continue to make thousands of gallons, three gallons at a time, filling orders from coast to coast and around the globe.

What makes Pat Mitchell's ice cream so good? Everyone has a different opinion, as the store offers more than 250 flavors, with treats such as banana delight, made with fresh banana ice cream, cashews, and a chocolate weave; fresh cantaloupe; coconut almond fudge; and, of course, chocolate chip.

Pat Mitchell's Homemade Ice Cream shops are at 231 Vestal Avenue in Endicott, and on Vestal Avenue in Binghamton. For information call (607) 785–3080 or 786–5501.

Places to Stay in the Finger Lakes

To receive a copy of the Finger Lakes Bed & Breakfast Association brochure, contact the organization at: Finger Lakes Bed & Breakfast Association 56 Cayuga Street Seneca Falls 13148 (877) 422–6327 www.flbba.org

AURORA

Aurora Inn
391 Main Street
(315) 364–8888
www.aurora-inn.com

CORNING

Hillcrest Manor
227 Cedar Street
(607) 936–4548
www.corninghillcrestmanor
.com

ELMIRA

The Painted Lady B&B
520 Water Street
(607) 732–7515
www.thepaintedlady.net

GENEVA

Belhurst Castle
4069 Route 14 South
(315) 781–0201
www.belhurst.com

HAMMONDSPORT

Elm Croft Manor Bed & Breakfast
8361 Pleasant Valley Road
(607) 569–3071 or (800) 506–3071
www.elmcroftmanor.com

ITHACA

Hilton Garden Inn
130 East Seneca Street
(607) 277–8900
www.ithaca.gardeninn.com

Statler Hotel
11 East Avenue
(800) 541–2501
www.statlerhotel.cornell.edu

SENECA FALLS

John Morrison Manor
2138 Route 89
(866) 484–4218
www.johnmorrismanor.com

SKANEATELES

Sherwood Inn
26 Genesee Street
(800) 374–3796
www.thesherwoodinn.com

WATKINS GLEN

Idlewilde Inn
1 Lakeview Avenue
(607) 535–3081
www.idlewildeinn.com

Places to Eat in the Finger Lakes

CANANDAIGUA

Bristol Harbour's Lodge Restaurant
5410 Seneca Point Road
(585) 394–3909
www.bristolharbour.com

London Underground
69 East Market Street
(607) 962–2345

ELMIRA HEIGHTS

Pierce's 1894 Restaurant
228 Oakwood Avenue
(607) 734–2022

HAMMONDSPORT

Crooked Lake Ice Cream Parlor
Village Square
(607) 569–2751

Village Tavern Restaurant & Inn
30 Mechanic Street
(607) 569–2528
www.villagetaverninn.com

ITHACA

Moosewood Restaurant
215 North Cayuga Street
DeWitt Mall
(607) 273–9610
www.moosewoodrestaurant
.com

LODI

Dano's Heuriger on Seneca
9564 Route 414
(607) 582–7555
www.danosonseneca.com

Suzanne Fine Regional
Cuisine
9013 Route 414
(607) 582–7545
www.suzannefrc.com

SKANEATELES

Doug's Fish Fry
8 Jordan Street
(315) 685–7343

The Krebs 1899
53 West Genesee Street
(315) 685–5714
www.thekrebs.com

TRUMANSBURG

Taughanock Farms Inn
2030 Gorge Road
(607) 387–7711
www.t-farms.com

WATKINS GLEN

Veraisons Restaurant
Glenora Wine Cellars
5435 Route 14
(607) 243–9500 or
(800) 243–5513
www.glenora.com

OTHER ATTRACTIONS WORTH SEEING IN THE FINGER LAKES

Elizabeth Cady Stanton Home
32 Washington Street
Seneca Falls
(315) 568–2991

**George Eastman House/International
Museum of Photography & Film**
900 East Avenue
Rochester
(585) 271–3361

Richardson-Bates House Museum
135 East Third Street
Oswego
(315) 343–1342

Seward House
33 South Street
Auburn
(315) 252–1283

Susan B. Anthony Home
17 Madison Street
Rochester
(585) 235–6124

Watkins Glen International Raceway
Route 16
Watkins Glen
(607) 535–2481

REGIONAL TOURIST INFORMATION— THE FINGER LAKES

Cayuga County Office of Tourism
131 Genesee Street
Auburn
(800) 499–9615
www.tourcayuga.com

Chemung County Chamber of Commerce
400 East Church Street
Elmira
(866) 946–3386
www.chemungchamber.com

A Finger Lakes Visitors Connection
(Ontario County)
20 Ontario Street
Canandaigua
(877) 386–4669
www.visitfingerlakes.com

Finger Lakes Trails Visitor Center
6111 Visitor Center Road
Mount Morris
(535) 658–9320
www.fingerlakestrails.org

Finger Lakes Tourism Alliance
309 Lake Street
Penn Yan
(800) 548–4386
www.fingerlakes.org

Hammondsport Chamber of Commerce
47 Shethar Street
Hammondsport
(607) 569–2989
www.hammondsport.org

Information Center of Corning
1 West Market Street
Corning
(607) 962–8997
www.corningny.com

Ithaca/Thompkins County Convention and Visitors Bureau
904 East Shore Drive
Ithaca
(800) 284–8422
www.visitithaca.com

Seneca Falls Heritage Area Visitor Center
115 Fall Street
Seneca Falls
(315) 568–2703
www.senecafalls.com/heritage

Steuben County Chamber of Commerce Visitor Center
100 North Franklin Street
Watkins Glen
(607) 535–4300
www.schuylerny.com

The Niagara-Allegany Region

Ever since the Erie Canal was opened a century and a half ago, New York City and Buffalo have assumed a front door–back door status in New York State. New York City became the Empire State's gateway to the world, a capital of international shipping and finance. The docksides and rail yards of Buffalo, meanwhile, were the portals through which the industrial output and raw materials of the Midwest flowed into the state. **Buffalo** became an important "border" city between the East Coast and the hinterlands, a center of manufacturing and flour milling whose fortunes have risen and fallen with the state of the nation's smokestack economy.

But don't write Buffalo off as an old lunch-bucket town that gets too much snow in the winter. Buffalo has some impressive architecture, from Louis Sullivan's splendid Prudential Building and the art deco City Hall downtown to the Frank Lloyd Wright houses described later in this section. South Park, with its conservatory, and Riverside Park on the Niagara offer welcome open spaces, and there are even culinary treasures like Buffalo chicken wings and beef on 'weck (hot sliced roast beef on a pretzel-salt–coated kimmelweck or kaiser roll).

The countryside at the western tip of New York provides further evidence as to why Niagara Falls isn't the only reason

to drive to the end of the thruway. The Pennsylvania border country boasts giant Allegany State Park, a hiking and camping paradise, and the byways along the Lake Erie shore wander through a picture-pretty territory dotted with vineyards, cherry orchards, and roadside stands selling delicious goat's milk fudge. Yes, goat's milk fudge. It's the little serendipities that make traveling fun.

Buffalo-Niagara Region

Just to mix things up a bit, we'll venture out into the sticks to begin our tour of the Niagara-Allegany region. Only 40 miles northeast of Buffalo is a pristine tract of some 19,000 acres, the core of which (11,000 acres) makes up the federal *Iroquois National Wildlife Refuge,* managed by the U.S. Fish and Wildlife Service. On either side of the refuge are the *Oak Orchard* (east) and *Tonawanda* (west) *Wildlife Management Areas,* operated by the state of New York's Department of Environmental Conservation.

Roughly two-thirds of Iroquois National Wildlife Refuge is made up of freshwater marshes and hardwood swamps that are fed by Oak Orchard Creek as it meanders east to west through the refuge. Forests, meadows, and fields slope up gently from the wetland's edge, attracting a wide variety of wildlife. The refuge maintains four scenic overlooks and three nature trails, which are open from sunrise to sunset year-round for self-guided visits and wildlife watching.

Both the Oak Orchard and the Tonawanda areas are primarily wetlands, with some grassland and forest habitat. The dikes surrounding the man-made impoundments, as well as several overlooks and parking areas, provide access that offers superb opportunities not only for hunters (during designated seasons) but for hikers and birders as well.

AUTHORS' FAVORITES— NIAGARA-ALLEGANY REGION

Burchfield-Penney Art Center	Q-R-S Music Rolls
Herschell Carrousel Factory Museum	Roger Tory Peterson Institute of Natural History
Luci-Desi Museum	
Old Fort Niagara	The Roycroft Inn
Panama Rocks Scenic Park	Theodore Roosevelt Inaugural National Historic Site
Pedaling History Bicycle Museum	

Stage One

The handsome French Renaissance home at 484 Delaware Avenue in Buffalo was built in 1894 for S. Douglas Cornell, the successful owner of a lead foundry. Cornell, an avid amateur actor, had architect Edward A. Kent install a theater in the attic story of his new mansion. Here, he and his prominent Buffalo friends staged frequent performances. Among the amateur players' most enraptured fans was Cornell's little granddaughter, Katherine. Years later, when she was one of the great ladies of the American stage, Katherine Cornell credited those Delaware Avenue theatricals with kindling her ambition to become an actress.

The best time for birders to visit the area is from early March to mid-May. That's when more than 100,000 Canada geese, along with smaller flocks of ducks—black, pintail, mallard, American widgeon, teal, shoveler, and ring-necked—pause on their northward migration, with some staying to nest. The transitional habitat along the borders of the marsh attracts shore and wading birds and migrating spring warblers.

The Iroquois National Wildlife Refuge headquarters, 1101 Casey Road, **Basom** (585–948–5445), is open year-round Monday through Friday from 7:30 A.M. to 4:00 P.M., except holidays, and mid-March through May, Saturday and Sunday 9:00 A.M. to 5:00 P.M. Maps and other information are available here and on the Internet at http://iroquoisnwr.fws.gov. There are self-guided exhibits and an observation tower at the Oak Orchard Education Center on Knowlesville Road, just north of the town of Oakfield. The center is open daily from sunrise to sunset and is the starting point for four nature trails. For information about Oak Orchard and Tonawanda WMA contact the New York State Department of Environmental Conservation, P.O. Box 422, Basom 14013; (585) 948–5182.

The **Asa Ransom House** is an 1853 farmhouse on the site of one of the country's early gristmills. All but one of the nine guest rooms have fireplaces, and several have private front porches and balconies. The inn is also a full-service restaurant and serves a "country dinner" Sunday through Thursday, with specialties such as raspberry chicken and smoked corned beef with apple raisin sauce, and a five-course fixed-price dinner ($40) Friday and Saturday. Lunch is served Wednesday, and afternoon tea is served Tuesday, Thursday, and Saturday from 1:00 to 4:00 P.M. Dinner is served daily except Monday.

The Asa Ransom House is at 10529 Main Street, **Clarence** (716–759–2315 or 800–841–2340; www.asaransom.com). A double room, including full breakfast, ranges from $220 to $285 MAP (or Modified American Plan, i.e., with breakfast and dinner included in the rate) Friday and Saturday night; Sunday through Thursday a B&B rate of $98 to $155 is available, as well as an MAP rate of $150 to $205. Prices do not include service and tax.

Thirty Mile Point Lighthouse, more than 60 feet high, was built in 1875 of hand-carved stone near the mouth of Golden Hill Creek to warn vessels of the sandbar and shoals jutting out into Lake Ontario. Visitors can climb the circular steel staircase to the top of the tower for magnificent views of the lake and Canada. The lighthouse, now part of ***Golden Hill State Park,*** is free to those who pay a park entrance fee. It's open Friday through Sunday and holidays, 2:00 to 4:00 P.M. The park is on Lower Lake Road, ***Barker*** (716–795–3885; www.nysparks.state.ny.us/parks).

It seems as if it isn't possible to tick off too many miles in this state without encountering one of the string of forts that once defended the thirteen colonies' northwestern frontier and played so prominent a role not only in the struggles between the British and the French for North American supremacy but in our own War of Independence as well. The westernmost of these (in New York, at least) is ***Old Fort Niagara,*** located in ***Fort Niagara State Park*** downstream from Niagara Falls at the point where the Niagara River flows into Lake Ontario.

Fort Niagara occupies what was, one of the most strategic locations in all of the interior of North America. The great "French Castle" erected here in 1726 served as the core of Fort Niagara's defenses through nearly a century of intermittent warfare and was in use as officers' housing as recently as World War I. Now restored to its eighteenth-century appearance, it is the focal point of Old Fort Niagara.

Restored between the years 1927 and 1934, the older buildings of Fort Niagara are maintained by the private, nonprofit Old Fort Niagara Association in cooperation with the State of New York. Beyond the silent military structures are broad vistas of Lake Ontario and, in clear weather, the rising mists of Niagara Falls 14 miles to the south.

Old Fort Niagara, Fort Niagara State Park, ***Youngstown*** (716–745–7611; www.oldfortniagara.org), is open year-round daily from 9:00 A.M. until sunset. Closed Thanksgiving, Christmas, and New Year's Day. During the

Drummer at Old Fort Niagara

summer there are frequent costumed reenactments of military drills, with musket and cannon firings. Admission is $10.00 for adults, $9.00 for senior citizens and AAA members, and $6.00 for children ages 6 to 12.

Scottish émigré Allan Herschell literally carved a place for himself in America's history when, in 1883, he produced the first steam-driven "riding gallery"—known today as a merry-go-round. By 1891, one machine a day was being shipped to places around the world; later the Herschell-Spillman Company became the world's largest producer of carousels and amusement park devices. And because merry-go-rounds need music, North Tonawanda also became a major producer of band organs.

The *Herschell Carrousel Factory Museum*, housed in a historic factory building, traces the history of Herschell, his hand-carved wooden animals, and the finished carousels. There are ongoing woodcarving demonstrations, and best of all for all us kids, an antique, hand-carved wooden carousel to ride. "Super Sunday" family performances are held at 2:00 P.M. from mid-June through mid-September.

thegoatsweregot

According to legend, Goat Island is named for the only survivor of a herd that was left to winter there in 1779 by a settler named John Stedman.

The Herschell Carrousel Factory Museum, 180 Thompson Street, *North Tonawanda* (716–693–1885), is open April through mid-June, Wednesday through Sunday noon to 4:00 P.M.; mid-June through August, daily from 10:00 A.M. to 4:00 P.M.; and September through December, Wednesday through Sunday noon to 4:00 P.M. Closed major holidays. Admission is $4.00 for adults and $2.00 for children ages 2 to 12 and includes one carousel ride. Extra rides cost just 50 cents.

Heading upriver (or more likely, down I–190) we come to Buffalo, the terminus town of the Erie Canal and gateway to the Midwest. For a quick introduction to this sprawling inland port, head downtown to reconnoiter the city and Lake Erie from the twenty-eighth-floor observatory of *City Hall* (open weekdays from 9:00 A.M. to 3:00 P.M.) and then visit the nearby historic neighborhood of *Allentown.*

The works of a number of important architects and the homes of several famous people are tucked into the compact Allentown neighborhood. Representative of the district's myriad building styles are the Kleinhans Music Hall on Symphony Circle, designed in 1938 by Eliel and Eero Saarinen; the 1869 Dorsheimer Mansion, 434 Delaware Avenue, an early work of the peerless Henry Hobson Richardson; Stanford White's 1899 Butler Mansion (672 Delaware) and 1895 Pratt Mansion (690 Delaware); and a lovely example of the Flemish Renaissance style at 267 North Street. As for the haunts of the famous, there are the childhood home of F. Scott Fitzgerald, 29 Irving Street; the home of artist Charles Burchfield (once a designer for a Buffalo wallpaper company) at 459 Franklin Street; and, at 472 Delaware Avenue, the carriage house formerly attached to the home of Samuel Langhorne Clemens, who was once the editor and part-owner of the *Buffalo Morning Express*, (though he always hated Buffalo). For information call the Allentown Association at (716) 881–1024 or see www.allentown.org.

The Greek Revival house at 641 Delaware Avenue is important not for its architecture, but its history; on September 14, 1901, the home of prominent Buffalo lawyer Ansley Wilcox became part of American history, when a vigorous young man who had just rushed from a vacation in the Adirondacks stepped into the library to take the oath of office as president of the United States. William McKinley was dead, the victim of an assassin; the era of Theodore Roosevelt was about to begin.

The story of that fateful day and the tragic event that preceded it is told at the ***Theodore Roosevelt Inaugural National Historic Site,*** as the Wilcox House has been known since its restoration and opening to the public in 1971. Perhaps the most interesting aspect of the tale concerns the mad dash Roosevelt made from the Adirondacks to Buffalo. He had gone to the city and stayed for a few days at the Wilcox House after McKinley was shot by an anarchist at the Pan-American Exposition but had left to join his family at their mountain retreat after being assured by the president's doctors that his condition had stabilized. Notified several days later of McKinley's worsening state, the vice president made an overnight journey by horse and wagon to the nearest train station, where he learned that the president was dead. Roosevelt and his party then raced to Buffalo in a special train. Within two hours after his arrival, he was standing in Wilcox's library, wearing borrowed formal clothes as he took the oath of office as the nation's twenty-sixth president.

The Theodore Roosevelt Inaugural National Historic Site, 641 Delaware Avenue, Buffalo (716–884–0095; www.nps.gov/thri), is open Monday through

Buffalo's Grassy Knoll

On September 6, 1901, President McKinley was in Buffalo attending the Pan-American Exposition. While he was shaking hands with the public, Leon F. Czolgosz walked up and shot him with a revolver he had hidden under a handkerchief. Today the site where McKinley was assassinated is marked with a bronze plaque. It's on the traffic island on Fordham Drive between Elmwood Avenue and Lincoln Parkway. (Czolgosz was put to death the following October.)

Friday 9:00 A.M. to 5:00 P.M., weekends noon to 5:00 P.M. Closed New Year's Eve, New Year's Day, Easter, Memorial Day, Independence Day, Labor Day, Thanksgiving, Christmas Eve, and Christmas Day. Admission is $5.00 for adults, $3.00 seniors and students, and $1.00 for children 6 to 14.

The residential neighborhoods north of the downtown and Allentown areas of Buffalo boast five examples of the work of America's greatest architect, Frank Lloyd Wright. Wright's residential architecture is generally distributed within the central and upper Midwest, where he brought his "prairie style" to maturity. The fact that there exists a pocket of the master's work in Buffalo is due to his having designed a house in Oak Park, Illinois, for the brother of John D. Larkin, founder of the Larkin Soap Company of Buffalo. Larkin liked his brother's house and brought Wright to Buffalo to design the company headquarters. The Larkin Building, a light, airy masterpiece of commercial architecture, stood on Seneca Street from 1905 until it was unconscionably demolished in 1950. But fate was kinder to the five Buffalo houses built for Larkin Soap Company executives following Wright's arrival in town, all of which survive to this day. Here is a list of the *Frank Lloyd Wright houses* in Buffalo and their locations:

William Heath House, 76 Soldiers Place, corner of Bird Avenue, completed in 1906 and landscaped by Frederick Law Olmsted. (Private; not open to visitors.)

Darwin D. Martin House, 125 Jewett Parkway, corner of Summit Avenue. Also completed in 1906, this expansive home was unfortunately left vacant for seventeen years prior to the mid-1950s, during which time half of the original Wright windows were lost. It was restored in 1970 by the State University of New York at Buffalo, which uses it for offices. For information regarding tours contact the School of Architecture and Planning, Hayes Hall, 125 Jewett Parkway, Buffalo (716–856–3858). Tour schedules vary with seasons. Tours last one hour, except for two-hour in-depth tours offered on the fourth Saturday of each month at 11:00 A.M. Prices for tours are $10.00 for adults, $8.00 for students; in-depth tour charge is $18.00. The George Barton House is included in all tours.

George Barton House, 118 Summit Avenue, is a smaller brick structure with distinctive top-story casement windows and a broad roof overhang built in 1903–4.

Gardener's Cottage, Martin Estate, 285 Woodward Avenue. Constructed in 1906, the cottage is one of the few surviving service buildings of the Martin Estate. (Private; not open to visitors.)

Walter Davidson House, 57 Tillinghast Place. With the exception of Darwin Martin's 1926 summer house, built south of the city on a bluff above Lake Erie, the 1909 Davidson House is the last of Wright's Buffalo residences. (Private; not open to visitors.)

ANNUAL EVENTS IN THE NIAGARA-ALLEGANY REGION

FEBRUARY

Olmstead Winterfest
Buffalo
(716) 838–1249
www.buffaloolmstedparks.org

APRIL

Buffalo in Bloom
Buffalo and Erie County
Botanical Gardens
(716) 851–5344
www.buffaloinbloom.com

MAY

Falls Fireworks and Concert Series
Niagara Falls, Ontario
(877) 642–7275
www.niagaraparks.com
(through mid-September)

JUNE

Shakespeare in Delaware Park
Buffalo
(716) 856–4533
www.shakespeareindelawarepark.org
(through mid-August)

JULY

Can-Am Arts Festival
Sackets Harbor
(315) 646–2321
www.sacketsharborny.com

AUGUST

National Buffalo Wing Festival
Buffalo
(716) 565–4141
www.buffalowing.com

SEPTEMBER

Niagara County "Fall Classic" Fishing Derby
Lake Ontario
(800) 338–7890

NOVEMBER

Lights in the Park
Buffalo
(716) 856–4533

Toy Fest
East Aurora
(716) 687–5151
www.toytownusa.com

Winter Festival of Lights
Niagara Falls, Ontario
(800) 563–2557
www.wfol.com
(till early January)

DECEMBER

First Night Buffalo
Buffalo
(716) 635–4959
www.firstnightbuffalo.org

Player pianos first became popular during the first decade of the twentieth century, and they are with us still. Nowadays the most complete line of rolls for player pianos is manufactured and sold by a Buffalo institution called *Q-R-S Music Rolls.*

Q-R-S is one of the last (and oldest) manufacturers of player-piano rolls in the United States, having been founded in 1900 by Melville Clark, the man who perfected the player. During the heyday of the instrument in the 1920s, Q-R-S had plants in New York, Chicago, and San Francisco, but by 1966 only a small facility in the Bronx remained. A new owner bought the company and moved it to Buffalo, where subsequent ownership has kept it.

A piano-roll company like Q-R-S doesn't stay in business simply by cranking out reprints of "Sweet Adeline" and "You Are My Sunshine." Today you can buy rolls for Norah Jones' "Come Away With Me," or Toby Keith's "I Love This Bar," and other current tunes. The company also makes a device that will enable any piano to play music programmed on special Q-R-S CDs. You can also order a copy of the company's current catalog through the mail.

Q-R-S Music Rolls, 1026 Niagara Street, Buffalo (716–885–4600), is open Monday through Friday 9:00 A.M. to 4:00 P.M., with tours at 10:00 A.M. and 2:00 P.M. Admission fees, refunded with a purchase, are $2.00 for adults and $1.00 for children.

Just minutes from downtown the ***Buffalo Museum of Science*** houses an extensive collection of natural science exhibits. The museum was built in the 1920s and features a blend of classic dioramas and modern museum exhibitry. A stunning glass-enclosed atrium connects the museum to the Charles R. Drew Science Magnet School, one of the first science magnet schools in the nation to be physically and programmatically linked to a museum.

The museum's main exhibit hall is filled with exciting temporary exhibitions. A visit to the permanent "Dinosaurs & Co." exhibit provides an exciting look at some of the favorite prehistoric giants. "Insect World" features insects six times life-size in two vastly different ecosystems—the cloud forest in the coastal Andean highlands of north central Venezuela and the Niagara frontier region of New York State. Two halls of space provide detailed information about our world and the worlds around us, and observatories provide views of stars, planets, and our sun. The museum also features exhibits on endangered species, zoology, flora and fauna, gems and minerals, and technology. "Camp Wee Explorers," for kids 2 to 7, offers interactive exhibits focused on discovering the natural world.

The Buffalo Museum of Science is located at 1020 Humboldt Parkway (Best Street exit off the Kensington Expressway), Buffalo (716–896–5200; www .sciencebuff.org). Open Thursday through Saturday, and on Monday of Presidents Day and Columbus Day weekends, from 10:00 A.M. to 5:00 P.M. and Sunday noon to 5:00 P.M. Closed January 1, July 4, Thanksgiving, and Christmas. Admission is $7.00 for adults, $6.00 for seniors, and $5.00 for students and children 3 to 18.

The Buffalo Museum of Science also operates ***Tifft Nature Preserve*** just 3 miles from downtown. Billed as an "Urban Nature Sanctuary," the preserve is a 264-acre habitat for animal and plant life, dedicated to environmental education and conservation. With miles of hiking trails, three boardwalks, and a self-guided nature trail, it's a wonderful place to spend the day hiking or fishing. For bird-watchers there's a 75-acre freshwater cattail marsh with viewing blinds. In winter the preserve rents snowshoes. "Wellness Walks" are offered on Thursday at 10:00 A.M. The Makowski Visitor Center has some wonderful exhibits on ecology, animals, and plant life.

The Tifft Nature Preserve, 1200 Fuhrmann Boulevard, Buffalo (716–825–6397 or 896–5200), is open daily from dawn to dusk; the Makowski Visitor Center is open November to April, Thursday through Saturday 10:00 A.M. to 4:00 P.M.; May to October, Wednesday through Saturday 9:00 A.M. to 4:00 P.M. Closed New Year's, Thanksgiving, Christmas Eve, and Christmas Day. There is no admission charge, but donations are appreciated.

The **Burchfield-Penney Art Center** exhibits the largest and most comprehensive collection of the works of Charles E. Burchfield, one of the country's foremost watercolorists, as well as the works of other western New York artists. The center, which serves the community as a multifaceted cultural and educational institution, also hosts numerous special exhibitions throughout the year.

One of the center's exhibits, "Access to Art," uses a unique assortment of interpretive tools such as hands-on art activities, interviews with artists, tactile works, and library resources to give visitors of all ages the skills to enjoy a museum without feeling intimidated.

The Burchfield-Penney Art Center, Rockwell Hall, Buffalo State College, 1300 Elmwood Avenue, Buffalo (716–878–6011; www.burchfield-penney.org), is open Tuesday through Saturday from 10:00 A.M. to 5:00 P.M. and Sunday from 1:00 to 5:00 P.M.; closed major holidays. Admission is $5.00 for adults, $4.00 for seniors, and $3.00 for students and children over age 3.

Cemeteries are not often thought of as places to go to for fun, but **Forest Lawn** is not a typical cemetery; it's more like a city park. The final resting place of prominent Buffalonians such as Red Jacket, the Seneca orator, and Millard Fillmore, the country's thirteenth president, is also a nature sanctuary, with 6,000 trees and 157 species of birds.

At this cemetery you'll *know* for whom the bell tolls: Upon request, attendants will ring the 6-foot, 3,000-pound solid bronze Oishei bell cast in France. Other highlights include the Blocher monument, with life-size figures carved in Italian marble, and numerous unique monuments and mausoleums.

Sundays in June, July, and August, the staff offers free tours. Several of the interred, such as President Fillmore, make guest appearances during the hour-long bus and walking tours that relate the cemetery's history. (Tours are not given in inclement weather.) Advance reservations are required.

The "Real Thing"?

The Buffalo chicken wings recipe below is reputed to be the genuine Anchor Bar version—but only they know for sure, and they're not talking. In any event, it sure is good:

6 tablespoons Durkee's Hot Sauce

½ stick margarine

1 tablespoon white vinegar

⅛ teaspoon celery seed

⅛ to ¾ teaspoon cayenne pepper

¼ teaspoon Worcestershire sauce

1 to 2 teaspoons Tabasco sauce

dash of black pepper

Mix ingredients in a small saucepan over low heat until margarine melts, stirring occasionally.

Fry wings at 375° F for 12–15 minutes in vegetable or peanut oil.

Drain for a few minutes on a brown paper bag or paper towels, then put them in a bowl. Pour the sauce over them, cover the bowl, and shake it to coat the wings. (An option here is to put the wings on a baking sheet and bake a few minutes for an extra-crispy coating.) Serve with carrot and celery sticks and blue cheese dressing.

Here's a second "authentic" recipe:

1 tablespoon butter

¼ cup Durkee Red Hot Cayenne Pepper Sauce

Melt the butter and combine it with the hot sauce, then follow the directions above. This recipe, however, calls for baking the wings at 350° F for 11–12 minutes.

Forest Lawn Cemetery & Garden Mausoleums, 1411 Delaware Avenue at Delavan, Buffalo (716–885–1600; www.forest-lawn.com), is open daily 8:00 A.M. to 7:00 P.M. in spring and summer; until 5:00 P.M. fall and winter.

Mark Twain aficionados will want to visit the **Buffalo & Erie County Public Library**'s Grosvenor Rare Book Room. Among the thousands of manuscripts and first editions dating back to the fifteenth century is the original manuscript of *The Adventures of Huckleberry Finn*. The room also contains other mementos of Twain, a one-time Buffalo resident.

Buffalo & Erie County Public Library, Lafayette Square, Buffalo (716–858–8900; www.buffalolib.org); call for hours.

Those buffalo-style chicken wings really were invented in Buffalo—at the **Anchor Bar and Restaurant,** which has been serving them up with celery and blue cheese dip since 1964. The restaurant has a reputation for good food, moderate prices, and large portions. It's at 1047 Main Street (716–886–8920; www.anchorbar.com).

Sample the city's other local specialty—beef on 'weck—at **Anderson's** or at **Charlie the Butcher;** both have several branches in the area.

More than 400 rare and unique bicycles and thousands of cycling-related collectibles span more than 185 years of bicycling history at the **Pedaling History Bicycle Museum,** the world's largest of its kind.

Among the exhibits are a reproduction of the very first bicycle (made in 1817), an Irish Mail four-wheel velocipede, some "boneshakers" dating back to the 1860s, a pneumatic highwheel safety American Star, an 1881 Marine bicycle and an electric bike from the year 2000. There are also extensive bicycle stein and lamp collections and ample photo opportunities.

The Pedaling History Bicycle Museum, 3943 North Buffalo Road (Routes 277 and 240), Orchard Park (716–662–3853), is open Monday through Saturday 11:00 A.M. to 5:00 P.M. and Sunday 1:30 to 5:00 P.M.; closed Tuesday through Thursday from January 15 to April 1. Admission is $6.00 for adults, $5.40 for seniors, $3.75 for children ages 7 to 15, and $17.50 for a family of up to four generations. Write or call for a listing of special free events, including antique bike parades on July 4 and other occasions.

Lake Erie Shore

The southwestern tip of New York State is packed with as eclectic a mix of off-the-beaten-path sights as can be found anywhere. Remember kazoos—those funny little musical instruments you could play just by humming into them? They're still being made in **Eden,** at **The Original American Kazoo Company Factory, Museum, and Gift Shop.** Established in 1916, it's now the only metal kazoo factory in the world—and it's still making them the same way they were made in 1916. The company used to produce everything from toy flutes and fishing tackle boxes to metal dog beds and peanut vending machines, but in 1965 the demand for kazoos became so great that the firm stopped manufacturing everything else.

The "working museum" at The Original American Kazoo Company, Factory, Museum, and Gift Shop shows how "America's only original musical instrument" is made, chronicles kazoo history, and regales visitors with such fascinating trivia as "'Far, Far Away' is the most requested tune played on the kazoo."

The Original American Kazoo Company, Factory, Museum, and Gift Shop, 8703 South Main Street, Eden (716–992–3960 or 800–978–3444; www.eden kazoo.com), is open Monday through Saturday 10:00 A.M. to 5:00 P.M., Sunday noon to 5:00 P.M. Self-guided tours can be taken Monday through Thursday from 9:30 A.M. to 2:30 P.M. Closed Thanksgiving, Christmas, New Year's, Memorial Day, Easter, Fourth of July, and Labor Day. Admission is free.

Although it's now just a short hop off I–90, it's easy to imagine how isolated the **Dunkirk Historical Lighthouse** must have been when the lantern in the square, 61-foot tower first began guiding ships into Dunkirk Harbor in 1876. Today an automated light in the tower does the job, and the two-story stick-style keeper's dwelling has been converted into a **Veterans' Park Museum.**

Five of the museum's rooms are devoted to displays of each branch of the military; five are preserved to show how the lighthouse keeper used to live; one is a memorial to the Vietnam era. An exhibit of maritime history and lake freighters is on display in the souvenir store. A separate building displays artifacts from the submarine service and Coast Guard.

Displays on the grounds include a 45-foot lighthouse buoy tender, a 21-foot rescue boat, and Civil War cannons. Visitors can take a tour of the lighthouse tower. An admission fee is charged for grounds tours and tours of the museum.

Dunkirk Historical Lighthouse and Veterans' Park Museum, off Point Drive North, Dunkirk (716–366–5050; www.dunkirklighthouse.com), are open May through June and September through October, Monday, Tuesday, Thursday, Friday, and Saturday, from 10:00 A.M. to 2:00 P.M. with the last tour at 1:00 P.M. July and August the complex is open from 10:00 A.M. to 4:00 P.M., with the last tour at 2:30 P.M. Admission is $5.00 for adults and $2.00 for children ages 4 to 12.

Ready for a little beef on 'weck? Or perhaps a fancier lunch entree, like angel hair pasta with grilled chicken breast or tortellini Provençal? For dinner, how about Dijon-grilled salmon or a filet mignon preparation that might include bacon and smoked gouda? Stop at the stately **White Inn** in **Fredonia.** Duncan Hines did, back in the 1930s, and was so taken with the food that he included it in his "Family of Fine Restaurants." Although the restaurant/inn has since undergone several transformations, it still proudly displays the Duncan Hines sign out front. And the building itself encompasses the original Victorian mansion built in 1868 and operated as an inn since 1919.

The White Inn, 52 East Main Street, Fredonia (716–672–2103 or 888–FREDONIA for reservations; www.whiteinn.com), is open daily year-round. Breakfast and lunch are served Monday through Saturday, and dinner is served nightly. Inn rates, from $79 to $179, include breakfast.

Owners John and Debra Zorazio and Jack and Marlene Gambino have made **Stockton Sales** one of Chautauqua County's favorite antiquing destinations. Casual browsers and serious antiques aficionados alike know that this is the place to look for items ranging from cobalt blue glassware to silver trays to Mikasa Japanese porcelain place settings. "We've had everything from a harp to a 1930s wicker wheelchair," says John, "and our library is one of our biggest attractions. We've got hardcovers for $2.00, and paperbacks for $1.00, and we're always restocking." The proprietors also run monthly auctions with big lots of antique furniture. Call for dates.

Stockton Sales, 6 Mill Street, Stockton (716–595–3516), is open 10:00 A.M. to 6:00 P.M. daily.

Locals dubbed the sixteen-room mansion completed by James McClurg in 1820 "McClurg's Folly." He designed it, made and baked his own bricks, prepared local timber for the interior woodwork, and landscaped the spacious grounds with ornamental trees and shrubs and a water fountain stocked with goldfish.

Today the Chautauqua County Historical Society operates the restored frontier mansion as a museum and library and has filled it with furnishings, fine art, and local artifacts from its collection.

McClurg Museum, Village Park, Routes 20 and 394, *Westfield* (716–326–2977), is open Tuesday through Saturday from 10:00 A.M. to 4:00 P.M. Admission is $3.00 for adults, children free.

At the northern tip of Chautauqua Lake in *Mayville,* the people at *Webb's Candy Factory* have been making goat's milk fudge since 1942. The goats are no longer out back and the milk now comes from cans, but the confection is just as rich and creamy as ever, and the chocolate fudge with pecans is a regional taste treat not to be missed. Webb's makes all its candies by hand, using the old-fashioned copper-kettle method, and has added a host of other treats to its repertoire, including "frogs," hard suckers, chocolate bars, divinity, and chocolate clusters. If you own a goat and want to start production, take a short tour of the candy factory between 10:00 A.M. and 4:00 P.M. Monday through Friday.

Webb's Candy Factory, Route 394, Mayville (716–753–2161; www.webbs world.com), is open daily year-round. In summer the hours are 10:00 A.M. to 9:00 P.M.; in winter noon to 5:00 P.M. Call for holiday hours.

Chautauqua Lake is also the home of a 133-year-old enterprise that exemplifies the American penchant for self-improvement. The *Chautauqua Institution* gave its name to an endless array of itinerant tent-show lyceums around the turn of the century. A lot of us have forgotten, though, that the original institution is still thriving right where it was founded in 1874. Bishop John Heyl Vincent and industrialist (and father-in-law of Thomas Edison) Lewis Miller orginally founded Chautauqua with the modest goal of establishing a school for Sunday-school teachers. *Chautauqua* grew to become a village unto itself, offering not only religious instruction but a program of lectures and adult-education courses.

The largely secularized Chautauqua of today bears little resemblance to the Methodist camp meeting of more than a hundred years ago, although services in the major faiths are held daily. The Chautauqua emphasis on culture and mental and spiritual improvement has led to an extensive annual summer calendar of lectures, classical and popular concerts, dramatic performances, and long- and short-term courses in subjects ranging from foreign languages to tap dancing to creative writing. It has its own 30,000-volume library.

To put it simply, Chautauqua is a vast summer camp of self-improvement, a place where you can rock (in chairs) on broad verandas, walk tree-lined streets that have no cars, and listen in on a chamber music rehearsal on your way to lunch.

The season at Chautauqua lasts for nine weeks each summer, but admission is available on a daily, weekend, or weekly basis.

For complete information on facilities and programs, contact Chautauqua Institution, 1 Ames Street, Chautauqua (716–357–6200 or 800–836–ARTS; www.ciweb.org).

Head south along the lake for a few miles to catch a ride on the ***Bemus Point–Stow Ferry.*** The cable-drawn ferry has traversed the "narrows" of the lake at these points since 1816. Unfortunately (or, for animal rights activists, fortunately), the oxen that once pulled the ferry with the aid of a treadmill and manila rope retired quite a while ago. But the pace and charm of the primitive open barge still remain. The six-minute ride debarks from North Harmony.

The Bemus Point–Stow Ferry, Stow (mailing address: 15 Water Street, Mayville 14757), (716–753–2403; www.bemuspoint.com/ferry.html), is open from 11:00 A.M. to 9:00 P.M. Saturday and Sunday in June and daily in July and August. Admission is $4.00 per car, $2.00 for motorcycles, and $1.00 for walk-ons.

The same folks who run the Bemus Point–Stow ferry also offer tours on the ***Chautauqua Belle,*** one of only six authentic stern-wheel steamboats operating east of the Mississippi. The *Belle* cruises Chautauqua Lake daily from Memorial Day through Labor Day, with departures at 11:00 A.M., 1:15 P.M., and 3:00 P.M.; limited schedule in May, June, and September. The trips last one-and-a-half hours. Fares are $14.00 for adults, $12.50 with AARP card, and $5.00 for ages 6 to 12; children under 6 are free. For information, call (716) 753–2403, or see www.chautauquabelle.com.

Geologists believe that more than 300 million years ago ***Panama Rocks***— reputed to be the world's most extensive outcropping of glacier-cut, ocean-quartz conglomerate rock—were islands of gravel and sand amid a vast inland sea that extended west toward what is now Utah. As layer after layer of these materials was deposited, the weight forced the water out, and a natural form of concrete called quartz conglomerate, or pudding stone, was created.

Approximately 165 million years ago, earthquakes and other geological upheavals raised what was to become Panama Rocks to its present altitude of 1,650 feet. The layers fractured, and water, carrying minerals such as iron and lead, seeped into the openings. A scant 10,000 years ago, during the last ice age, a passing glacier widened these fractures, creating thousands of crevices and alley passageways.

Today visitors can thread through these crevices and passageways along a mile-long trail that winds through a world of towering rocks, past cavernous dens and small caves. Most hikers take one-and-a-half hours to follow the route, although the more adventurous can leave the trail and explore at their own pace. Because there are no railings, adults are required to sign a waiver of liability and are warned that the upper part of the trail can be dangerous for children; the lower trail, which has the most dramatic scenery, is safer. Persons under the age of eighteen must be with an adult to enter the rock area. No pets are allowed.

Panama Rocks Scenic Park, 11 Rock Hill Road (County Route 10), ***Panama*** (716–782–2845), is open mid-May through late October, 10:00 A.M. to 5:00 P.M. Admission is $6.00 for adults, $4.00 for ages 13 through 21, $4.00 for children ages 6 to 12, and $5.00 for seniors. There is a picnic area with grills for guests. For more information check its Web site: www.panamarocks.com.

Jamestown, birthplace of one of the country's leading naturalists, is home to his ***Roger Tory Peterson Institute of Natural History,*** housed in a handsome wood and stone building designed by architect Robert A. M. Stern on twenty-seven acres of woods and meadows.

The institute's mission is to train educators to help children discover the natural world around them. Part of this program involves changing exhibitions of wildlife art and nature photography at the institute, and the public is invited to visit, hike the surrounding trails, and stop in the Butterfly Garden and gift shop.

The Roger Tory Peterson Institute of Natural History, 311 Curtis Street, Jamestown (716–665–2473 or 800–758–6841; www.rtpi.org), is open Tuesday through Saturday 10:00 A.M. to 4:00 P.M. and Sunday 1:00 to 5:00 P.M. Admission is $4.00 for adults, $3.00 for students, and $12.00 for families. The grounds are open daily dawn to dusk.

In ***Jamestown,*** everyone loves Lucy. The ***Lucy-Desi Museum*** stands in the heart of the city's theater district, between the Lucille Ball Little Theatre of Jamestown—the largest community theater in New York—and the former Palace Theater (now the Reg Lenna Civic Center), where little Lucy went with her grandfather to see vaudeville.

Among the exhibits are a computer program with Lucy trivia questions, an audio clip from the *My Favorite Husband* radio show, which preceded *I*

Love Lucy, and exclusive clips from *Lucy and Desi: A Home Movie* produced by their daughter, Lucie Arnaz. The gift shop carries over 600 *I Love Lucy* licensed products.

The Lucy-Desi Museum, 212 Pine Street, Jamestown (877–LUCY FAN [582–9326] or 716–484–0800; www.luci-desi.com), is open Monday through Saturday 10:00 A.M. to 5:30 P.M. and Sunday 1:00 to 5:00 P.M.; Admission is $6.00 for adults and $4.00 for children ages 6 to 18.

Jones Bakery, across the street from the museum, still makes the Swedish limpa bread that remained one of Lucy's favorites throughout her life. And if you're strolling through downtown Jamestown, look for the three outdoor wall murals depicting scenes from *I Love Lucy*—they're all within walking distance of the museum.

Great music at unbeatable prices draws lovers of gospel, bluegrass, and country to **The Mountain Depot.** Every Sunday between 2:00 and 7:00 P.M. from the end of April through October, families flock to the alcohol-free establishment on a hill above Ellington to hear The Mountain Railroad Band and guest musicians rock the halls. Admission is just $6.00 for adults and free for children under 12. The Depot is on Gerry-Ellington Road, Ellington (716–287–2316).

Ellington borders on **Amish Country,** which encompasses several towns to the north and east. The Amish first came to Cattaraugus County from Ohio in 1949. Although they usually keep to themselves, they're friendly people who generally welcome questions about their way of life. (They do request, however, that you not photograph them.) There are a number of small shops on Route 62 in the town of **Conewango Valley** that offer products made by, or about, the Amish. **Franklin Graphics** sells Amish photos, books, and postcards. Stop at **Mueller's Valley View Cheese Factory** to sample Swiss cheese and forty other varieties made in Amish country. **Amish Country Fair** carries furniture and crafts.

Allegany Heartland

Salamanca is the only city in the United States located on a Native American reservation; it is also home to the largest park in the state's park system. The **Seneca-Iroquois National Museum** on the Allegany Indian Reservation traces the cultural and historical heritage of the Seneca, known as "Keeper of the Western Door of the Iroquois Confederacy." The museum exhibits collections of artifacts beginning with prehistoric times and re-creates the culture and history of the Seneca people.

The Seneca-Iroquois National Museum, Broad Street Extension, Salamanca (716–945–1760; www.senecamuseum.org), is open November through April,

Monday through Saturday 9:00 A.M. to 5:00 P.M. and Sunday noon to 5:00 P.M.; call for hours between April and November. Admission is $5.00 for adults and $3.00 for children.

With 65,000 acres, two 100-acre lakes, and 80 miles of hiking trails, **Allegany State Park,** "the wilderness playground of western New York," is the largest of the state parks. It's a mecca for both summer and winter outdoor enthusiasts. There are lakes for boating and swimming, ballfields, tennis courts, picnic areas, playgrounds, bike paths, and miles of cross-country and snowmobile trails. Rowboats and paddleboats can be rented at the Red House boathouse; you will also find a tent and trailer area, and bicycle rental. The park has seasons for small game, turkey, and deer (archery only). There's an extensive campground as well as more than 370 cabins—163 winterized. Some are "turn-key," offering many amenities.

Allegany State Park, off Route 17, Salamanca (716–354–9121; www.nys .state.ny.us/parks), is open daily year-round. There is an entrance fee of $7.00 per car when the lake is open for swimming, and $6.00 per car when the lake is closed. The gate is closed weekdays off-season.

Before you leave Salamanca, stop at the **Salamanca Rail Museum,** a fully restored passenger depot constructed in 1912 by the Buffalo, Rochester, and Pittsburgh Railroad. The museum uses exhibits, artifacts, and video presentations to re-create an era when rail was the primary means of transportation from city to city.

Salamanca Rail Museum, 170 Main Street, Salamanca (716–945–3133), is open Monday through Saturday from 10:00 A.M. to 5:00 P.M. and Sunday from noon to 5:00 P.M. April through December. Admission is free, but donations are welcomed.

It's the pleasant surprises that make traveling off the beaten path rewarding—like discovering that in addition to more than 260 species of rare and unusual trees and herbs and perennial gardens, **Nannen Arboretum** is home to Roanji Temple Stone Garden (an abstract garden of stone and sand) and Amano-Hashidate Bridge (bridge to heaven). The arboretum (716–699–2377 or 800–897–9189) is on Parkside Drive, directly behind Cornell Cooperative Extension, in Ellicottville. It is open daily from dawn to dusk. Donations are welcomed.

Head north on Route 219 a short distance to **Ashford Hollow** to see one of the most unconventional sculpture "gardens" ever. For almost forty years, local sculptor Larry Griffis has been integrating his art with nature, placing his monumental abstract/representational creations throughout a 400-acre woodland setting/nature preserve. More than 200 of his pieces, most made of steel and between 20 and 30 feet high, are on exhibit at **Griffis Sculpture Park.** Ten nudes ring a pond, sharing the banks with live swans and ducks. A

Griffis Sculpture Park

towering mosquito awaits unwary hikers along one of the 10 miles of hiking trails. Giant toadstools grow in a field, waiting to be climbed on.

Griffis Sculpture Park, Route 219, Ahrens Road, Ashford Hollow (mailing address: 6902 Valley Road, East Otto 14729) (716–667–2808; www.griffispark.org), is open daily, May through October, from sunup to sundown; closed November through April. Admission to the Mill Valley Site is $5.00 for adults and $3.00 for seniors and students; admission to the Rohr Hill Site is free but donations are welcome. Tours are given by appointment.

About 320 million years ago, river and delta sediments were deposited on the eroded surface of Devonian shoals. Crystalline igneous and metamorphic rocks with milky quartz veins were exposed, and long transportation of the sediments selectively weathered and eroded the nonquartz minerals.

What all this means is that **Rock City Park** is one of the world's largest exposures of quartz conglomerate (pudding stone), a place where you can wander through crevices and past towering, colorfully named formations like Fat Man's Squeeze, Tepee Rock, and Signal Rock, with its 1,000-square-mile view.

Rock City Park, 505A Route 16 South, **Olean** (716–372–7790; www.rock citypark.com), is open daily May through October from 9:00 A.M. to 6:00 P.M. Admission is $4.50 for all 12 years and older, $3.75 for seniors, and $2.50 for ages 6 to 12; a season pass is $8.95.

If you were heading off to a summer at Chautauqua three generations ago, you would have gotten there by rail—specifically by a steam-hauled train of the Erie, Pennsylvania, or New York Central Railroad. Of course, Amtrak can get you there today (nearest station: Erie, Pennsylvania), but if you want steam, you'll have to head to a nostalgia operation like the **Arcade and Attica Railroad,** headquartered just southeast of Buffalo in **Arcade.**

Maybe *nostalgia* isn't the right word, since the Arcade and Attica is a real working railroad with a healthy freight clientele. But the company's passenger operation is an unabashed throwback, relying for motive power on a pair of circa 1920 coal burners pulling old, open-window steel coaches that once belonged to the Delaware, Lackawanna, and Western. Arcade and Attica passengers enjoy a ninety-minute ride through some of upstate's loveliest farm country, ending right where they started by way of a trip back through time.

The Arcade and Attica Railroad, 278 Main Street, Arcade (585–492–3100), operates weekends from Memorial Day through the end of October, with Wednesday and Friday trips during July and August. Special excursions using a diesel engine, including an Easter Bunny run, a Santa Claus Express, and nature ride/hikes are scheduled off-season. Call for information. Tickets cost $12.00 for adults and $7.00 for children ages 3 through 11 and are available at the 278 Main Street office, or in advance by phone using a credit card.

Horse lovers can roll out of bed and onto a mount for a trail ride through the Colden Hills at *Pipe Creek Farm B&B,* a working equine farm. The four-bedroom inn has shared baths (private baths available on request) and an in-ground pool. Rates range from $75 to $125 and include a continental breakfast. In addition to trail rides, owners Phil and Kathy Crone give lessons in hunt seat, stock seat, and saddle seat. In the winter there are 200 acres of cross-country ski trails to enjoy.

Pipe Creek Farm B&B, 9303 Falls Road, *West Falls* (716–652–4868), is open all year-round.

One of the most interesting personalities of turn-of-the-century America was a self-made philosopher named *Elbert Hubbard.* In addition to writing a little "preachment" (as he called it) titled "A Message to Garcia" that dealt with the themes of loyalty and hard work, and publishing his views in a periodical called the *Philistine,* Hubbard was famous for having imported the design aesthetic and celebration of handcrafts fostered in England by the artist and poet William Morris. Elbert Hubbard became the chief American proponent of the Arts and Crafts movement, which touted the virtues of honest craftsmanship in the face of an increasing tendency in the late nineteenth century toward machine production of furniture, printed matter, and decorative and utilitarian household objects.

Visually, the style absorbed influences as diverse as art nouveau and American Indian crafts and is familiar to most of us in the form of solid, oaken, slat-sided Morris chairs and the simple "Mission" furniture of Gustav Stickley. Elbert Hubbard not only wrote about such stuff but also set up a community of craftspeople to turn it out—furniture, copper, leather, even printed books. He called his operation The Roycrofters, and it was headquartered on a "campus" in *East Aurora.*

There are several ways the modern traveler can savor the spirit of Elbert Hubbard in modern East Aurora. One is by visiting the *Roycroft Campus,* on

South Grove Street. The campus grounds, now a National Historic Site, feature a gift shop, working pottery, art gallery, and several antiques dealers, all housed in Hubbard-era buildings. The site also includes the East Aurora Town Museum, housed in the Town Hall Building—the former Roycroft Campus chapel. For information contact the East Aurora Chamber of Commerce, 431 Main Street, East Aurora 14052 (716–652–8444 or 800–441–2881; www.eanycc.com).

Another window on the Roycroft era is the **Elbert Hubbard–Roycroft Museum,** recently located in a 1910 bungalow built by Roycroft craftsmen and now on the National Register of Historic Places. Part of the furnishings, including the superb Arts and Crafts dining room, are original and were the property of centenarian Grace ScheideMantel when she turned the house over to the museum in 1985. (ScheideMantel's husband, George, once headed the Roycroft leather department.) Other Roycroft products on display at the house include a magnificent stained-glass lamp by Roycroft designer Dard Hunter and a saddle custom-made for Hubbard just prior to his death on the torpe- doed *Lusitania* in 1915.

There is a wonderful period garden, complete with a sundial and a "gazing ball," maintained by "The Master Gardeners" of the Erie County Cooperative Extension Service.

The Elbert Hubbard–Roycroft Museum (ScheideMantel House), 363 Oak- wood Avenue, East Aurora (716–652–4735; www.roycrofter.com/museum), is open from June 1 to mid-October on Wednesday, Saturday, and Sunday 1:00 to 4:00 P.M.; by appointment the rest of the year. Admission is $5.00 for adults; free for children under 12. Private or group tours also can be arranged, year- round, by appointment.

Elbert Hubbard opened *The Roycroft Inn* in 1903 to accommodate the people who came to visit his community of craftsmen. When Hubbard and his wife died in 1915, their son, Elbert II, assumed leadership of the Roycroft enter- prises. Beginning in 1938, the ownership of the inn passed from the Hubbard family through a series of owners. In 1986 the inn was granted National Land- mark status, and it reopened in 1995 after extensive restorations by the Mar- garet L. Wendt Foundation.

All of the inn's charm and history have been preserved. Although the suites have all of the modern-day amenities, each has been meticulously restored and furnished with historically accurate elements, including Stickley furniture, Roy- croft lamps and wall sconces, and wallpaper in the style of William Morris.

The Roycroft Inn, 40 South Grove Street, East Aurora (716–652–5552; for reservations only, 877–652–5552; www.roycroftinn.com), rents three-, four-, and five-room suites ranging from $120 to $230 a night, including continental breakfast. The restaurant is open for lunch Monday through Saturday, for din- ner nightly, and for Sunday brunch.

Toy Town Museum is a must for anybody traveling with kids. The museum/children's activity center displays a large collection of antique toys (including many by local manufacturer Fisher-Price), as well as ToyWorks, a learning center for lots of "hands-on" fun. The museum hosts its annual three-day Toyfest at the end of August.

Toy Town Museum, 636 Girard Avenue, East Aurora (716–687–5151; www.toytown.usa.com), is open Monday through Saturday 10:00 A.M. to 4:00 P.M. Donations are welcome.

Before taking leave of East Aurora, we should stop in at the home of one of our least-appreciated presidents, ***Millard Fillmore.*** Fillmore, who was born in the Finger Lakes town of Genoa in 1800, came to East Aurora to work as a lawyer in 1825. He built this house on Main Street with his own hands, and it it the only presidential residence to make that claim. He moved it to its present Shearer Avenue location the same year and lived here with his wife until 1830. As restored and furnished by previous owners and the Aurora Historical Society, the ***Millard Fillmore House National Landmark*** contains country furnishings of Fillmore's era, as well as more refined pieces in the Greek Revival, or "Empire," style of the president's early years. A high desk to be used while standing was part of the furnishings in Fillmore's law office; the rear parlor, added in 1930, showcases furniture owned by the Fillmores in later years, when they lived in a Buffalo mansion. The large bookcase was used in the White House during the Fillmore presidency.

The Millard Fillmore House National Landmark (Aurora Historical Society), 24 Shearer Avenue, East Aurora (716–652–8875; www.millardfillmore house.org), is open the same times and at the same admission fees as the Elbert Hubbard–Roycroft Museum.

The village of ***Wyoming,*** settled in the early 1800s, has more than seventy buildings on the Historic Register. Gaslight Village Shops, in the historic landmark district, include the ***Gaslight Christmas Shoppe, Silas Newell's Provisions, Eccentricities,*** and ***Carney's Antiques.*** Stop for a cappuccino at the ***Gaslight Village Cafe and Pub*** or for lunch, dinner, or the night at Wyoming Inn B&B.

If you want to stay a bit out of town, ***Hillside Inn,*** on forty-eight acres of woods, streams, hills, and ravines, has twelve guest rooms. Built in 1851 as a health spa, the classic Greek Revival mansion serves an innovative American cuisine featuring entrees such as charred yellowfin tuna and sautéed tournedos of beef in a cabernet and black pepper sauce. All vegetables are grown in the inn's organic garden. Rates, which include a continental breakfast, begin at $100 for a room in Hollyhock Cottage and go up to $249 for a deluxe room with a whirlpool bath in the mansion. Water from the inn's mineral spring, in use since 1851 without even running dry, is used in whirlpools and for drinking throughout the property. Business customers are most welcome. Hillside Inn is located at 890 East Bethany Road, Wyoming (585–495–6800 or 800–544–2249; www.hillsideinn.com).

We know everyone loves Jell-O, but we bet you didn't know it was invented in the village of *Le Roy,* where there is a museum dedicated to it, and housed in the oldest house in town. In 1897 Le Roy was already known as the Patent Medicine Capital of the world. But it was the gelatinous creation of P. B. Waite, which his wife named Jell-O, that earned it a place in history. Two years later, Mr. Waite sold his recipe to the Genesee Pure Food Company for $450, but it was not until 1964, when Jell-O was sold to the Postum Company (which later became General Foods), that Jell-O ceased being made in Le Roy.

Today, the *Jell-O Gallery,* in the Historic Society's Le Roy House, documents the creation and rise of Bill Cosby's—and America's—favorite dessert. Seven rooms of the 1823 building are furnished with period pieces of the nineteenth century, and there's an extensive exhibit of Morganville redware pottery made here by Fortunatus Gleason, Jr., in the nineteenth century.

The Jell-O Gallery, in the Le Roy House, 23 East Main Street, Le Roy (585–768–7433; www.jellomuseum.com), is open April through December, Monday through Saturday 10:00 A.M. to 4:00 P.M.; January through March, Monday through Friday 10:00 A.M. to 4:00 P.M. Admission is $3.00 for those 12 years of age and older, and $1.50 for children 6 through 11.

Places to Stay in the Niagara-Allegany Region

ALBION

Tillman's Historic Village Inn
Corner Route 104 West & 98
(585) 589-9151
www.tillmansvillageinn.com

BUFFALO

Beau Fleuve
242 Linwood Avenue
(800) 278-0245
www.beaufleuve.com

Hampton Inn
220 Delaware Avenue
(716) 855-2223

The Mansion on Delaware
414 Delaware Avenue
(716) 886-3300
www.mansionondelaware
.com

Red Coach Inn
2 Buffalo Avenue
Niagara Falls
(800) 282-1459 or (716)
282-1459
www.redcoach.com

CHAUTAUQUA

Athenaeum Hotel
South Lake Drive
(800) 821-1881

Brasted House B&B
4833 West Lake Road
(888) 753-6205
www.brastedhouse.com

The Spencer Hotel
25 Palestine Avenue
(716) 357-6250
www.thespencer.com

DUNKIRK

Clarion Hotel Marina and Conference Center
30 Lake Shore Drive East
(716) 366-8350
www.clariondunkirk.com

ELLICOTTVILLE
Ellicottville Inn
8 Washington Street
(716) 699–2373

WESTFIELD
Brick House B&B
7573 East Route 20
(716) 326–6262
www.brickhousebnb.com

The William Seward Inn
6645 South Portage Road
(716) 326–4151
www.williamsewardinn.com

Places to Eat in the Niagara-Allegany Region

ALBION
Tillman's Historic Village Inn
Corner Route 104 West & 98
(585) 589–9151
www.tillmansvillageinn.com

BUFFALO
Chef's
291 Seneca Street
(716) 856–9187

Left Bank
511 Rhode Island Street
(716) 882–3509

Mother's Restaurant
33 Virginia Place
(716) 882–2989

Red Coach Inn
2 Buffalo Avenue
(800) 282–1459 or
(716) 282–1459
www.redcoach.com

EAST AMHERST
La Scala Ristorante
9210 Transit Road
(716) 213–2777

KENMORE
O'Connell's Hourglass Restaurant
981 Kenmore Avenue
(716) 877–8788

TONAWANDA
Saigon Bangkok
512 Niagara Falls Boulevard
(716) 837–2115
www.saigonbangkok.net

WILLIAMSVILLE
Tandoori's
7740 Transit Road
(716) 632–1112
www.tandooris.com

Trattoria Aroma
5229 Main Street
(716) 631–2687

REGIONAL TOURIST INFORMATION— THE NIAGARA-ALLEGANY REGION

Buffalo-Niagara CVB
617 Main Street
Buffalo 14203
(716) 852–0511
www.visitbuffaloniagara.com

Niagara County Tourism
139 Niagara Street
Lockport 14094
(800) 338–7890
www.niagara-usa.com

Wyoming County Tourist Promotion Agency
30 North Main Street
P.O. Box 502
Castile 13327
(800) 839–3919
www.wyomingcountyny.com

OTHER ATTRACTIONS WORTH SEEING IN THE NIAGARA-ALLEGANY REGION

Amherst Museum
3755 Tonawanda Creek Road
Amherst
(716) 689–1440
www.amherstmuseum.org

Artpark
South Fourth Street
Lewiston
(716) 754–9000
www.artpark.net

Broadway Market
999 Broadway
Buffalo
(716) 893–0705
www.broadwaymarket.com

Colonel William Bond House
143 Ontario Street
Lockport
(716) 434–7433

**Davis Memorial Carillon
Alfred University**
Saxon Drive
Alfred
(607) 871–2562

Fredonia Opera House
9–11 Church Street
Fredonia
(716) 679–1891
www.fredopera.org

Lily Dale Assembly
5 Melrose Park
Lily Dale 14752
(716) 595–8721
www.lilydaleassembly.com

**Lockport Cave and Underground
Boat Ride**
21 Main Street
Lockport
(716) 438–0174
www.lockportcave.com

Maid of the Mist Boat Tour
151 Buffalo Avenue
Niagara Falls
(716) 284–4233
(in season) or 284–4122
www.maidofthemist.com

**Miss Buffalo, Niagara Clipper
Cruise Boats**
Erie Basin Marina
Buffalo
(800) 244–8684
www.missbuffalo.com

The Catskills

To generations of New Yorkers, the Catskills were the "Borscht Belt," summers filled with shuffleboard and table tennis at sprawling vacation colonies like the Nevele, Grossinger's, and the Concord. While some of these resort hotels survive as golf destinations, the era of highballs and "Bésame Mucho" evoked in the movie *Dirty Dancing* is but a memory.

Today towns along the New York State Thruway like Kingston, New Paltz, Woodstock, Hudson, and Saugerties are rife with chic shops and fine dining, and the whole area is dotted with wineries, organic food co-ops, inns, and spas.

Clearly, what draws so many ex-urbanites, many of whom migrated to their former weekend homes, is the area's incredible natural beauty, largely unspoiled despite 300-odd years of European incursion. This is mostly thanks to the creation of the Catskill Park and Forest Preserve, 700,000 acres of mountains and valleys, forests and farms, rivers, streams, and waterfalls. The park is not only ground zero for fly-fishing, but it is a vital watershed, supplying half the state, including New York City, with clean drinking water. With thirty-five peaks topping out at more than 3,500 feet, the Catskills have long attracted skiers, and now they are fast becoming a haven for mountain bikers, rock climbers, and other extreme sports fans.

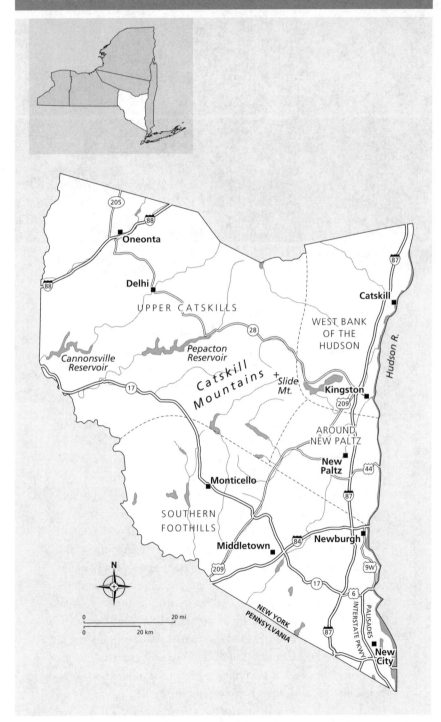

Oneonta

Delhi

UPPER CATSKILLS

Catskill

WEST BANK
OF THE
HUDSON

Cannonsville
Reservoir

Pepacton
Reservoir

Catskill
Mountains

Slide
Mt.

Kingston

Hudson R.

AROUND
NEW PALTZ

New
Paltz

Monticello

SOUTHERN
FOOTHILLS

Middletown

Newburgh

N

NEW YORK
PENNSYLVANIA

PALISADES INTERSTATE PKWY

New
City

0   20 mi
0   20 km

So if you think you've been-there, done-that, it's time to rediscover the Catskills, which are actually parts of the Appalachian range. In this chapter, we'll start in the southeast and expand our horizons to the north and west.

Southern Foothills

During World War II more than 1.3 million soldiers shipped out from Camp Shanks to fight in North Africa and Europe. They lived and trained in 2,500 buildings sprawled across 1,300 acres; today a small exhibit, vintage training films, and memorabilia at *Camp Shanks WWII Museum* tell the story of the men and women who passed through here on their way to the front. The museum, on South Greenbush Road State Routes 303/340, Orangeburg (845–638–5419), is open Memorial Day to Labor Day, Saturday and Sunday 10:00 A.M. to 3:00 P.M.

The *Edward Hopper House,* birthplace and boyhood home of the realist painter famous for works such as *Night Hawk,* is now a New York State Historic Site. One room of the home, built in 1858, documents his life and work in Nyack. Three other rooms exhibit works by local artists. Jazz concerts are presented in the restored garden in the summer. The house and gallery, at 82 North Broadway, *Nyack* (845–358–0774), is open Thursday through Sunday from 1:00 to 5:00 P.M. in summer. There is a suggested donation of $1.00.

Just about everyone knows where West Point is, but how many Hudson Valley travelers or military buffs can locate Constitution Island? Though it's practically on the east shore of the Hudson, separated from the mainland only by marshes, we include it here, since visitors have to take a boat to get to the island, and the boat leaves from West Point.

AUTHORS' FAVORITES—CATSKILLS

Catskill Corners Festival Marketplace	Mohonk Mountain House
Catskill Fly Fishing Center and Museum	Onteora, The Mountain House
Gomez Mill House	Saugerties Lighthouse
Inn at Lake Joseph	Slabsides
Minnewaska State Park Preserve	Sugar Loaf Arts and Craft Village

West Point Washouts

Not everyone is cut out for the rigors of cadet life at West Point. In 1831, after eight months, Edgar Allan Poe was dismissed for insubordination. Artist James A. McNeill Whistler washed out in his third year when he failed chemistry. He later commented, "Had silicon been a gas, I would have been a major general."

Although **Constitution Island** never served any military purpose after the Revolutionary War, it had an important part to play in General Washington's strategy for keeping British naval traffic out of the upper Hudson River. During the earlier part of the war, the fortifications on the island were relatively ineffectual; begun in 1775, **Fort Constitution** was still unfinished when it was captured by the British two years later. Largely destroyed by its American defenders before they retreated, the fort was never rebuilt.

By the following year, however, the island was back in American hands and was more valuable than ever in view of its position opposite the new American defenses constructed at West Point. Here was a place where British ships could be stopped dead in the water, and the way to do it was to stretch an immense iron chain across the river from **West Point** to Constitution Island. The chain was forged of stout New Jersey iron (a portion of it can be seen at the state reservation at Ringwood, New Jersey), floated across the river on rafts of logs, and securely anchored at either shore. Three redoubts and a battery were constructed on Constitution Island to protect the eastern end of the chain.

The chain did its job, and Constitution Island saw no further hostilities throughout the remaining five years of the war.

Constitution gained fame in the nineteenth century as the home of the Warner sisters, Susan (1819–85) and Anna (1824–1915). Under pseudonyms the two sisters wrote a total of 106 books, collaborating on 18 of them. Part of the present-day tour of the island is a visit to the **Warner House,** fifteen rooms of which are furnished in the Victorian style of the Warner sisters' heyday.

Constitution Island is open to guided two-hour tours from late June through mid-October. Boats leave West Point South Dock Wednesday and Thursday afternoons at 1:00 and 2:00 P.M., and reservations are required. Fare and admission to the house and fort are $9.00 for adults, senior citizens, students, and children 6 and over; $6.00 for children 3 to 5. For information contact the Constitution Island Association at (845) 446–8676 or visit www .constitutionisland.org.

Manitoga, Algonquin for "Place of the Great Spirit," was the home of Russel Wright, one of the country's foremost designers of home furnishings and a proponent of American design. His designs reflected his love of natural, organic shapes, and he would extend this respect for the earth and nature to the grounds where he built his home, Dragon Rock.

When he bought the property for his home in 1942, it had been damaged by 150 years of logging and quarrying. Over the next 30 years, Mr. Wright worked to restore the land, designing a living theater—a carefully designed backdrop of native trees, ferns, mosses, and wildflowers that appears as if it grew naturally.

A year before he died, the designer-naturalist opened his land to the public, and today programs at Manitoga teach ecology, science, art, and design. Visitors are invited to wander several one-way paths that Mr. Wright designed as journeys into the secrets of the forest. In building each, he would study the landscape and the land's natural contour to determine its direction. The main path passes by his home, designed to blend into the landscape of the quarry.

The grounds of Manitoga, Route 9D, *Garrison* (845-424-3812; www.russel wrightcenter.org), are open from April through October, Monday through Friday 9:00 A.M. to 4:30 P.M. and Saturday and Sunday 10:00 A.M. to 6:00 P.M. The grounds are open the rest of the year on weekdays only. Ninety-minute tours of Dragon Rock, Mr. Wright's home built on the rock ledge of an abandoned quarry, and of the woodland gardens, are given daily in season at 11:00 A.M. Visitors can take self-guided hikes on weekdays from 9:00 A.M. to 4:00 P.M.; and weekends from 10:00 A.M. to 6:00 P.M. April through October. A donation is requested if visitors hike the grounds. Admission for the tour is $15 (call for times).

In the 1830s John Jaques emigrated from Europe to the small town of *Washingtonville.* Trained as a shoe and bootmaker, he planned to support

A Magnifico's Bequest

The town of Harriman and Harriman State Park, a unit of the Palisades Interstate Park system, are now just names on the map to most travelers, though some New Yorkers may remember the late diplomat and one-time New York governor W. Averell Harriman. But the town and the park were named for the governor's father, E.H. Harriman, at one time the most powerful railroad baron in the United States. Edward Henry Harriman (1848–1909) controlled some 60,000 miles of American railways, including the Union Pacific. The present-day park consists of much of the 20,000-acre estate he acquired northwest of New City, and which he left to his wife with the intention that it would one day be transferred to state ownership.

ANNUAL EVENTS IN THE CATSKILLS

JANUARY

Hudson Valley Rail Trail Winterfest
New Paltz
(845) 691–8151
www.hudsonvalleyrailtrail.com

FEBRUARY

Winter Carnival Weekend
Monticello
(845) 796–3161
www.holidaymtn.com

MARCH

Women's History Month
New Paltz
(845) 255–1403

APRIL

Pennsylvania Dutch Festival
Port Ewen
(845) 338–0356

MAY

Hudson Valley Mayfaire
New Paltz
(845) 338–3468

Irish Festival
East Durham
(800) 434–FEST

JUNE

Arts on the Bridge Festival
New Paltz
(845) 255–2871

JULY

Belleayre Music Festival
Highmount
(800) 254–5600
www.belleayremusic.org
(through August)

Hurley Stone House Tour
Hurley
(845) 331–4121

New Paltz Gardens Plus Tour
New Paltz
(845) 255–0243

Peaceful Valley Bluegrass Festival
Shinhopple
(607) 363–2211 or 746–2281

Windham Chamber Music Festival
Windham
(518) 734–3868
www.windhammusic.com
(through August)

himself with his trade. To augment his income he purchased ten acres of land on Main Street and planted grapes in the rich, loamy Hudson Valley soil to sell at market. When he became a church elder, he used some of his grapes to make sacramental wine.

Today ***Brotherhood*** is America's oldest winery, and the church where Mr. Jaques's wine was first served is the winery's gift shop. Brotherhood has been making wine continuously since 1839, having survived Prohibition by once again reverting to the sale of sacramental wine. Its vast underground cellars,

AUGUST

Colonial Street Festival
New Paltz
(845) 255–1660

Daniel Nimham International Pow Wow
Carmel
(800) 470–4854
www.nimham.com

International Celtic Festival
Hunter
(518) 263–4223

Maverick Concert Series
Woodstock
(845) 679–8217
www.maverickconcerts.org
(through early September)

SEPTEMBER

Great Catskill Mountain Quilt Show
Windham
(800) SKI–WINDHAM or (518) 734–4300

Hudson River Valley Ramble
Two weekends, various locations
(800) 453–6665

Turn-of-the-Century Day
Roxbury
(607) 326–3722

OCTOBER

Hudson Valley Fall Festival
Milton
(845) 464–2789

Oktoberfest
Hunter
(518) 263–4223

NOVEMBER

Annual Greek Festival
Kingston
(845) 331–3522

Rosendale International Pickle Festival
Rosendale
www.picklefest.com

DECEMBER

Woodstock's Holiday Open House
Woodstock
(845) 679–6234

comparable to those of famous European wineries, are the largest in the country and, in addition to sacramental wine, Brotherhood now makes specialty, table, dessert, and premium vintage wines, including Grand Monarque champagne. A tour of the winery includes a visit to the underground cellars and a sampling of a half-dozen wines.

Brotherhood, 100 Brotherhood Plaza, Washingtonville (845–496–3661; www.brotherhoodwinery.net), offers guided half-hour wine-tasting tours daily at noon and 2:30 P.M.; weekends only January through March. The store is open from 11:00 A.M. to 5:00 P.M. Admission is $5.00 per person (free for those under 15). Call for a calendar of weekend events.

Orange County is known for its fine standardbred horses—the horses of the harness track. Hambletonian, sire of virtually all of today's trotters, was born here. For years it has been home to the Trotting Horse Museum, Home of the Hall of Fame of the Trotter, now officially the *Harness Racing Museum & Hall of Fame.*

Visitors to the museum can experience the thrill of harness racing—without the horse. One of the museum's newer permanent exhibits is the "Ready to Ride Racing Simulator." Participants sit on a twelve-seat motion-based platform (there are six stationary seats for those who want to see the film but not experience the motion) and watch a film that utilizes a variety of advanced techniques to create what amounts to a virtual harness race.

There are a host of other activities and exhibits, including the opportunity to call and judge a race, and a historic collection of photographs, ephemera, and fine art.

The Harness Racing Museum & Hall of Fame, 240 Main Street, *Goshen* (845–294–6330; www.harnessmuseum.com), is open daily from 10:00 A.M.to 6:00 P.M.; November to March it closes at 5:00 P.M. Admission is $7.50 for adults, $5.50 for seniors, and $3.50 for children 6 to 12.

Across the way is *Goshen Historic Track,* the oldest active harness track in the country and the first sporting site in the nation to be designated a National Registered Historic Landmark by the National Park Service.

The hamlet of *Sugar Loaf* has enjoyed a reputation as a crafts community for more than 250 years. Today more than fifty artisans live and work in the

Harness Racing Museum & Hall of Fame

original barns and buildings, creating a variety of goods ranging from stained glass to pottery to hand-tooled leather products. Visitors are invited to watch the artists at work in their studios and browse through a variety of specialty and gift shops peppered throughout the town.

There is an extensive program of concerts, festivals, and special events at **Sugar Loaf Arts and Craft Village** throughout the year. The 700-seat theater, Lycian Center (www.lycian.com/centre), offers a venue for performances by national and international touring companies in Broadway musicals, drama, dance, concerts, and children's shows.

Sugar Loaf Arts and Craft Village, Sugar Loaf Chamber of Commerce, Inc., P.O. Box 125, Sugar Loaf 10981 (845–469–9181), is open year-round. Days and hours vary from shop to shop; request a brochure from the Chamber of Commerce or visit www.sugarloafartsvillage.com on the Internet.

The next time you eat an onion, consider this: It might well have been grown in black dirt formed 12,000 years ago in a glacial lake in an area now known as **Pine Island.** As the glaciers melted and the climate warmed, vegetation grew, died, and sank to the bottom of the lake. The lake area earned the nickname "the drowned lands" and remained a swamp until the early 1900s, when immigrants came, bought the land cheap, drained the lake by hand, built drainage ditches, and then planted onions in the rich black dirt. Today, with thousands of acres planted, the "black dirt" region is one of the country's leading producers of onions.

The cream of onion soup at **Ye Jolly Onion Inn** is made from Pine Island onions. So are the deep-fried onion blossoms, the onion rings, and the onion gravy on the Pine Island steak. And the vegetables on the salad bar are all from farms in the area (in season). After a visit to the "black dirt" region and Ye Jolly Onion Inn, you'll never again think lightly of the humble onion.

Ye Jolly Onion Inn, corner of Route 517, Pulaski Highway and Orange County Route 1, Pine Island (845–258–4277; www.yejollyonion.com), is open

Black Tie, No Tails

Toward the end of the nineteenth century, in the gated community of millionaires' estates called Tuxedo Park in the Ramapo Mountains near the New Jersey border, daring young fashion plates scandalized their elders by abandoning traditional full evening dress with its cutaway tailcoats in favor of a shorter black jacket cut like a daytime suit coat. Despite initial resistance the new style caught on, and the new semiformal men's uniform came to be known as the tuxedo.

Wednesday and Thursday 5:00 to 9:00 P.M., Friday and Saturday 5:00 to 10:00 P.M., and Sunday noon to 7:30 P.M.

If your interest in horses has been piqued by the Harness Racing Museum & Hall of Fame, head over to **New Hope Farms Equestrian Park** in **Port Jervis.** With eighty acres it's one of the largest equestrian facilities in the nation and features indoor and outdoor arenas and permanent stabling for one hundred horses. Visitors are invited to stop by at any time to watch thoroughbreds and warmbloods being trained for show jumping competitions.

Throughout the year there are events such as a tri-state rodeo, a family festival, polo matches, and a championship dressage; musical events are also presented. The indoor arena, which seats 2,500, is one of the largest in the country.

New Hope Farms Equestrian Park, 500 Neversink Drive, Port Jervis (845–856–8384), is open daily year-round from 8:00 A.M. to 5:00 P.M. From the end of January through March 15, most of the horses are moved south and there's very little activity. For a list of events, check www.webusers.warwick.net.

The **Inn at Lake Joseph** is a Victorian country estate high in the Catskill Mountains. It nestles against a 250-acre lake and is surrounded by thousands of acres of forest and wildlife preserve.

Built by Thomas Hunt Talmadge in the latter part of the nineteenth century, the estate served as a retreat for the Dominican Sisters, as a vacation home of Cardinals Hayes and Spellman of New York, and finally as a sumptuous inn.

Rooms are available in the Manor, the Carriage House, and The Cottage. Several of the inn's ten guest rooms in the Manor have working fireplaces and whirlpool baths. If you yearn for even more privacy, request a room in the recently restored turn-of-the-century Adirondack-style Carriage House (where pets are welcome). Each has its own entrance, a working fireplace, and a whirlpool bath. Some have lofted ceilings and private sundecks. Pets are also welcome in The Cottage, which has three rustic, Adirondack–style guest rooms with stone fireplaces, full kitchens, whirlpool baths, and private sundecks. Meals are served, and there are plenty of outdoor sporting activities, including paddling around in a Victorian-style swimming pool. Lake Joseph has a reputation as one of the finest largemouth bass lakes in the state.

Inn at Lake Joseph, 400 St. Joseph Road, **Forestburgh** (845–791–9506, www.lakejoseph.com), is open year-round. Weekend rates range from $170 to $385. There is a $20-per-day fee for pets.

From December through March (eagle time), Sullivan County becomes home to a large concentration of migrant **bald eagles**—mostly from Canada. A few of their favorite nesting places include Mongaup Falls Reservoir and Rio Reservoir in Forestburgh and the Rondout Reservoir in Grahamsville. For an update and complete list of sites, contact the **Audubon Society of New York State,** P.O. Box 111, **Eldred** 12732, (845) 557–8025.

If the sight of our majestic national bird inspires you to take wing, visit **Wurtsboro Airport.** Established in 1927, Wurtsboro bills itself as the oldest soaring site in the nation. The airport's Flight Service is the largest soaring school in the United States, offering lessons for people with no flight experience as well as for those licensed to fly power planes. For the casual visitor, however, the big attraction is the demonstration rides. After being towed aloft by a single-engine Cessna, you'll glide high above the Catskills with an FAA-rated commercial pilot at the stick. A demonstration ride or an introductory lesson costs $75. Be sure to call in advance for a reservation.

Wurtsboro Airport and Flight Service, Route 209, Wurtsboro (845–888–2791; www.wurtsboroairport.com), is open daily all year from 9:00 A.M. to 5:00 P.M. or dusk (weather permitting), whichever comes first. Closed major holidays.

According to the folks at **Memories,** buyers searched five states and three countries to fill their 20,000-square-foot building with more than 25,000 unique items covering every style and taste from the early 1800s to the 1950s. Stock includes furniture, lamps, clocks, rocking horses, decoys, glass, china, magazines, and, as they say, "who knows what's coming in?"

Memories, Route 17 Quickway, **Parksville** (845–292–4270; www.memories antiques.com), is open daily year-round from 10:00 A.M. to 5:00 P.M.

Many devotees of fly-fishing believe that, in North America, the sport began in the Catskills. And seeing the streams that run along the Beaverkill and Willowemoc Valleys, it's hard to imagine a more suitable location for a center devoted to preserving the heritage and protecting the future of fly-fishing in the United States. That's the mission of the **Catskill Fly Fishing Center and Museum/Hall of Fame,** on the shores of the Willowemoc River between Roscoe and Livingston Manor.

Founded in 1891, the new facility, which opened in May 1995, illuminates the contributions and lives of the great names associated with the Catskill era—Gordon and Hewitt, Dette and Darbee, LaBranche and Flick—as well as Lee Wulff, Poul Jorgensen, and others from the world of fly-fishing. Interpretive exhibits on the evolution of the sport, as well as hundreds of meticulously crafted rods, flies, and reels are on display. Special guest fly tyers demonstrate their craft every Saturday afternoon throughout the season. The center offers a variety of educational and recreational programs year-round, including courses in stream ecology and angling, fly tying, and rod building.

Catskill Fly Fishing Center and Museum/Hall of Fame, 1031 Old Route 17, **Livingston Manor** (845–439–4810), is open daily 10:00 A.M. to 4:00 P.M. from April through October; Tuesday through Friday 10:00 A.M. to 1:00 P.M. and Saturday 10:00 A.M. to 4:00 P.M. November through March. Closed holidays. A $3.00 donation is requested.

Feeling stressed? Consider escaping for a peaceful weekend at *Dai Bosatsu Zendo,* a Zen Buddhist monastery on 1,400 acres in the Catskill Mountain Forest Preserve. All are welcome here, whether it be for a three-day weekend for novices who want to learn basics, such as sitting, breathing, and chanting; a longer stay for those steeped in the way of Rinzai Zen Buddhism; or even those just looking for an overnight retreat. The grounds are open to day visitors March through November.

As expected, accommodations are simple but comfortable and include three vegetarian meals a day. Rooms with private and shared baths are available. Rates for the three-day weekend begin at under $200.

Dai Bosatsu Zendo, 223 Beecher Lake Road, Livingston Manor (845–439–4566; www.daibosatsu.org), requests that guests reserve at least two weeks in advance.

More than one hundred varieties of cheese and fifty flavors of jelly beans make *The Cheese Barrel* a popular stop for kids of all ages. The shop specializes in gourmet goodies and breads from Bread Alone. The old stockroom has been turned into an ice-cream parlor, and the dining area serves continental breakfasts and light lunches with homemade soups, salads, and sandwiches. The latest innovation: an espresso bar.

The Cheese Barrel, 880 Main at Bridge Street, *Margaretville* (845–586–4666; www.cheesebarrel.com), is open daily. The ice-cream parlor is open until 8:00 p.m.; later during the summer.

Around New Paltz

The 90,000-acre Northern Shawangunk mountain range, whose cliffs, summits, and plateaus are home to almost forty rare plant and animal species, has been designated a "Last Great Place on Earth" by the Nature Conservancy.

Minnewaska State Park Preserve, high in the Shawangunk Mountains, is an outdoor paradise of hiking trails, waterfalls, and scenic vistas. A network of carriageways accessible to bicyclists, hikers, and horseback riders links many of the park's major highlights. It will require a hike of approximately 3 miles, however, to reach one of the park's greatest draws: lovely Lake Awosting, a mile-long swimming lake rimmed by pine trees. Although it's a popular spot on a hot summer day (a lifeguard is on duty), those used to the crowds at ocean beaches will feel almost as if they're at a private party. For the less ambitious there's also swimming at the more accessible Lake Minnewaska, nestled amid white sandstone cliffs (it's easy to see why the Indians named it "floating waters").

Minnewaska State Park Preserve, off Route 44/55, New Paltz (914–255–0752; www.lakeminnewaska.org), is open year-round. There is a $7.00 parking fee.

Not far from Minnewaska is a 4,600-acre tract of land that contains one of the world's best examples of a ridgetop dwarf pine barrens: **Sam's Point Dwarf Pine Ridge Preserve**. According to the Nature Conservancy, managers of the barrens, one of Earth's most endangered ecosystems thrives here for several reasons: "limited water during the growing season; exposure to direct sun and wind; shallow, highly erodible soils; and the regular occurrence of fires. All of these processes, and perhaps yet unknown factors, have historically worked together to shape the plant and animal communities that thrive there today."

Several trails wind through the preserve. One of the most popular, Verkeerderkill Falls/Long Path, meanders through the barrens to the falls and offers panoramic views to the southeast.

For information contact the Nature Conservancy, Eastern New York Chapter, 265 Chestnut Ridge Road, Mt. Kisco, 10549, (914) 244–3271.

In 1714 Louis Moses Gomez, a refugee from the Spanish Inquisition, purchased 6,000 acres of land along the Hudson highlands and built a fieldstone blockhouse. Today the **Gomez Mill House** is the earliest surviving Jewish residence in North America.

Over the ensuing years subsequent owners of the house made changes to the original structure. The most famous twentieth-century owner was the Craftsman-era designer Dard Hunter, who rebuilt the old gristmill on "Jew's Creek" into a paper mill and then made paper by hand, cut and cast type, and handprinted his own books.

Today the house, continuously inhabited for almost 300 years, is preserved by the Gomez Foundation for Mill House; the foundation is made up of friends and descendants of families who lived here.

The Gomez Mill House, 11 Mill House Road, **Marlboro** (845–236–3126; www.gomez.org), is open from the Wednesday after Easter and Passover through October, Wednesday through Sunday 10:00 A.M. to 4:00 P.M., with tours at 10:00 and 11:30 A.M. and 1:00 and 2:30 P.M. Admission is $7.50 for adults, $5.00 for seniors, and $2.00 for children. On Sundays the museum sponsors a lecture series.

Fast becoming the next "in" weekend retreat, the **Buttermilk Falls Inn and Spa** in Milton is a seventy-acre estate overlooking the Hudson River just 75 miles north of New York City. Dating from 1764, the sophisticated inn has thirteen rooms, three carriage houses, the North Cottage, and a new, two-story, 3,500-square-foot spa.

"The spa at Buttermilk Falls Inn embraces a total holistic philosophy," says spa director Heidi Weaver. Guests unwind with a stroll on the estate's tranquil grounds past cascading waterfalls, winding brooks, flowering terraces, a peacock and chicken rookery, and a pre-Revolutionary cemetery. The spa lunch, prepared from organically grown produce from the estate's garden and from local farms and orchards, is served up with a charming river view.

The spa offers deep-tissue and hot-stone massages and purifying facials using organic skin care products. Buttermilk Spa's couples massage and spine-realigning "raindrop technique" are two of its signature treatments. Various sixty-minute sessions are priced from $75 and higher. Four spacious massage rooms even have river views. The spa is also adding a saltwater pool, a steam room, and a Jacuzzi.

Buttermilk offers midweek Gourmet Spa Getaway packages (for two or three nights) starting at $575 per room based on double occupancy; included are accommodations, breakfast and afternoon tea daily, two sixty-minute massages, entrance to one of several of the Hudson Valley's area attractions and coupons for savings at nearby Woodbury Commons Premium Outlets. For more information call (845) 795–1310 or visit www.buttermilkfallsinn.com.

Back in the old Hudson Valley town of New Paltz, **Huguenot Street** is the oldest street in America that still has its original houses. Think about it: Find a street where each building lot has had only one house upon it, and chances are you're in a modern subdivision. But the stone houses on Huguenot Street were built between 1692 and 1712, and they'll look good for at least another 300 years.

Persecuted by the Catholic majority in their native France, many Huguenots came to New York in pursuit of freedom and tolerance. In 1677 twelve of their number purchased the lands around present-day New Paltz from the Esopus Indians and built log huts as their first habitations.

As the twelve pioneers and their families prospered, they decided to build more permanent dwellings. And permanent they were. Here are five perfectly preserved houses, with additions that were built by the settlers' descendants over the years. All of the houses are maintained by the Huguenot Historical Society, which gives tours Tuesday through Sunday from May 1 through October 31.

Tours of the houses are available for $10.00 for adults, $9.00 for students and seniors, $5.00 for ages 6 to 17; free for under 5. Family rate is $24.00. For information contact the Huguenot Society, 18 Broadhead Avenue, New Paltz (845–255–1660 or 255–1889).

Just north of New Paltz, at High Falls, is a museum dedicated to a great work of engineering brought about by an energy crisis—a disruption in coal supply brought about by America's 1812–14 war with Great Britain. Two brothers, Maurice and William Wurts, envisioned a canal to bring Pennsylvania anthracite (hard coal) from the mines to New York City and vicinity. In 1825, they formed the Delaware and Hudson Canal Company with the goal of linking Honesdale, Pennsylvania, with the Hudson River port of Eddyville, New York.

The surveying and engineering of the 108-mile route was handled by Benjamin Wright, chief engineer of the Erie Canal. The Delaware and Hudson Canal, completed in 1828, was the first million-dollar enterprise in America. Between 1847 and 1852 it was enlarged and deepened to accommodate heavier traffic. A lot of coal barged along that route, yet in 1829, the company also began to work its gravity-operated rail line between Honesdale and Carbondale, Pennsylvania, with a new English steam locomotive. Except for a few weedy stretches, the canal is gone, but the Delaware and Hudson Railroad survives to this day as the oldest transportation company in the United States.

The **Delaware and Hudson Canal Museum** is a private institution established to tell the story of the old canal, and it does so not merely through glassed-in exhibits but by preserving the extant structures, channel, and locks in the **High Falls** vicinity. Visitors learn about the canal through sophisticated dioramas, photos, and technological exhibits, including models of a working lock and gravity railroad. There are five locks at High Falls. The Delaware and Hudson Canal Historical Society has done whatever restoration and preservation work is possible on them and has linked canal sites in the area with a system of hiking trails. Self-guided tours take in nearby canal segments as well as the remains of John Roebling's suspension aqueduct.

The Delaware and Hudson Canal Museum, Mohonk Road, High Falls (845–687–9311; www.canalmuseum.org), is open May through October, Thursday, Friday, Saturday, and Monday 11:00 A.M. to 5:00 P.M., and Sunday 1:00 to 5:00 P.M. Admission is $4.00 for adults, $2.00 for children.

Originally built to serve canal workers, the **Depuy Canal House** is a 1797 stone tavern right on the Delaware and Hudson Canal. It still has its original fireplaces and wooden floors, and diners can watch meals being prepared from a second-floor balcony that overlooks the kitchen.

From these dizzy heights, foodies revel in watching chef John Novi, whom *Time* magazine called "The Father of Nouvelle Cuisine," prepare a delicate appetizer of quail cutlet with hazelnut crust or a plate of rare venison medallions with maitake mushroom risotto. You might even want to order the roast poussin with truffle mashed potato just to see how it's done!

The menu might come with a warning—indulging in the multi-course prix fixe carries a risk of satiety—but that's no problem if you've planned to overnight at the **Locktender's Cottage** right next door. The variety of comfortable accommodations includes the Chef's Quarters, a suite with a hot tub and, of course, a kitchenette. Reservations are recommended for both dining and overnight stays; contact the Depuy Canal House, Route 213, High Falls at (845) 687–7700 or www.depuycanalhouse.net. Dinner is served Friday through Sunday; brunch is also offered on Sunday.

Even as canals and railroads were changing the face of America, the first conservationists started speaking out against the dangers of the Industrial Revolution. Among them was John Burroughs, a native New Yorker who wrote twenty-five books on natural history and the philosophy of conservation. In 1895 Burroughs built a rustic log hideaway in the woods outside the village of **West Park,** barely 2 miles from the west bank of the Hudson. He called it **Slabsides,** and it is a National Historic Landmark today.

Burroughs, whose permanent home was only a mile and a half away, came to his little retreat to write and to quietly observe his natural surroundings. John Muir came here to talk with Burroughs, as did Theodore Roosevelt and Thomas Edison. They sat around the fire on log furniture of Burroughs's own manufacture, much of it still in the cabin.

Slabsides, which was deeded to the John Burroughs Association after the author's death in 1921, now stands within the 191-acre *John Burroughs Sanctuary,* a pleasant woodland tract that forms a most fitting living monument to his memory. The sanctuary is open all year; on the third Saturday in May and the first Saturday in October, the John Burroughs Association holds an open house from noon to 4:00 P.M. In addition to an opportunity to see the cabin, the special days include informal talks and nature walks. Admission is free. The sanctuary has 2½ miles of hiking trails open to the public daily from dawn to dusk. For further information write the association at 15 West 77th Street, New York City 10024, or call (845) 384–6320 or (212) 769–5169.

Nestled in the heart of a 24,000-acre natural area in the Shawangunk Mountains, overlooking Lake Mohonk, is a sprawling Victorian castle resort called **Mohonk Mountain House.** Built in 1869, the castle is a National Historic Landmark whose facilities include 251 guest rooms, 5 guest cottages, 150 working fireplaces, and 200 balconies. Above the Mohonk Mountain House stands **Sky Top Tower**, an observation tower built in 1923 of Shawangunk conglomerate that was quarried at its base. From the top of Sky Top Tower, on a clear day, you can see forever—or at least as far as the Rondout and Wallkill valleys, New Jersey, Connecticut, Vermont, Pennsylvania, and Massachusetts. (The tower is also known as the Albert K. Smiley Memorial Tower in tribute to the cofounder of the Mohonk Mountain House.) Guests, of course, have use of the resort's spacious grounds and many amenities, but even if you're not an overnight guest, you can pay a day-visitor fee (under $15) that will give you access to the tower; 85 miles of hiking trails, paths, and carriage roads; and the lovely landscaped grounds with their formal show gardens, herb garden, and new Victorian maze.

Day visitors are also invited to visit the **Barn Museum,** in one of the largest barns in the Northeast. Built in 1888, it houses more than fifty nineteenth-century horse-drawn vehicles and many working tools made more than one hundred years ago. The Barn Museum (845–255–1000, ext. 2447), is open Wednesday, Saturday, and Sunday during the winter and daily in summer and fall. In the winter, day visitors can cross-country ski on more than 35 miles of marked, maintained cross-country ski trails. In the summer and fall, a shuttle ($5.00 per person round-trip) runs to and from Picnic Lodge—the day-visitors' center, which serves sandwiches and pizza—and the parking lot.

Mohonk Mountain House, Lake Mohonk, New Paltz (845–255–1000; www.mohonk.com; for reservations, 800–772–6646). Overnight rates vary according to view and decor, but all include three meals. They range from $379 a night for a double in one of the traditional-style rooms to $735 for a tower room.

West Bank of the Hudson

When mayonnaise king Richard Hellmann was told, at the age of fifty-five, that he had only six months to live unless he moved to the country, he did what any sane millionaire would do. (No, he didn't go to the Mayo Clinic.) He built a magnificent estate on the side of Mount Ticetonyk overlooking the Esopus River valley, moved there with his family, and lived to be ninety-four.

Now a B&B, **Onteora, The Mountain House** (Onteora is the Mohican name for the Catskills, which translates to "the land and the sky") is surrounded by 225 acres of forest and features a magnificent multiwindowed 20- by 30-foot Great Room with a massive stone fireplace; a 40-foot covered dining porch with Adirondack-style tree-trunk columns and railings; and a 60-foot southwest deck. All five guest rooms have private baths. The house is filled with an eclectic collection of antiques and Japanese and Korean art.

Onteora, The Mountain House, Piney Point Road, **Boiceville** (845–657–6233; www.onteora.com), is open year-round. Rates, which include a full breakfast (with items such as crepes with three fillings and Eggs Hellmann), range from $165 a weekday night to $240 a weekend night; there is a two-night minimum on weekends.

Totem Indian Trading Post, one of, if not *the* oldest trading post in the state, is a New York State Historic Site. It's also the site of numerous megalithic sculptures done by Emil Brunel, founder of the New York Institute of Photography, who died in Boiceville in 1944. The ashes of the man who perfected the one-hour film developing process seventy years before it became popular are interred in one of his cement pieces here.

Totem Indian Trading Post, Sacred Ground, Route 28, Boiceville (845–657–2531), is open daily from 10:00 A.M. to 6:00 P.M.

Floating down Esopus Creek on a lazy afternoon as it winds through the Catskill Mountains is the ultimate vacation: relaxing, scenic, and fun. *The Town Tinker* rents tubes, helps chart your course, provides instruction as needed, and arranges transportation. There are separate 2½-mile routes for beginner and expert tubers. Each route takes approximately two hours, and transportation is provided by either Town Tinker Tube Taxis on weekdays or the Catskill Mountain Railroad on weekends.

The Town Tinker, Bridge Street (Route 28), *Phoenicia* (845–688–5553; www.towntinker.com), is open daily mid-May through September from 9:00 A.M. to 6:00 P.M. (last rentals are at 4:00 P.M.). Basic inner tubes rent for $12.00 a day. A full-gear package for $25.00 includes a tube with seat, life vest, wetsuit, and helmet as well as one-time transportation. Children must be 12 years old and good swimmers. Taxi transportation is $5.00 per trip.

On weekends and holidays *Catskill Mountain Railroad* transports novice tubers back to Phoenicia at the end of their run (one-way fare is $5.00). But if you'd rather tour Esopus Creek by rail, the railroad offers a 6-mile round-trip ride, stopping at Phoenicia at a circa 1900 train depot.

Catskill Mountain Railroad Company, Route 28, *Mt. Pleasant* (845–688–7400; www.catskillrailroad.com), operates weekends and holidays Memorial Day weekend through late October with trains running hourly 11:00 A.M. to 5:00 P.M. Fare is $14.00 round-trip for adults, $8.00 for children ages 4 to 11. Call ahead to verify schedules.

Back in the summer of '69, thousands of music fans gathered at Max Yasgur's farm in Bethel to hear Jimi Hendrix, Janis Joplin, and other voices that defined the Woodstock era; psychedelic visions were also common. Today visitors can enjoy their visions chemical-free at the world's largest kaleidoscope, located at Emerson Place, an upscale hotel and spa complex on Route 28 in Mt. Tremper.

Housed in an old farm silo, the *Emerson Kaleidoscope* is more than 60 feet high with three 38-foot mirrors, creating a total immersion in color and light. Three specially designed shows are presented throughout the year: "America, The House We Live In," is a history in music and light; "Hexagon Holiday" is a winter wonder that is shown from Christmas through Presidents' Day weekend; and "Metamorphosis" is a show that opens in early spring, just as the buds are popping, and traces the progress of the seasons through the Catskills. Entry is $7.00 per person; children under 12 get in free.

Emerson Place also has a country store and other shops, including the *Kaleidostore,* where handmade, one-of-a kind kaleidoscopes are on sale. The recently rebuilt *Emerson Resort and Spa* now has twenty-five new suites in addition to the Adirondack-style accommodations at the old *Lodge at Emerson Place.* Rates for a standard double start at $190 a night; call (877) 688–2828 or go to www.emersonplace.com for particulars.

If you're looking for a different dining experience, **Catskill Rose** is an excellent option. How about appetizers such as smoked shrimp with ginger black beans and entrees like smoked duckling with apricot tamarind chutney? The restaurant, on Route 212 in Mt. Tremper (845–688–7100), begins serving dinner at 5:00 P.M. Thursday through Sunday. Reservations are appreciated.

One of the country's first art colonies was founded in **Woodstock** in 1903, and today Ulster County is still a haven for artists. The **Woodstock Guild,** a multiarts center, displays and sells works of some of the area's best. It's at 34 Tinker Street, Woodstock (845–679–2079; www.woodstockguild.org, and is open Friday through Sunday from noon to 5:00 P.M.; closed January and February.

The baguette is a work of art at **Bread Alone,** 22 Mill Hill Road, Woodstock (845–679–2108). Workers at the European-style bakery shape the breads by hand and then bake the loaves in the wood-fired ovens. Among the house specialties: brioche, challah, and sourdough currant buns. The bakery is open daily from 7:00 A.M.. to 5:00 P.M. (Friday and Saturday until 6:00 P.M.); see www.breadalone.com for locations in Boiceville, Rhinebeck, and Kingston.

There are numerous excellent restaurants in the Woodstock area. Among the more unusual is **New World Home Cooking Company,** 1411 Route 212, Saugerties (845–246–0900), featuring "New Wave" cooking—an eclectic assortment of ethnic dishes often pepped up with hot peppers and Asian spices. House specialties include Jamaican jerk chicken, cajun-peppered shrimp, and *ropa vieja.* There's a lovely outdoor patio and a great selection of beers to extinguish the fire. Open for dinner nightly, and lunch Friday through Monday in fall and winter. Reservations are highly recommended.

For almost forty years until his death in 1976, Harvey Fite created a monumental environmental sculpture out of an abandoned Saugerties bluestone quarry. **Opus 40,** made of hundreds of thousands of tons of finely fitted stone, covers more than six acres. Visitors can walk along its recessed lower pathways, around the pools and fountains, and up to the nine-ton monolith at the summit. To create his Opus, Fite worked with traditional tools that were used by quarrymen here. The **Quarryman's Museum** houses his collection of tools and artifacts.

Opus 40 and Quarryman's Museum, 50 Fite Road, **Saugerties** (845–246–3400; www.opus40.org), is open Memorial Day weekend through Columbus Day weekend, Friday, Saturday, and Sunday and most Monday holidays (call in advance) noon to 5:00 P.M. Admission is $10.00 for adults, $7.00 for students and senior citizens, and $3.00 for children.

If you've ever looked longingly at a distant lighthouse, wishing you could escape Wal-Mart, McDonald's, and the Internet for a bit, check into the **Saugerties Lighthouse,** an 1869 stone structure at the mouth of Esopus Creek on the Hudson River.

Deactivated by the U.S. Coast Guard in 1954, the lighthouse has since been restored by the Saugerties Lighthouse Conservancy, which operates it as a museum and inn. In 1990 the Coast Guard installed a fourth-order solar-powered light, and the lighthouse once again aids mariners.

Two second-floor bedrooms are for rent. Guests share a kitchen and bath. Guests get to the lighthouse via a half-mile nature trail (at low tide only) or by private boat. From April through November the rooms rent for $160 week-nights, $175 weekends. Reservations are essential.

The museum at Saugerties Lighthouse Conservancy, 168 Lighthouse Drive, Saugerties (845–247–0656), is open Saturday, Sunday, and holidays from 2:00 to 5:00 P.M. Memorial Day through Labor Day. There is a suggested donation of $3.00 for adults and $1.00 for children.

New York's highest waterfall is actually 3 miles east of *Tannersville*—it's *Kaaterskill Falls.* (As you drive on Route 23A up the winding road, watch for the vehicle pullout and park there. Follow the sign that says TRAIL back down the road a short distance to the bridge to view the falls.) Kaaterskill Falls leaps from a rock ledge as a narrow curtain of white water, plunging past a natural grotto to a second scooped-out shelf at which it gathers force to finish its plunge toward the floor of Kaaterskill Clove.

Now little known outside of hikers' guidebooks, the falls was once the Catskills' most celebrated natural wonder. Thomas Cole, founder of the Hudson River School of art, immortalized the falls in his painting *View of Kaaterskill Falls* in the early 1800s. Washington Irving described the cove as "wild, lonely, and shagged, the bottom filled with fragments from impending cliffs, and scarcely lighted by the reflected rays of the setting sun."

The path to the base of the falls is not particularly difficult, although in the spring, when its snow cover has melted and refrozen into glare ice, it requires a ginger step. But it is a short trail, and it follows the ravine gouged by Kaaterskill Creek for less than a mile before reaching the base.

Now we're going to the Broncks. No, it's not the wrong chapter—or the wrong spelling. Bronck was the family name of one of the original clans of Swedish settlers in New Amsterdam and the Hudson Valley. The farmstead of Pieter Bronck, who settled on the west bank of the Hudson near what is now *Coxsackie,* today makes up the *Bronck Museum.*

Eight generations of Broncks lived in the seventeenth-century house before it passed to the Greene County Historical Society, along with the entire farm settled in those early years. The Broncks' property had come down virtually intact until Leonard Bronck Lampman willed the acreage and buildings to the historical society. Thus, we get to appreciate not only the oldest of the farm buildings but also all of the barns, utility buildings, and furnishings acquired over two centuries of prosperity and familial expansion. What it all amounts to is an object lesson in the changes in style, taste, and sophistication that took place between the seventeenth and nineteenth centuries.

The Bronck Museum, 45 Lafayette Avenue, Coxsackie (518–731–6490), is open Memorial Day until mid-October, Tuesday through Saturday and holiday Mondays 10:00 A.M. to 4:00 P.M. and Sunday 1:00 to 5:00 P.M. Call for admission fees.

Upper Catskills

The clear, cold streams of the Catskills—Beaver Kill, Esopus Creek, the east and west branches of the Delaware River—are among the most hallowed waterways in the history of American trout fishing. Not surprisingly, the Catskills have a rich tradition of handcrafted trout flies. If you're headed up this way to do some fishing, be sure to stop in at Mary Dette's home, where she sells flies hand-tied by artisans from around the Catskills region. (Mary also ties some herself, but we hear the wait for these is up to a year.) *Dette Trout Flies,* a local institution, is at 68 Cottage Street, Roscoe (607–498–4991). Look for the sign out front: DETTE TROUT FLIES: WALT, WINNIE, MARY. It's open daily from 8:00 A.M. until 8:00 P.M.

If you're heading west from the Hudson Valley into the upper Catskills, a stop at the *Durham Center Museum* in *East Durham* provides an instructive look at the things a small community finds important—in many ways this museum is archetypal of the "village attics" that dot the land, and travelers could do worse than to take an occasional poke into one of these institutions. At the museum, which is housed in a circa 1825 one-room schoolhouse and several newer adjacent buildings, the collections run to Indian artifacts, portions of local petrified trees, old farm tools, and mementos of the 1800 Susquehanna Turnpike and the 1832–40 Canajoharie-Catskill Railroad, both of which passed this way. There is also a collection of Rogers Groups, those plaster statuette tableaux that decorated Victorian parlors and played on bourgeois heartstrings before Norman Rockwell was born. Finally, don't miss the collection of bottled

The Bridges of Delaware County

Three historic covered bridges are among the rural attractions of Delaware County. The Hamden and Fitches Bridges span the west branch of the Delaware River, while the Downsville Bridge, crossing the Delaware's east branch, is at 174 feet the longest covered bridge still in use in New York State.

The Long Good Night

Literature's greatest snoozer, Rip Van Winkle, hailed from Palenville and took his twenty-year nap in a ravine halfway up Catskill Mountain. Hikers still search for the spot where Rip sat, drank from a keg offered to him by an old man with thick, bushy hair and a grizzled beard, and watched odd-looking fellows playing ninepins before he drifted off.

sand specimens from around the world, sent by friends of the museum. If you're planning a trip to some far-off spot not represented on these shelves, don't hesitate to send some sand.

The Durham Center Museum, Route 145, East Durham (518–239–8461), is open the third weekend in May through Columbus Day, Thursday through Sunday from 1:00 to 4:00 P.M. and Thursday from 7:00 to 9:00 P.M. (winter by appointment). Admission is $2.50 for adults and $1.00 for children under 12. Groups are welcome by appointment. Genealogical researchers are welcome year-round by appointment.

Two 1876 Queen Anne boarding houses were restored and joined to create **Albergo Allegria,** a luxurious sixteen-room inn with an elegant Victorian flavor and modern-day amenities. There is also a carriage house with five suites. Rates, which range from $73 for a weekday room in the inn to $299 (in high season) for the Millenium Suite, include afternoon tea (served alfresco on warm days) and a gourmet breakfast, with treats such as stuffed French toast, Belgian waffles, and honey-cured bacon. The B&B is on Route 296, Windham (518–734–5560; www.albergousa.com).

In 1824 a young man named **Zadock Pratt** came to a settlement called Schoharie Kill to establish a tannery. He bought some land, surveyed it, and set up his factory. Over the next twenty years, more than 30,000 employees, using hides imported from South America, tanned a million sides of sole leather, which were shipped down the Hudson River to New York City. And in the meantime Mr. Pratt established **Prattsville,** one of the earliest planned communities in New York State.

Mr. Pratt went on to become a member of the U.S. Congress elected in 1836 and 1842. He sponsored a bill that created the Smithsonian Institution. One of the most enduring legacies he left behind was **Pratt Rocks Park** (518–299–3395), on Main Street, which he donated to the town in 1843. Carved into the park's cliffs are symbols of Mr. Pratt's life, including a huge bust of his son who was killed in the Civil War, a horse, a hemlock tree, an uplifted hand, his tannery, a wreath with the names of his children, and an unfinished tomb where Pratt was to be buried overlooking the village (he was buried in a conventional grave at the other end of town). There's also a grave site with a stone bearing the names of his favorite dogs and horses.

While you're in Prattsville, take time to visit the **Zadock Pratt Museum** (518–299–3395; www.prattmuseum.com), located in Zadock Pratt's restored homestead in the center of town. The museum, on the National Register of Historic Places, is just a half mile from the rocks: It focuses on the history and culture of the northern Catskills in the mid-nineteenth century and is open Memorial Day to Columbus Day, Thursday through Sunday 1:00 to 4:00 P.M. There is an admission fee. Nearby, the National Register **Reformed Dutch Church,** with its handsome three-tiered tower, was built in 1804.

Roxbury, New York, is where we again come into contact with the naturalist **John Burroughs.** He may have spent much of the last decades of his life at Slabsides, down on the Hudson, but it was here in Roxbury that he was born in 1837 and here where he spent the last ten summers of his life at Woodchuck Lodge. He was buried here, in a field adjacent to the lodge, on April 2, 1921. The grave site and the nearby "Boyhood Rock" that he had cherished as a lad are now part of **Burroughs Memorial State Historic Site.**

The Burroughs Memorial is unique among historic sites in that its chief feature (apart from the grave and the rock) is simply a field surrounded by forests and the rolling Catskill hills. This is as fine a memorial as one could possibly imagine for a man who once said about the Catskills, "Those hills comfort me as no other place in the world does—it is home there."

Burroughs Memorial State Historic Site, off Route 30 (take Hardscrabble Road to Burroughs Road), north of Roxbury, is open during daylight hours. Admission is free. For information call (518) 827–6111 or see www.nysparks.com/sites.

Many of John Burroughs's modern-day spiritual descendants use the term *appropriate technology* to refer to renewable, nonpolluting sources of energy.

Breaking "Legs"

The tiny town of Acra was once home to one of Prohibition's most infamous criminals. Jack "Legs" Diamond heard about a potent applejack that the locals made from cider and decided to move in and "organize" the stills. He bought a farmhouse just north of the village for his gang headquarters and began calling on the mountain bootleggers. Unfortunately for "Legs," the locals didn't want to be organized, and he was gunned down. Wounded, he had the trunks of the trees around his house painted white to hinder a possible ambush and was eventually killed in an Albany rooming house.

Over in the northwestern Catskills town of *East Meredith,* the *Hanford Mills Museum* celebrates one of the oldest of these so-called alternative-energy sources, the power of running water harnessed to a wheel. Kortright Creek at East Meredith has been the site of waterpowered mills since the beginning of the nineteenth century, and the main building on the museum site today was built in 1846.

The old mill became the Hanford Mills in 1860, when David Josiah Hanford bought the operation. During the eighty-five years in which it owned the mill, the Hanford family expanded its output to include feed milling and the manufacture of utilitarian woodenware for farms and small industries. The mill complex grew to incorporate more than ten buildings on ten acres, all clustered around the millpond. The mill continued in operation until 1967.

Much of the original nineteenth-century equipment at Hanford Mills is still in place and in good working order. Today's visitors can watch lumber being cut on a big circular saw and shaped with smaller tools, all powered by the waters of Kortright Creek. At the heart of the operation is a 10-by-12-foot waterwheel, doing what waterwheels have done for more than 2,000 years. Visitors may explore at their leisure, or take a guided tour.

The Hanford Mills Museum, intersection of County Routes 10 and 12, East Meredith (607–278–5744 or 800–295–4992), is open May 1 to October 31, daily 10:00 A.M. to 5:00 P.M. Admission is $6.00 for adults, $5.00 for senior citizens, and $3.00 for children. Group rates are available.

Places to Stay in the Catskills

GREENVILLE

Greenville Arms 1889 Inn
Routes 32 & 81
(888) 665–0044
www.greenvillearms.com

HIGH FALLS

Captain Schoonmaker's 1760 House
913 Route 213
(845) 687–7946
www.captainschoonmakers.com

HIGHLAND

Jingle Bell Bed & Breakfast
302 Swartekill Road
(845) 255–8458

MONROE

Roscoe House
45 Lakes Road
(845) 782–0442

NEWBURGH

Morgan House
12 Powelton Road
(845) 561–0326

SAUGERTIES

The Villa at Saugerties
159 Fawn Road
(845) 246–0682
www.thevillaatsaugerties.com

WALDEN

Heritage Farm
163 Berea Road
(845) 778–3420
www.heritagefarminn.com

OTHER ATTRACTIONS WORTH SEEING IN THE CATSKILLS

Byrdcliffe Historic District
Glasgow Turnpike and Lark's Nest Road
Woodstock
(845) 679–2079

Catskill Game Farm
400 Game Farm Road
Catskill
(518) 678–9595

Fort Delaware Museum of Colonial History
6615 Route 97
Narrowsburg
(845) 252–6660

Hudson River Cruises
Rondout Landing
Kingston
(845) 340–4700 or (800) 843–7472
www.hudsonrivercruises.com

Hunter Mountain Skyride
Route 23A
Hunter
(518) 263–4223
www.huntermtn.com

Knox's Headquarters State Historic Site
Forge Hill Road, Route 94
Vails Gate
(845) 561–5498

Last Encampment of the Continental Army
Route 300
Vails Gate
(845) 561–5073

Museum Village in Orange County
Route 17M, Museum Village Road
Monroe
(845) 782–8247
www.museumvillage.org

New Windsor Cantonment State Historic Site
Temple Hill Road, Route 300
Vails Gate
(845) 561–1765

Rondout Lighthouse
One Rondout Landing
Kingston
(845) 338–0071

Thomas Cole House
218 Spring Street
Catskill
(518) 943–7465
www.thomascole.org

Tomsco Falls
Mountaindale
(845) 434–6065

Trolley Museum
Route 89 East Strand
Kingston
(845) 331–3399

Washington's Headquarters State Historic Site
84 Liberty Street
Newburgh
(845) 562–1195

West Point Museum
Main Street
USMA Visitor Center
West Point
(845) 938–3590
www.usma.edu/museum

WALKILL

Audrey's Farmhouse
2188 Brunswyck Road
(845) 895–3440
www.audreysfarmhouse.com

WINDHAM

Hotel Vienna
105 Route 296
(518) 734–5300
www.thehotelvienna.com

Places to Eat in the Catskills

DELHI

Quarter Moon Cafe
53 Main Street
(607) 746–8886

HIGHLAND

The Would Restaurant
120 North Road
(845) 691–9883
www.thewould.com

KINGSTON

Armadillo Bar and Grill
97 Abeel Street
(845) 339–1550
www.armadillos.net

Le Canard Enchainé
278 Fair Street
(845) 339–2003
www.le-canardenchaine.com

Ship to Shore
15 West Strand
(845) 334–8887
www.shiptoshorehudson
valley.com

PHOENICIA

Sweet Sue's
Main Street
(845) 688–7852

ROSENDALE

Rosendale Cement
Company
419 Main Street
(845) 658–3210

SAUGERTIES

Cafe Tamayo
89 Partition Street
(845) 246–9371
www.cafetamayo.com

WALTON

Miller's Barbecue and
Apple Place
29735 State Highway 10
(607) 865–4721

WOODSTOCK

The Bear Cafe
Route 212
(845) 679–5555
www.bearcafe.com

Mountain Gate Indian
Restaurant
4 Deming Street
(845) 679–5100

REGIONAL TOURIST INFORMATION– THE CATSKILLS

CATS
(518) 943–3223 or (800) NYS–CATS
www.catskillgetaways.com

**Delaware County Chamber
of Commerce**
114 East Main Street
Delhi 13753
(800) 642–4443
www.delawarecounty.org

**Greene County Promotion
Department**
Route 23B
Catskill 12414
(800) 355–2287
www.greene-ny.com

Sullivan County
100 North Street
City Government Center
Monticello 12701
(800) 882–2287
www.scva.net

New York City

The first-time visitor to New York City can easily be overwhelmed. There are so many things to see and do—the Empire State Building, the Statue of Liberty, the Museum of Modern Art, the Met, Carnegie Hall, Broadway shows, the shops on Madison Avenue. It's clear that unless your time, energy, and budget are unlimited, you can't do it all; just consider that the city has some 150 world-class museums and 18,000 restaurants on its 6,374.6 miles of streets.

We hope that *New York Off the Beaten Path* helps you discover some of our favorite places, the places that most tourists would never find—the independent bookstores, the neighborhood pizzerias, the neighborhoods themselves. While Manhattan can keep you busy for a lifetime or more, get out to the boroughs, too. Brooklyn, Queens, the Bronx, and Staten Island all have changed in recent years, in many cases much for the better.

The fast-paced capital of finance and culture, New York City is also a place with nearly 400 years of history, a place where Dutch farmers and great writers and poets and presidents have lived. All these sites are here, waiting to be discovered.

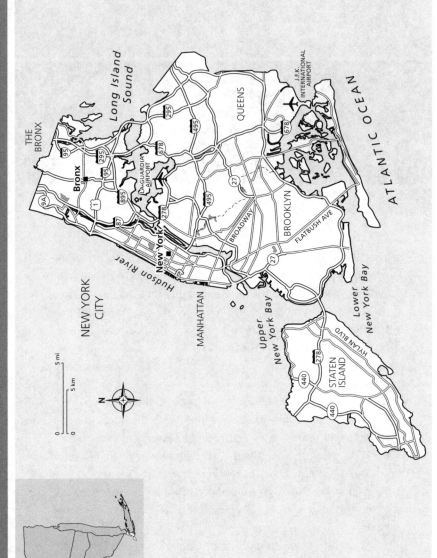

NEW YORK CITY

THE
BRONX

Long Island Sound

QUEENS

J.F.K.
INTERNATIONAL
AIRPORT

ATLANTIC OCEAN

LAGUARDIA
AIRPORT

Bronx

Hudson River

New York

NEW YORK
CITY

MANHATTAN

BROADWAY

BROOKLYN

FLATBUSH AVE

Upper
New York Bay

Lower
New York Bay

HYLAN BLVD

STATEN
ISLAND

N

0   5 mi
0   5 km

Manhattan

First-time visitors may wish to take one of the bus tours listed on New York's official Web site, www.nycvisit.com, simply to get acquainted with the geography of the city. For those who prefer to explore on foot, the same Web site includes a good selection of walking tours (see the "Things to Do" section).

A number of interesting walks are offered by **Big Onion tours** (212–439–1090; www.bigonion.com). Priced between $10 and $15, the tours cover many areas of the city, from Harlem to the Upper West Side to Greenwich Village and beyond to Brooklyn.

Noteworthy—and free—are the walking tours offered by the **Central Park Conservancy** (212–360–2726; www.centralparknyc.org). You'll see gardens, woodlands, and meadows and learn about the park's history and design.

Also free: a ninety-minute walking tour of downtown New York that meets on the steps of the National Museum of the American Indian every Thursday at noon (212–606–4064).

Where to stay in Manhattan can be an issue. Although there are accommodations to fit most budgets, the nicer places (and we're not talking about luxury digs, where the prices are astronomical) are priced considerably higher than comparable accommodations in smaller cities. Many hotels, especially the chains, offer discounts to members of AAA or AARP; inquire about such discounts when you check for rates. Also ask for the best possible rate or current promotions, as this information generally will not be volunteered.

Bed-and-breakfast inns often can cost less than a hotel room, and for that reason we include a booking service listing at the end of this chapter. Manhattan has a number of college and university clubs, so if you attended one of the places represented in the city—or have a family member or friend who did—you may find this a good option.

If you aren't particular about such features as a private bath and hotel amenities, there are no-frills rooms at the city's YMCAs. The **West Side YMCA,** for example, has a prime location at 5 West 63rd Street (212–875–4100;

AUTHORS' FAVORITES—NEW YORK CITY

Isamu Noguchi Garden Museum	Studio Museum in Harlem
Jacques Marchais Museum of Tibetan Art	Una Pizza Napolitana
Lower East Side Tenement Museum	

The Big Apple

The city's nickname was first coined in the 1920s, when John Fitzgerald, a sportswriter for the *Morning Telegraph,* overheard stable-hands in New Orleans refer to New York City's racetracks as "the Big Apple." He named his column "Around the Big Apple." A decade later jazz musicians, who used the slang world *apple* for any city they were touring, adopted the term to refer to New York City, and especially Harlem, as the jazz capital of the world. The meaning: There are many apples on the tree of success, but when you pick New York City, you pick the Big Apple.

www.ymcanyc.org) and offers single rooms with shared baths at well under $100. There are two other YMCA locations: one on the west side, the other in Harlem.

One of the more attractive options among Manhattan's boutique hotels is *The Shoreham* at 33 West 55th Street (212–247–6700; www.shorehamhotel .com). The Shoreham provides guests convenient access to a number of attractions, designer boutiques, department stores, jewelers, and some of the city's best restaurants. The rooms have a European style; they are functional and well laid out, with marble and slate bathrooms and a nice selection of Aveda toiletries. The pillow-top beds are excellent, as are the high-end linens, plasma-screen televisions, and superior music systems in select rooms. The hotel has an intimate bar, a superior restaurant, and a fitness room. Especially appealing: the complimentary continental breakfast; free twenty-four-hour espresso, cappuc-

Get a Discount

Those people you see in line at *TKTS* at Duffy Square, 47th Street and Broadway (or, while Duffy Square is being renovated, at the temporary location at the Marriott Marquis Hotel, West 46th Street between Broadway and Eighth Avenue) are queuing up for half-price tickets to Broadway shows. Tickets are available Monday through Saturday, 3:00 P.M. till 8:00 P.M.; Sunday from 3:00 P.M. until one half-hour before curtain time. For matinee tickets, on Wednesday and Saturday, tickets are sold between 10:00 A.M. and 2:00 P.M.

There is a second (and less crowded) TKTS booth downtown, at the South Street Seaport, 199 Water Street, at the corner of Front and John Streets. Here you can buy matinee tickets the day before, Monday through Friday, from 11:00 A.M. till 6:00 P.M. and also on Saturday from 11:00 A.M. till 7:00 P.M. For evening performances, the hours are from Monday through Friday, from 11:00 A.M. till 6:00 P.M. For more information visit www.tdf.org.

cino, or tea; and free Internet access. (Most NYC hotels add significant charges for these.) In-room spa services are available. Depending on the time of year, rooms start at about $300.

When you're in the Times Square area, stop by the **Times Square Information Center** for free brochures and citywide information from the multilingual tourist counselors. Here you can also access the Internet free via Yahoo. For more information check www.times squarenyc.org.

Of the first-rank museums in the city of New York, perhaps the least well-known is the Smithsonian Institution's **National Museum of the American Indian, George Gustav Heye Center.** George Heye was an heir to an oil fortune who worked as a railroad construction engineer in the Southwest. In 1897 he bought the first of his Indian artifacts, a contemporary Navajo buckskin shirt, and from that point he went on to develop a collection that encompassed all things native, from Alaska to Tierra del Fuego. He bought items that had just

been made (including, it is said, the clothes off Indians' backs), and archaeological finds dating from long before the European discovery of America. Heye founded his museum in 1916, and it opened to the public six years later. At that stage the collector had owned some 400,000 objects; today the museum has more than a million individual items.

Throughout the year Native American musicians, dancers, artists, and elders present both formal and informal programs designed to help visitors better understand Indian cultures.

The National Museum of the American Indian, George Gustav Heye Center, Smithsonian Institution, Alexander Hamilton U.S. Custom House, One

eatnewyork— it'sabargain!

Twice a year, once in winter and once in summer, scores of the city's restaurants—including many fine dining (and expensive) places—participate in **Restaurant Week.** For two weeks only they offer three-course lunches and dinners at bargain prices. (In 2007 it was $24.07 for lunch, $35.00 for dinner.) Check www.nycvisit.com for details.

Beaded Buckskin Dress, National Museum of the American Indian

Among the Earliest Arrivals

The country's oldest Jewish congregation, **Congregation Shearith Israel** ("Remnant of Israel"), dates to September 12, 1654, when a group of newly arrived Jews from Spain and Portugal held a New Year service in New Amsterdam. The oldest gravestone in the congregation's first cemetery, at 55–57 St. James Place, bears the date 1683. The remains of many colonial-era Jews interred here had to be moved to newer cemeteries in Manhattan to make room for road construction.

Bowling Green (212–514–3700; www.nmai.si.edu), is open daily except Christmas from 10:00 A.M. to 5:00 P.M. and Thursday until 8:00 P.M. Admission is free.

More than 2,000 photographs, a large collection of artifacts, original documentary films, and individual narratives are utilized to create a picture of Jewish life and culture from the late 1880s to the present at the **Museum of Jewish Heritage,** A Living Memorial to the Holocaust. The museum is in Battery Park City overlooking the Statue of Liberty and Ellis Island. The Museum of Jewish Heritage, A Living Memorial to the Holocaust, 36 Battery Place (646–437–4200; www.mjhnyc.org), is open Sunday through Tuesday and Thursday 10:00 A.M. to 5:45 P.M.; Wednesday 10:00 A.M. to 8:00 P.M.; Friday and the eve of Jewish holidays 10:00 A.M. to 3:00 P.M. Admission is $10.00 for adults, $7.00 for seniors, and $5.00 for students. Admission is free on Wednesday from 4:00 to 8:00 P.M.

In the mid-1800s Lucas Glockner, a German-born tailor, bought a lot at 97 Orchard Street on the Lower East Side that measured 25 by 100 feet. The lot was originally intended for single-family town houses, but Glockner erected a six-story tenement with apartments for twenty-two families, as well as two storefronts in the basement. Each floor featured four three-room apartments with a total of 325 square feet each. Only one of the three rooms had windows.

Although 1,100 people have been documented as living at 97 Orchard Street between 1863 and 1935, a more realistic estimate is that 10,000 people from more than twenty-five nations lived there during its seventy-two-year residential service.

Ninety-seven Orchard Street is the first tenement to be preserved in America, and it is the site of the **Lower East Side Tenement Museum.** The museum's mission is to "promote tolerance through the presentation and interpretation of the variety of urban immigrant experiences on Manhattan's Lower East Side, a gateway to America." The museum also hosts a series of weekend walks through the historic Orchard Street area. "The Streets Where We Lived" helps visitors learn how different immigrant groups shaped, and continue to shape, the Lower East Side.

All programs at the Lower East Side Tenement Museum (212–431–0233; www.tenement.org) begin at the Visitor Center, 90 Orchard Street, at the corner of Broome Street. Public tours are offered Tuesday through Friday from 1:20 to 4:45 P.M., Saturday and Sunday from 11:00 A.M. to 4:00 P.M. Tickets are $15 for adults; $11 for students and seniors.

More Lower East Side history—and a good pastrami sandwich—can be found nearby at **Katz's Deli,** 105 East Houston Street (212–254–2246). Not only are sandwiches terrific, but the huge dining room also evokes memories of the neighborhood's good old days, when egg creams cost a nickel.

The **Lesbian, Gay, Bisexual and Transgender Community Center,** located in Greenwich Village, is the largest of its kind on the East Coast and second largest in the world. Among the services offered are a free welcome packet with maps and community information; an information and referral staff on duty throughout the center's open hours; and Internet access at the David Bohnett Cyber Center. The center also runs social service, public policy, educational, and cultural/recreational programs. The National Archive of Lesbian, Gay, Bisexual, and Transgender History, also located at the center, sponsor regular exhibits, publications, and scholarly research activities.

The Lesbian, Gay, Bisexual, and Transgender Community Center, 208 West 13th Street (212–620–7310; www.gaycenter.org), is open daily from 9:00 A.M. to 11:00 P.M.

Back in Buffalo, we saw the house where Theodore Roosevelt was inaugurated president of the United States. Here in the city you can see where his

Taxi Tips

Yellow medallion cabs are the only authorized taxis in New York City. There are more than 12,000 yellow medallion cabs in the city, driven by cabbies from some eighty-five different nations. If the cab's center roof light is not lit, it's not available.

One fare covers all passengers. The fare starts at $2.50 for the first ⅕ mile, 40 cents for each ⅕ mile thereafter, and 40 cents for each minute in slow traffic or not in motion. A $1.00 surcharge is added to rides begun between 4:00 and 8:00 P.M., and a 50-cent surcharge is added between 8:00 P.M. and 6:00 A.M. Bridge or tunnel tolls are paid by the passenger. Cabs can issue printed receipts, which are especially helpful if you leave something behind. There's a flat rate of $45 plus tolls and tip (generally 15 to 20 percent) to transport passengers between Manhattan and John F. Kennedy Airport.

If you've wondered how New York's cabs came to be yellow, it's because John Herz, who founded the Yellow Cab Company in 1907, chose the color after he read a study by the University of Chicago indicating that it was the easiest to spot.

ANNUAL EVENTS IN NEW YORK CITY

JANUARY

Three Kings Day Parade
Spanish Harlem
(212) 831–7272
www.elmuseo.org

Winter Antiques Show at Seventh Regiment Armory
(718) 292–7392
www.winterantiquesshow.com

FEBRUARY

Chinese New Year
(212) 484–1222
Note: As this annual event is based on the lunar calendar, the dates change from year to year; in 2008 it will take place in February.

Westminster Kennel Club Dog Show
(800) 455–3647
www.westminsterkennelclub.org

MARCH

Manhattan Antiques Triple Pier Expo
(212) 255–0020

St. Patrick's Day Parade
(212) 484–1222

APRIL

Macy's Flower Show
(212) 494–4495

MAY

Fleet Week
(212) 245–0072
www.fleetweek.com

Great Five-Boro Bike Tour
(212) 932–0778

Ninth Avenue Food Festival
(212) 581–7217

Washington Square Outdoor Art Exhibit
(212) 982–6255

JUNE

JVC Jazz Festival
(212) 501–1390

Lesbian and Gay Pride Week and March
(212) 807–7433
www.hopinc.org

Metropolitan Opera in the Parks
(212) 362–6000

Museum Mile Festival
(212) 606–2296
www.museummilefestival.org

life began, at the *Theodore Roosevelt Birthplace National Historic Site.* The building that stands here today is a faithful reconstruction of the brownstone row house in which T.R. was born on October 27, 1858. It was built following the former president's death in 1919, replacing a nondescript commercial building that had gone up only three years before, when the original Roosevelt home was torn down.

Puerto Rican Day Parade
(212) 484–1222

Shakespeare in the Park
(212) 539–8500
www.publictheater.org

JULY

Brooklyn Independence Day Parade
(718) 921–3403

Fourth of July Fireworks Spectacular
(212) 484–1222 or (212) 494–2922

AUGUST

Harlem Week
(212) 484–1222

U.S. Open Tennis Championships
(718) 760–6200
www.usopen.org or www.usta.com

SEPTEMBER

African-American Day Parade
(212) 862–8497

Feast of San Gennaro
(212) 768–9320

New York Film Festival
(212) 875–5050

Pulaski Day Parade
www.pulaskiparade.org

West Indian-American Day Parade
(212) 484–1222 or (718) 625–1515

OCTOBER

Columbus Day Parade
(212) 249–9923

Greenwich Village Halloween Parade
www.halloween-nyc.com

NOVEMBER

Macy's Thanksgiving Day Parade
(212) 484–1222 or (212) 494–2922

New York City Marathon
(212) 423–2249 or (212) 860–4455
www.nyrrc.org

DECEMBER

New Year's Eve in Times Square
(212) 768–1560 or (212) 484–1222
www.timessquarebid.org

Radio City Music Hall's Christmas
Spectacular
(212) 247–4777
www.radiocity.com

Rockefeller Center Tree-Lighting
Ceremony
(800) NYC–VISIT
www.nycvisit.com

Open to the public since 1923, and a National Historic Site since 1963, the reconstructed Roosevelt home is furnished in the same style—and with many of the same articles—familiar to the sickly lad who lived here for the first fourteen years of his life. The president's widow and his two sisters supervised the reconstruction, recalling room layouts, furniture placement, and even interior color schemes. The result is a careful study not only of the environment that

Qui Plantavit Curabit

The Roosevelt Arms, Theodore Roosevelt Birthplace

produced the scholar and improbable athlete who would become a rancher, police commissioner, Rough Rider, New York governor, and president but also of the lifestyle of New York's more comfortable burghers in the middle of the nineteenth century.

The "new" Roosevelt house stands in stubborn contrast to the modern buildings that surround it, reminding us of just how completely the neighborhoods of New York have changed over the years. The Theodore Roosevelt Birthplace National Historic Site, 28 East 20th Street (212–260–1616; www.nps.gov/thrb/), is open Tuesday through Saturday 9:00 A.M. to 5:00 P.M.; closed on federal holidays. Admission is $3.00 for adults; children under 18 are admitted free.

Book lovers will find bliss at the ***Strand Bookstore,*** 888 Broadway (12th Street) (212–473–1452; www.strandbooks.com). With an inventory that includes "18 miles of books" (their count, not ours), the Strand stocks everything from best sellers to dollar books to rare editions that sell for thousands of dollars. (There is a Strand Annex at 95 Fulton Street and a Central Park kiosk at 60th Street and Fifth Avenue, across the street from the Pierre Hotel.)

One of Manhattan's quirkier Institutions is the ***Museum of Sex,*** dedicated to the "history, evolution, and cultural significance of human sexuality." Its holdings include the Ralph Whittington collection of erotica, assembled by a distinguished former curator of a prestigious museum, and artifacts from the nearby Harmony Theater, formerly known as the Melody Burlesque. Recent special exhibitions have included offerings such as "Stags, Smokers, and Blue Movies" and "Mapping Sex in America."

The Museum of Sex, 233 Fifth Avenue (at 27th Street) (212–689–6337; www.mosex.com), is open Sunday to Friday, 11:00 A.M. to 6:30 P.M.; Saturday

Over and Underground

When not exploring New York on foot (or splurging on a taxi), visitors will be using the services of the MTA, the most efficient and economical way to get around. The MTA is a vast transportation network, the largest in North America. It includes 656 miles of subway tracks, 8,590 subway cars, 734 rail and subway stations, and 5,113 buses—and provides some 2.4 billion rides a year. People with disabilities can comfortably ride the buses, which have wheelchair lifts located near the middle of the vehicles.

The subway network does not service Staten Island, but there is a ferry that runs between Whitehall Street in lower Manhattan and St. George on Staten Island. Though the ferry exists to transport commuters, it offers visitors a 5-mile, twenty-five-minute ride with majestic views of New York Harbor—free! Visit www.siferry for details.

As of early 2007, a single ride on a bus or subway was $2.00; buy a MetroCard with a value of $4.00 to $80.00. When you buy a card worth $10 or more, you get a 20 percent bonus; for example, a $10 purchase gives you $12 in rides. You get an automatic (free) transfer between buses or between subways and buses). Children under 44 inches ride free when accompanied by an adult.

Money-saving options that are popular with visitors include:

- The one-day Fun Pass ($7), good for unlimited rides on subways and local buses, from first use until 3:00 A.M. the following day. The Fun Pass is available at MetroCard vending machines and neighborhood stores, but not at subway station booths.

- The seven-day Unlimited Ride MetroCard ($24), good for unlimited rides on subways and local buses, for seven days, until midnight from day of first use.

- For other options, visit www.mta.info/metrocard. Seniors age 65 and over may also apply for a card that allows them to buy rides at half price; without the card it is necessary to show the red, white, and blue Medicare card as identification.

11:00 A.M. to 8:00 P.M.; closed Thanksgiving and Christmas. Admission is $14.50; $13.50 for students and seniors.

While midtown Manhattan may seem like it's all glass and steel, at the **American Folk Art Museum** the homey and handmade are cherished, too. Founded by a group of collectors in 1961, the museum is devoted to preserving the country's rich folk heritage. Its expansive collection includes paintings, drawings, sculpture, textiles, furniture, functional and decorative arts, photographs, and contemporary environmental works. With pieces dating from the mid-eighteenth century to the present, the collection reflects the museum's increasingly broad definition of the field of folk art. The museum presents special exhibitions and events throughout the year and publishes *Folk Art*

Object of Desire:
The Search for the Perfect Pizza

Confident that every visitor to New York might crave a mouth-watering "tomato pie" at least once, we include a few of our personal favorites. To us and to many pizza aficionados, the very best is to be found at **Una Pizza Napoletana** (212–477–9950) in the East Village, where master pizzaolo Anthony Mangieri makes his dough by hand with no yeast and allows it to rise for two days. After topping his *pizze* with the finest ingredients, including fresh buffalo mozzarella, fresh basil, and San Marzano tomatoes, he bakes it in a wood-burning oven. The result is a pie that's both rich and light, bursting with the tang of Sicilian sea salt. As Master Mangieri is a purist, you will find only the Neapolitan classics here: marinara, margherita, bianca (white), and filetti (with cherry tomatoes).

We also like the pies at **Totonno's,** a Coney Island establishment dating back to 1924. Today Totonno's has four locations. Two are on Second Avenue in Manhattan, one between 26th and 27th Streets (212–213–8800), the other between 80th and 81st Streets (212–213–8800). The other two are in Coney Island (718–372–8606) and Yonkers (914–476–4446).

Another old-timer is **Lombardi's** (212–941–7994) on Spring Street, where the crusts are chewy and charred and the cheese is always creamy.

In Brooklyn pizzerias are numerous, but the pies at **Di Fara** (718–258–1367) consistently please. Bronx favorites include the **Tosca Cafe** (718–239–3300) on East Tremont Avenue and **Full Moon** (718–584–3451) off Arthur Avenue. Staten Islanders are fortunate to have **Denino's Pizzeria** (718–442–9401) on Port Richmond Avenue.

magazine, the only publication in the country covering the growing field of American folk art.

American Folk Art Museum, 45 West 53rd Street (212–265–1040; www.folk artmuseum.org), is open Tuesday through Sunday 10:30 A.M. to 5:30 P.M. and Friday until 7:30 P.M. Closed Monday, Christmas Day, New Year's Day, and Thanksgiving, and closes early on July 4th. Admission is $9.00 for adults, $7.00 for seniors and students. There is a branch location, the Eva and Morris Field Gallery at 2 Lincoln Square.

Is it possible to tour a building that no longer exists? The answer is yes, sort of, if the building is Pennsylvania Station—not the dreary modern terminal that crouches beneath Madison Square Garden, but the mighty neoclassical edifice that the Pennsylvania Railroad and McKim, Mead, and White built in 1910 to evoke the Baths of Caracalla and stand, perhaps, for centuries. Demolished barely more than fifty years later in what the *New York Times* rightly called a "monumental act of vandalism," the old Penn Station was nevertheless too deeply embedded in the sinews of Manhattan to have disappeared altogether. Like the Roman edifices that inspired it, its ghostly fragments lurk beneath its modern successor; see them when you take the 34th Street Partnership's **Penn Station Tour,** a ninety-minute walk through time that reveals the physical remains of what was once, along with still-glorious Grand Central Station, one of the grand entrances to New York City.

You'll see the pink granite and herringbone brickwork that once paved the station's carriage drive, peeking through fake modern tile; discover the last of the iron-and-brass staircases that preceded escalators as a means of accessing the train platforms; stand opposite the only remaining original elevator cage; and look down at a patch of the original glass bricks that allowed sunlight to filter from the upper levels of the station to the tracks below. Along the way, architectural historian John Turkeli will tell the story of the rise and demise of the New York terminus of "The Standard Railroad of the World."

The free tour is offered on the fourth Monday of each month; participants gather at the main Visitor Information kiosk in main rotunda at Penn Station. To confirm tour schedule, call (212) 719–3434 or visit www.34thStreet.org.

Looking for an unusual souvenir? Perhaps the horn of an impala (*Aepyceros melampus*), the skeleton of the lookdown fish (*Selene vomer*), or the skull of a tokay gecko will do. **Maxilla & Mandible, Ltd.,** the world's only osteological store, is a natural-history and science emporium with 19,000 square feet of showroom, laboratory, workshop, and storage facilities. All of their specimens are unique, anatomically accurate, and obtained from legal and ethical sources. They're at 451 Columbus Avenue (212–724–6173; www.maxillaand mandible.com), and are open Monday through Saturday 11:00 A.M. to 7:00 P.M. and Sunday 1:00 to 5:00 P.M. Closed on major holidays.

El Museo del Barrio is dedicated to highlighting the art and culture of Puerto Rico and Latin America. Its collection includes more than 8,000 works

An Act of God

In 1870 the American actor Joseph Jefferson went to a church near the spot where the Empire State Building now stands to arrange for a friend's burial service. Upon learning that the deceased was an actor, the rector suggested that Jefferson make arrangements at a church around the corner. Jefferson is said to have replied, "Thank God for the little church around the corner," and that's how the **Church of the Transfiguration** at 1 East Twenty-ninth Street got its nicknames, "Little Church Around the Corner" and the "Actors' Church." Over the years grateful thespians, including Sarah Bernhardt, have worshipped here, and there are memorial windows to actors such as John Drew, Edwin Booth, and Richard Mansfield.

freeforall

Though New York may be one of the world's most expensive cities, a great many fine things are free. Visit http://nyc.freecityevents.com and you will find movies, concerts, and more at the city's libraries; jazz at St. Peter's church; chamber music at the Juilliard School; and lectures and signings by famous authors at bookstores.

of art, from pre-Columbian vessels to contemporary pieces. Among the holdings are the second-largest collection of Taino objects in the country; secular and religious pieces, including an outstanding collection of 360 *santos de palo* (carved wooden saints used for household devotions); and an exhibit documenting the history of print- and poster-making in Puerto Rico from the 1940s to the present.

El Museo del Barrio, Heckscher Building, 1230 Fifth Avenue at 104th Street (212–831–7272; www.elmuseo.org), is open Wednesday through Sunday from 11:00 A.M. to 5:00 P.M. Suggested donation is $6.00 for adults and $4.00 for seniors and students. Free admission for seniors all day Thursday.

Rich in history, tradition, music, and food, Harlem is enjoying yet another renaissance, reflected in strong property prices and the influx of new businesses. A number of companies now offer specialized tours of the area; among the options offered by *Harlem Spirituals* are "Harlem Gospel on Sunday," which includes a church service and a soul-food brunch, and "Soul Food and Jazz." Multilingual tours are available; reservations are required. Harlem Spirituals, 690 Eighth Avenue (between 43rd and 44th Streets), (800–660–2166 or 212–391–0900; www.harlemspirituals.com).

For information on some of the lodging options in Harlem, as well as events and tours, visit www.harlemonestop.com. For dining options in the area, check www.eatinharlem.com.

The *Studio Museum in Harlem* was founded in 1967 as a working and exhibition space for African-American artists. Today, in a 60,000-square-foot

Key to the City

The first-time visitor may wish to see some of the city's most popular attractions, and for this we recommend the *CityPass,* a $106 value priced at $53 (ages 6 to 17, $44). The pass includes admission to the *American Museum of Natural History* and the Space Show in the *Hayden Planetarium,* the *Museum of Modern Art,* the *Empire State Building Observatory,* the *Guggenheim Museum,* and a choice of two-hour excursions aboard *Circle Line Sightseeing Cruises.* For more information call (888) 330–5008 or (707) 256–0490 or visit www.citypass.com.

building, the country's first accredited African-American fine arts museum houses an extensive collection of nineteenth- and twentieth-century African-American art, twentieth-century Caribbean and African art, and traditional African art and artifacts. But this building is more than a museum. It's a center for interpreting its contents to both children and adults. In addition to an artists-in-residence program and an outreach program for Harlem's public schools, the museum hosts numerous workshops, arts and humanities programs, and special exhibits throughout the year.

The Studio Museum in Harlem, 144 West 125th Street (212–864–4500; www.studiomuseum.org), is open Wednesday to Friday noon to 6:00 P.M.; Saturday 10:00 A.M. to 6:00 P.M.; Sunday noon to 6:00 P.M. Suggested donation is $7.00 for adults; $5.00 for students and seniors; free for those under 12.

Manhattan's only lighthouse—nestled underneath the George Washington Bridge on Jeffrey's Hook—served as a beacon to ships for twenty-six years. Built in 1880 on Sandy Hook, New Jersey, the 40-foot-tall **Little Red Lighthouse** was dismantled in 1917 and reconstructed in 1921 on Jeffrey's Hook, where it continued to operate until 1947. The lighthouse was made famous by the 1942 children's book *The Little Red Lighthouse and the Great Gray Bridge* by Hildegarde Swift and Lynd Ward. In 1951, the Coast Guard decided to dismantle it, but supporters (mainly fans of the book) rallied to save it.

whereforethe eggcream?

There are no eggs or cream in the egg cream, though some sources say that the original fountain drink, still beloved by New Yorkers, used a syrup made with eggs, mixed with cream to give a richer taste. But the egg cream as we know it today is a mixture of milk, chocolate syrup, and seltzer—and costs more than the nickel originally charged.

Today the lighthouse, with its forty-eight brightly painted cast-iron plates, is a part of the Historic House Trust of New York City. Visitors can climb the spiral staircase to an observation deck that looks out across the river at the Palisades. Exhibition panels at the base provide information about the river. The Little Red Lighthouse, in Fort Washington Park at 178th Street (212–304–2365; www.lighthousemuseum.org), is open for public tours. If you're in the city, just dial 311 for information on Parks Department programs.

The Bronx

Now we come to the only borough of the city of New York not located on an island: the Bronx. It was named for Swedish commercial sea captain Jonas

Bronck, who, in 1639, became the first European settler to establish himself in this area.

With a population of 1.4 million, the Bronx claims a number of famous people who have lived here: performers Anne Bancroft, Tony Curtis, Robert Klein, Hal Linden, Penny and Gary Marshall, Rita Moreno, Chaz Palminteri, Roberta Peters, Regis Philbin, and Carl Reiner; athletes Lou Gehrig and Jake La Motta; authors E.L. Doctorow, Theodore Dreiser, Edgar Allan Poe, Mark Twain, and Herman Wouk; statesmen John Adams, John F. Kennedy, and Colin Powell; designers Calvin Klein and Ralph Lauren; and the conductor Arturo Toscanini.

The Bronx's golden age in the 1920s saw the building of the "El," an elevated subway line; Yankee Stadium; the mile-long Grand Concourse (which many likened to the Champs Elysées); and a population boom.

Artifacts of that history—and earlier, all the way back to the eighteenth century—can be found in the *Museum of Bronx History.* The museum is located in a fieldstone house built in 1758, which looks as if it would be more at home on a farm in Bucks County, Pennsylvania, than in the borough of endless row houses and apartment buildings.

The Museum of Bronx History, 3266 Bainbridge Avenue at 208th Street, Bronx (718–881–8900), is open Saturday from 10:00 A.M. to 4:00 P.M., Sunday from 1:00 to 5:00 P.M., and weekdays by appointment. Admission is $2.00. The Bronx County Historical Society, which administers the museum and the Poe Cottage, offers tours of the Bronx, as well as a lecture series. Call for a schedule or visit www.bronxhistoricalsociety.org.

An important chapter in Bronx history and in the history of literature relates to a thirty-seven-year-old poet, short-story writer, and critic named Edgar Allan Poe. In 1846 Poe rented a small wooden cottage, now known as the Poe Cottage, in Poe Park, East Kingsbridge Road and the Grand Concourse, not far from the campus of Fordham University. (In Poe's day the school was known as St. John's College.) Poe's wife was in fragile health and it was thought that the Bronx was a more salubrious environment than the couple's former home, New York City. But Virginia Clemm Poe, who was also the writer's cousin, died of tuberculosis early in 1847, leaving Poe in the state of despondency reflected in his poem, "Annabel Lee," and other melancholy verse.

Poe maintained his residence in the Bronx after his wife's death, drinking heavily and trying to keep up with his bills by delivering an occasional lecture. While returning from one of his lecture trips, he died in Baltimore in 1849.

Sometimes the world takes better care of dead poets' residences than it does the poets while they are alive, and such was the case with Edgar Allan Poe. Though the rapidly growing Bronx enveloped the Poe Cottage during the latter half of the nineteenth century, in 1902 the city dedicated a park in his honor across the street from the house. The house was moved to the park eleven years later and has been open as a museum since 1917.

The **Edgar Allan Poe Cottage,** Grand Concourse and East Kingsbridge Road, Bronx (718–881–8900), is open Saturday 10:00 A.M. to 4:00 P.M. and Sunday 1:00 to 5:00 P.M. throughout the year. Admission is $3.00 for adults and $1.00 for children under 12.

Not all of the Bronx was gobbled up by developers, though; 24 percent of its 42 square miles is still green space, a greater percentage than any other urban area in the country.

Discover some of the borough's 6,000 acres of green space at the **New York Botanical and Zoological Gardens, Van Cortlandt Park,** and **Pelham Bay Park.** But a visit to the borough should also include a stop at **Wave Hill,** a twenty-eight-acre preserve in the Riverdale neighborhood at the northwest corner of the Bronx. Wave Hill is not wilderness but a section of the borough that remained in its natural state until the middle of the last century, when it was first acquired as a country estate. Today, Wave Hill is the only one of the great Hudson River estates within the city limits preserved for public use.

In 1836 New York lawyer William Morris bought fifteen acres of riverbank real estate and built Wave Hill House, one of the two mansions that today grace the property, as a summer retreat. Thirty years later the Morris tract was acquired by publisher William Appleton, who remodeled the house and began developing the gardens and conservatories for which the property would become famous. The gardens were brought to their apogee, however, by financier George Perkins, who bought the estate in 1893 and increased its size to eighty acres, with a scattering of six fine houses, including not only Wave Hill but also Glyndor, which had been built by Oliver Harriman. Burned in 1927, Glyndor was rebuilt by Perkins's widow, and Glyndor II, as it is known, is still a part of the Wave Hill property.

Today, the attractions of Wave Hill include art exhibits, concert series, outdoor dance performances, and special events. But the star is still the landscape, with some grounds manicured and some remaining relatively wild.

acityofislands

Look at a map and you'll see that Manhattan and Staten Island are islands; Queens and Brooklyn are on the western tip of Long Island. That means that of New York City's five boroughs, only the Bronx is part of the mainland. However, there is an island that's part of the Bronx: City Island, a marine-based community that feels like a New England fishing village. In 1898 the five boroughs were incorporated into a single entity, known as Greater New York.

There are 350 varieties of trees and shrubs, plus the wild and cultivated flowers planted in three greenhouses, in formal and informal gardens, and along the pathways of the estate. A ten-acre section of woods has been restored as a native Bronx forest environment, complete with elderberries, witch hazel, and native grasses.

Wave Hill, 249th Street and Independence Avenue, Bronx (718–549–3200; www.wavehill.org), is open Tuesday through Sunday, mid-April through mid-October, 9:00 A.M. to 5:30 P.M., and Wednesday (June and July only) until 9:00 P.M. In fall and winter Wave Hill is open Tuesday through Sunday 9:00 A.M. to 4:30 P.M. The greenhouses are open from 10:00 A.M. to noon and 2:00 to 4:00 P.M. Wave Hill is closed Christmas and New Year's Day. Admission is free all day Tuesday, until noon Saturday, and during December, January, and February. Other days, admission is $4.00 for adults, $2.00 for seniors and students, and free for children 6 and under. Tours are given each Sunday at 2:15 P.M. The cafe is open for lunch and snacks.

While Manhattan's museums boast grand collections of artists from days gone by, the permanent collection at the *Bronx Museum of the Arts,* now located in a stunning new building, focuses on the work of contemporary artists of African, Asian, and Latin American descent. It has presented hundreds of critically acclaimed exhibitions featuring works by culturally diverse and under-recognized artists.

The Bronx Museum of the Arts, 1040 Grand Concourse (at 165th Street), Bronx (718–681–6000; www.bronxmuseum.org), is open Wednesday through Sunday from noon till 6:00 P.M. Admission is $5.00 for adults, $3.00 for seniors and students, free on Friday.

And since man does not live by culture alone, the Bronx's Little Italy, Belmont and Arthur Avenues, offers a feast for the eyes and the stomach. You'll find colorful and delicious food in markets overflowing with fruits, vegetables, salamis and sausages, homemade mozzarella, a rainbow of olives, luscious pastries, and breads. Our personal favorite: the mouthwatering sandwiches—the Michelangelo made of mozzarella and prosciutto, for example—at *Mike's Deli* at 2344 Arthur Avenue, Bronx (718–295–5033; www.arthuravenue.com).

Brooklyn

Not so long ago, few tourists would have put Brooklyn on their to-do list; today, the *QM2* brings 'em in by the boatload, docking at the new cruise terminal in the once-gritty Red Hook neighborhood. And with new hotels and more than two dozen restaurants listed in the Michelin guide to fine dining, the borough prides itself on being a destination.

You can get a postcard view of Brooklyn if you travel there on foot from lower Manhattan, walking across the iconic 1883 Brooklyn Bridge, which ranks as one of the world's great suspension bridges. You'll arrive in Brooklyn Heights, an upscale and quite beautiful 50-block historic district that has been seen in such films as *Moonstruck* and *Prizzi's Honor.* Among the famous people who have lived here are Truman Capote, Walt Whitman, Arthur Miller, Benjamin Britten, and Gypsy Rose Lee.

If you're traveling with children between the ages of two and ten, head over to the **Brooklyn Children's Museum,** founded in 1899, the first museum in the world designed expressly for youngsters. Here, the philosophy is "touch and learn," so kids can have (relatively) uninhibited fun with a collection of more than 27,000 artifacts and specimens in ten galleries. Housed in a unique 35,000-square-foot underground structure, the museum features a turn-of-the-twentieth-century kiosk entrance and a "stream" running the length of the "people tube," a huge drainage pipe that connects four levels of exhibit space. However, as of 2007, a $39-million expansion was under way, which would double the museum's size to 102,000 square feet, add new galleries and a Kid's Cafe—and bring it above ground for the first time in twenty-five years. New technologies will make it the first "green" museum in New York City.

The Brooklyn Children's Museum, 145 Brooklyn Avenue, Brooklyn (718–735–4400; www.brooklynkids.org), is open during the school year Wednesday through Friday 1:00 to 6:00 P.M.; Saturday and Sunday 11:00 A.M. to 6:00 P.M. (Open longer hours during school vacations.)

After a $3-million restoration, the country's first public Japanese garden provides an exotic refuge in the middle of Brooklyn. Designed in 1915 by Takeo Shiota, the Japanese Hill-and-Pond Garden at the **Brooklyn Botanic**

A Brooklyn Bargain

There is so much to see and do in Brooklyn that the cultural partnership known as the Heart of Brooklyn offers the **Brooklyn Pass,** a two-day passport to the borough's top attractions. Priced at $25 ($15 for children), the pass provides admission to the Brooklyn Museum, Brooklyn Botanic Garden, Brooklyn Children's Museum, Prospect Park (Carousel and Independence Electric Boat), Prospect Park Zoo, New York Aquarium, New York Transit Museum, Weeksville Historic Hunterfly Road Houses, and the Jewish Children's Museum. Also included: discounts on food and retail outlets. The pass can be purchased at the South Street Seaport, the Brooklyn Bridge Marriott, and the Brooklyn Tourism and Visitors Center at Brooklyn Borough Hall (209 Joralemon Street)—or online at www.brooklynpass.com.

Garden, is an urban retreat like no other in the metropolitan area. Visitors enter through an orange-red Torii gate into a magical world of azaleas, pines, and weeping cherry trees, where dwarf bamboo and irises edge a pond inhabited by bronze cranes and waterfalls cascade gently from recessed grottoes.

The Brooklyn Botanic Garden, 1000 Washington Avenue, Brooklyn (718–623–7200; www.bbg.org), is open in spring and summer, Tuesday through Friday 8:00 A.M. to 6:00 P.M.; weekends and holidays 10:00 A.M. to 6:00 P.M. Fall and winter, hours are Tuesday through Friday 8:00 A.M. to 4:30 P.M.; weekends and holidays 10:00 A.M. to 4:30 P.M. Closed Monday, except on holiday Mondays, and closed major holidays. Admission is $5.00 for adults, $3.00 for seniors and students, and free for children 16 and under. Admission is free on Saturday from 10:00 A.M. to noon, on weekdays from mid-November through February, on Tuesday from March through mid-November; senior citizens are admitted free on Friday.

Explore a different kind of green space in *Sunset Park's Green-Wood Cemetery,* 500-25th Street, Brooklyn (718–728–7300; www.green-wood.com). Not only is it one of the world's most beautiful cemeteries, with a harbor view and 478 acres rich with flowering shrubs, trees, and lakes, but Green-Wood is a cemetery with star power. Among the some 600,000 people buried here (nearly double the population of Pittsburgh) are Leonard Bernstein, Samuel Morse, Louis Comfort Tiffany, F.A.O. Schwarz, "Boss" Tweed, and mob boss Joey Gallo. Guided tours are offered during the Halloween season and at other times during the year; call to check schedule.

At the *Brooklyn Museum,* 200 Eastern Parkway, Brooklyn (718–638–5000; www.brooklynmuseum.org), which has one of the finest Egyptian collections in the world, there's an outdoor sculpture garden devoted to artwork and architectural details removed from vanished New York City buildings. Here you'll find Adolph Weinmann's Night, an allegorical female figure carved from pink granite. Along with a companion named Day, she once drowsed against a massive clock at one of the entrances to McKim, Mead, and White's magnificent Pennsylvania Station, built in 1910 and lost to developers in 1963. Museum hours are Wednesday through Friday, from 10:00 A.M. to 5:00 P.M. and on Saturday and Sunday from 11:00 A.M. to 6:00 P.M. Suggested contribution is $8.00 for adults; seniors and students, $4.00.

Museum-going always gives us an appetite, and after a few hours at the Brooklyn Museum, we always head to Atlantic Avenue for some of the best Middle Eastern food in the city. We get fresh-baked pita bread and baklava from the *Damascus Bakery,* 195 Atlantic Avenue, Brooklyn (718–625–7070), and olives and sumac and all sorts of prepared delicacies from *Sahadi's,* 187 Atlantic Avenue (718–624–4550; www.sahadis.com). Then it's lunch or dinner at the ***Tripoli Restaurant*** at 156 Atlantic Avenue (718–596–5800; www .tripolirestaurant.com), where authentic Lebanese dishes are modestly priced; entrees start at under $10.00 and the traditional *mazza,* consisting of twenty mouth-watering dishes, is $41.95.

The ***Grand Prospect Hall*** is a building with a history.

- When it was built in 1892, it was the tallest building in Brooklyn.
- Its French birdcage elevator was Brooklyn's first passenger elevator.
- William Jennings Bryan appeared on stage when he was stumping for the presidency.
- *The Cotton Club* and *Prizzi's Honor* were filmed here.
- Enrico Caruso, Mae West, Lena Horne, and Fred Astaire performed here.

The French Empire–style Victorian confection features a breathtaking lobby, marble grand staircase, rococo-style gold-leafed opera theater, a domed ceiling, and a grand ballroom that can accommodate up to 2,000 people.

Throughout the years the hall has served as a music hall, a German opera house, a vaudeville theater, a dance hall, a boxing arena, and a professional basketball court. Today it is used as a convention center as well as a venue for weddings, meetings, and bar mitzvahs. The Grand Prospect Hall, 263 Prospect Avenue, Brooklyn (718–788–0777; www.grandprospect.com).

The Wildlife Conservation Society's ***New York Aquarium,*** in Coney Island, is the oldest continuously operating aquarium in the country. It houses more than 10,000 specimens, including the only California sea otters outside of California, and the only aquarium-born beluga whales to survive past their first birthday.

The aquarium's Sea Cliffs, a 300-foot-long re-creation of the rocky Pacific coast, is now home to walruses; harbor, grey, and fur seals; sea otters; and black-footed penguins. Exhibits in Conservation Hall focus on the society's efforts to protect marine species around the world, replicating habitats in areas such as the Belize Barrier Reef, the Amazon River, the Coral Reef, and Lake Victoria. The Aquatheater features a 200,000-gallon pool where marine mammal demonstrations are held throughout the day.

The New York Aquarium, Surf Avenue and West 8th Street, Brooklyn (718–265–FISH), is open daily at 10:00 A.M.; closing hours vary, from 4:30 P.M. to 7:00 P.M. Call ahead or check the Web site at www.nyaquarium.com. Admission is $12.00 for adults and $8.00 for senior citizens and children ages 2 to 12. Parking is $10.00 per car.

The amusement park that made Coney Island famous in the 1920s is gone. The boardwalk and rides that remain are dim reminders of its glory days, as are the famous freak shows that used to titillate the throngs on a summer's night. But ***Sideshows by the Seashore*** makes a valiant effort to re-create the thrill of a traditional ten-in-one circus sideshow, with ten live acts and attractions in every show. Actors and performance artists have replaced the two-headed man and bearded lady with wonders like Robbie the Indian Rubber Boy, a twenty-year-old contortionist from Calcutta; and Eak "the illustrated man," an escape artist, geek, and snake charmer.

atreegrows inbrooklyn

The **Brooklyn Botanic Garden** was founded in 1910 on the site of an ash dump. It now features 12,000 plant species from throughout the world.

Sideshows is in a historic 1917 building that, in the 1950s and 1960s, was home to Dave Rosen's Wonderland Circus Sideshow, where oddities including Sealo the Seal Boy once performed. The Freak Bar in the lobby serves beer, and there's a gift shop.

Sideshows by the Seashore, Surf Avenue and West 12th Street, Coney Island (718–372–5159), is open with varying hours from April through early September. Call ahead or visit www.coneyisland.com/sideshow.shtml for specific information. Admission is $6.00 for adults and $4.00 for children under 12. Tickets can be purchased at the door only on the day of performance.

Next door to Sideshows is the **Coney Island Museum,** a small but engaging collection of Coney Island memorabilia, a hodgepodge of antiques and old rides. It offers a great view of landmark rides, including the Wonder Wheel (which offers fabulous views of Manhattan) and the legendary Cyclone roller coaster. The museum is small, a work in progress, but it gives visitors a glimpse into the Coney Island of long ago. Admission is just ninety-nine cents, and the museum is open Saturday and Sunday from noon to 5:00 P.M. (longer hours in summer). For information call (718) 372–5159 or visit www.coneyisland.com/museum.shtml.

Queens

Queens may well be the most ethnically diverse 115 square miles on earth, with the number seven subway line nicknamed "The International Express" and designated a National Millennium Trail for its representation of the immigrant experience.

Dine on superb Greek food in Astoria, or Indian food and Peruvian grilled chicken in Jackson Heights. Asian restaurants in Flushing reflect the large Chinese and Korean population, while Sunnyside offers visitors nightlife at a Spanish theater or a Romanian nightclub. In Woodside, you can rent a Thai video or hear traditional music at an Irish pub. Add a population of Italians, Japanese, Colombians, Puerto Ricans, Israelis, Maltese, Asian Indians—and there you have Queens.

The borough has also become an important cultural destination. Some of the metropolitan area's most exciting international art exhibits are hosted at the **P.S. 1 Contemporary Art Center** in Long Island City (where most of the borough's cultural attractions are located). Housed in a former elementary school, the center is affiliated with Manhattan's Museum of Modern Art (MOMA), but has a much edgier atmosphere. Known for avant-garde exhibits, the recently remodeled facility includes sculpture, a theater, and many modern installations. During exhibition openings, artists who are receiving free workspace in the buildings open their studios to the public, and in summer, DJs spin on the roof. The P.S. 1 Contemporary Art Center is located at 22–25 Jackson Avenue, Long Island City (718–784–2084; www.ps1.org), and is open Monday through Thursday noon to 6:00 P.M. Suggested donation is $5.00; $2.00 for seniors and students.

"It is said that stone is the affection of old men," said American-Japanese sculptor Isamu Noguchi, explaining his obsession with the medium. Caress the smooth, cold stone of his pieces, and perhaps you'll understand. They're at the **Isamu Noguchi Garden Museum,** a brick factory building the artist converted for use as a warehouse in the 1970s. Prior to the museum's opening, he added a dramatic open-air addition and an outdoor sculpture garden. Today more than 250 of his works are exhibited in twelve galleries in the building. They include stone, bronze, and wood sculptures; models for public projects and gardens; elements of dance sets designed for choreographer Martha Graham; and Noguchi's Akari lanterns.

Noguchi's major granite and basalt sculptures are displayed in the garden, as is his tombstone, under which half of his ashes are interred. The other half are buried in his garden studio in Japan.

The Isamu Noguchi Garden Museum, 9–01 33rd Road (at Vernon Boulevard), Long Island City (718–204–7088; www.noguchi.org), is open Wednesday through Friday 10:00 A.M. to 5:00 P.M., Saturday and Sunday 11:00 A.M. to 6:00 P.M. Admission is $10.00 for adults and $5.00 for seniors and students. On the first Friday of every month, you may pay what you wish.

Since the 1920s Queens has been home to hundreds of jazz musicians,

akindcut, indeed

The first tree to be designated an official landmark by the New York City Landmarks Preservation Commission was the weeping beech tree now in **Weeping Beech Park,** Thirty-seventh Avenue between Parson Boulevard and Bowne Street, in Flushing. It was grown from a cutting taken from a tree at an estate at Beersal, Belgium.

OTHER ATTRACTIONS WORTH SEEING IN NEW YORK CITY

American Museum of Natural History
Central Park West at 79th Street
(212) 769–5100
www.amnh.org

Bronx Zoo/Wildlife Conservation Park
Bronx River Parkway–Fordham Road
Bronx
(718) 220–5100
www.bronxzoo.org

Central Park
Fifth Avenue at 64th Street
(212) 861–6030
www.centralpark.com

Empire State Building
350 Fifth Avenue (34th Street)
(212) 736–3100
www.esbnyc.com

Forbes Magazine Galleries
62 Fifth Avenue (12th Street)
(212) 206–5548
www.forbesgalleries.com

Hispanic Society of America Museum and Library
613 West 155th Street
(212) 926–2234
www.hispanicsociety.org

Jewish Museum
1109 Fifth Avenue (92nd Street)
(212) 424–3200
www.thejewishmuseum.org

Metropolitan Museum of Art
1000 Fifth Avenue
(212) 535–7710
www.metmuseum.org

Museum of the City of New York
1220 Fifth Avenue (103rd Street)
(212) 534–1672
www.mcny.org

Museum of Modern Art
11 West 53rd Street
(212) 708–9400
www.moma.org

National Academy Museum and School of Fine Arts
1083 Fifth Avenue (89th Street)
(212) 369–4880
www.nationalacademy.org

Neue Gallerie
1048 Fifth Avenue (86th Street)
(212) 628–6200
www.neuegallerie.org

New York Botanical Garden
200th Street and Southern Boulevard
(Kazimiroff Boulevard)
Bronx
(718) 817–8700
www.nybg.org

New York Public Library
Fifth Avenue and 42nd Street
(212) 869–8089
www.nypl.org

North Wind Undersea Institute
610 City Island Avenue
Bronx
(718) 885–0701

St. Patrick's Cathedral
Fifth Avenue at 50th Street
(212) 753–2261
www.saintpatrickscathedral.org

including such icons as Dizzy Gillespie, Fats Waller, Billie Holiday, Ella Fitzgerald—and the late, great Louis Armstrong. Armstrong trumpeted his way out of New Orleans as a young man, traveling the world and performing. But for nearly thirty years, "Satchmo" did have a quiet place where he rested, rehearsed, and spent time with friends and family between recording sessions, club gigs, and concert tours.

The *Louis Armstrong House* in Corona was the legend's modest, two-story home. He and his wife, Lucille, bought the house in 1943, and he lived there until his death in 1971. (Lucille passed away in 1983.)

Now completely restored and open to visitors, the 1910 house holds a collection of Armstrong memorabilia, including scrapbooks, photos, and gold-plated trumpets. The home's furnishings remain much as they were during Louis and Lucille's lifetimes. A gift shop on the premises sells Armstrong CDs, books, postcards, T-shirts, red beans and rice, and other items.

The Louis Armstrong House, 34–56 107th Street, Corona (718–478–8274; www.satchmo.net), is open Tuesday through Friday 10:00 A.M. to 5:00 P.M., Saturday noon to 5:00 P.M. (last tour at 4:00 P.M. each day). Admission is $8.00 for adults, and $6.00 for students and seniors.

Home of the New York Mets and the U.S. Open Tennis Championship, not to mention two World's Fairs (1939 and 1964), Flushing (a neighborhood of Queens) is nonetheless the butt of many bad jokes. Though Queens is now home to hundreds of thousands of immigrants, among the earliest was John Bowne, who built *Bowne House* in 1661. To get some idea of what the future outlying boroughs of New York were like in those days, consider that two years after the Bowne House was built, the town meeting of nearby Jamaica offered a bounty of seven bushels of corn for every wolf shot or otherwise disposed of. But wolves weren't the only threat John Bowne faced. A Quaker, he openly challenged Governor Peter Stuyvesant's edict banning that religion by holding meetings of the Society of Friends in his kitchen. He was arrested and sent back to Europe in 1662 but returned to New York two years later, after having been exonerated by the Dutch West India Company, managers of the New Amsterdam colony.

Now the oldest house in Queens, the Bowne House reflects not only the Dutch/English colonial style in which it was originally built but also all of the vernacular styles with which it was modified over the years. Everything here belonged to the Bownes, making this property a unique documentation of one family's experience in New York virtually from the time of its founding to the beginning of the modern era.

In 1694 the Friends of Flushing Village moved their meeting out of member John Bowne's house to a newly erected *Quaker Meeting House.* By 1717 the membership had grown so large that the Quakers built an addition onto the Meeting House, doubling the size of the original structure. Since then the house has remained virtually unchanged—a perfectly preserved early American structure still being used as its builders intended.

The Quaker Meeting House, 137–16 Northern Boulevard, Flushing (718–358–9636; www.nyym.org/flushing), is open for worship every Sunday from 11:00 A.M. to noon. All are invited to attend. Tours are conducted by appointment.

Staten Island

A seventeenth-century Quaker attending a clandestine meeting at the Bowne House might seem to have little in common with a twentieth-century Tibetan Buddhist, but the two share a bond of persecution. One of the uglier aspects of the Maoist period in China was the annexation of Tibet and the suppression of its ancient culture and religion. Despite some recent liberalization on the part of the Chinese occupiers of Tibet, it is still an extremely difficult place to visit; and ironically, those Westerners interested in Tibetan art and religious artifacts have learned to rely on foreign rather than native Tibetan collections. One such collection is the *Jacques Marchais Museum of Tibetan Art.* The museum houses more than a thousand examples of Tibetan religious art— paintings, carved and cast statues, altars, ritual objects, and musical instruments—each of which was created to aid in the meditation that is such an important part of Buddhism, especially as practiced in Tibet.

And who was Jacques Marchais? "He" was a woman named Jacqueline Coblentz Klauber, who operated a Manhattan art gallery under the masculine French pseudonym. Klauber/Marchais had a lifelong interest in things Tibetan, an interest that she said originated in her childhood, when she would play with Tibetan figures her great-grandfather had brought back from the Orient. She never traveled to Tibet, but she carefully added to her collection until her death in 1947.

With its terraced gardens, lily pond, and air of detachment and serenity, the Marchais Museum is a sublime setting for the religious objects that make up the collection, representing centuries of Tibetan culture.

The Jacques Marchais Museum of Tibetan Art, 338 Lighthouse Avenue, Staten Island (718–987–3500), is open 1:00 to 5:00 P.M. Wednesday through Sunday. Admission is $5.00 for adults, $3.00 for senior citizens and students, children under 6 free. Group tours are available by appointment. Check www.tibetanmuseum.org for current exhibits and programs and for information on holiday closings.

Within walking distance of the Marchais Museum is a unique attraction, a Colonial Williamsburg-like living history restoration, complete with a general store, an old county courthouse, and America's oldest elementary school. It's called **Historic Richmond Town.**

Many of the buildings are staffed by craftspeople working with period equipment. White clapboard farmhouses dot the property's one hundred acres, and a central museum houses exhibits of Staten Island–made products that reveal the history and diversity of New York's least populous borough.

Crowned Buddha, Jacques Marchais Museum of Tibetan Art

Historic Richmond Town, 441 Clark Avenue, Staten Island (718–351–1611; www.historicrichmondtown.org), is open Wednesday through Sunday 1:00 to 5:00 P.M. from the day after Labor Day to June 30, with guided tours given at 2:30 P.M. on weekdays and at 2:00 and 3:30 P.M. on weekends (visitors must be on tours to enter buildings). From July 1 through Labor Day, hours are Wednesday through Friday 10:00 A.M. to 5:00 P.M.; Saturday and Sunday 1:00 to 5:00 P.M. In summer, tours are self-guided, with costumed interpreters along the way. Closed major holidays. Admission is $5.00 for adults, $4.00 for seniors, and $3.50 for children ages 5 to 17.

An authentic Chinese Scholar's Garden is one of the highlights at the lovely eighty-acre **Staten Island Botanical Garden** on the grounds of **Snug Harbor Cultural Center.** It's an environment of wood, rocks, water, a variety of plants, and nineteenth-century furniture in the style of the Ming Period, all carefully composed to create an air of quiet meditation. Other displays include a Pond Garden; Heritage Rose, White, and Perennial Gardens; and a Sensory Garden designed to provide physically challenged persons with a garden experience. The garden, at 1000 Richmond Terrace, Staten Island (718–273–8200; www.snug-harbor.org), is open from dawn to dusk. The Chinese Scholar's Garden is open Tuesday through Sunday, 10:00 A.M. to 5:00 P.M. Admission to all facilties, including the Newhouse Galleries, is $6.00 for adults; $5.00 for seniors and students with I.D.; half-price for children under 12.

southbeach—
butnotinmiami

South Beach on Staten Island (718–816–6804), has a superb view of the Verrazano-Narrows Bridge; a 7,500-foot-long boardwalk (the fourth largest in the world); and a playground, *bocce* courts, a roller hockey rink, shuffleboard, ball fields, and picnic areas.

The 260-acre *Clay Pit Ponds State Park Preserve,* New York City's only State Park Preserve, allows visitors to step back in time to a Staten Island of 200 years ago. Preserved because of its unique geological, botanical, and historical significance, sands and clays were deposited here during the Cretaceous period nearly 70 million years ago. These, along with glacial deposits approximately 12,000 years old, provide a soil that supports a fascinating assemblage of plants such as black jack oaks, American chestnuts, and a variety of ferns in numerous habitats, including ponds, bogs, sandy barrens, freshwater wetlands, and fields. The park is also home to a large number of animals and birds, including raccoons, screech owls, box turtles, and rufous-sided towhees.

During the 1800s a man named Abraham Ellis and his partner, Balthaser Kreischer, mined clay here. The men dug it out of a huge bare pit with shovels and pick axes, and donkeys hauled it on rails to the brickworks to the southwest. The clay was used to make such products as paints, dyes, and laundry bluing. When the mines closed, the pit filled with water and marsh plants thrived. Today, Ellis Swamp is home to vegetation, such as cattails and yellow pond lilies, and a mecca for wildlife, such as red-winged blackbirds, spring peepers, and, in early winter, mallard ducks.

The preserve has an excellent printed trail guide, which outlines several walks of varying duration of a half-hour to an hour. They begin at the picnic area behind the Park Preserve Headquarters.

Clay Pit Ponds State Park Preserve, 83 Nielsen Avenue, Staten Island (718–967–1976; www.nysparks.com/parks), is open daily from dawn to dusk. Educational programs, such as nature walks, pond ecology, bird-watching and tree and flower identification, are offered.

Fort Wadsworth, one of the country's oldest military installations, was first used during the American Revolution and was a key component of the New York Harbor defense system until the early 1970s. It became a National Park site and Lighthouse Center and Museum in 1995. Start your visit by viewing the introductory video at the visitor center before heading out on the 1½-mile trail around the site.

The Visitor Center at Fort Wadsworth, Bay Street, Staten Island (718–354–4500), is open Wednesday through Sunday, 10:00 A.M. to 5:00 P.M. Call for information on ranger-led tours.

In 1857, while Alexander Graham Bell was a ten-year-old boy living in Scotland, Antonio Meucci developed the first working telephone, transmitting a human voice over a copper wire charged with electricity. While he was busy inventing, he played host to his friend, the great Italian patriot Giuseppe Garibaldi. The globe-trotting Garibaldi, who not only campaigned to drive foreign powers from his beloved Italy but had also fought on behalf of Uruguay in its struggle for independence from Argentina, worked as a candlemaker on Staten Island. He was yet to achieve his greatest victory, as the leader of the "red shirts" who liberated Sicily and southern Italy from Bourbon dynastic rule and set the stage for the ultimate defeat of the pope's temporal power and the incorporation of the Papal States into a secular Kingdom of Italy under the House of Savoy.

All this and more is explained at the *Garibaldi-Meucci Museum,* 420 Tompkins Avenue, Staten Island (718–442–1608; www.garibaldimeucci museum.org). The museum, owned and operated by the Order of the Sons of Italy in America, the oldest organization of Italian-American men and women in the United States and Canada, is open year-round, Tuesday through Sunday 1:00 to 5:00 P.M. Admission is $5.00.

The oldest cultural institution on Staten Island is the *Staten Island Institute of Arts and Sciences* (Staten Island Museum) founded in 1881 and headquartered in the small community of St. George just 2 blocks from the Staten Island Ferry Terminal. The institute's collection has been described as "eclectic"—and eclectic it is. Exhibits focus on the art, natural science, and cultural history of Staten Island and its people, drawing from the institute's collections of more than two million artifacts and specimens.

The art collection includes many fine works from ancient to contemporary periods, including works by Staten Island artists such as Jasper Cropsey, Guy Pene duBois, and Cecil Bell. Also included are pieces by internationally acclaimed talents such as Marc Chagall, Reginald Marsh, and Robert Henri, as well as decorative arts, furniture, clothing, and more. The natural history collections include 500,000 insects, 25,000 plant specimens, and geologic, shell, and archaeological specimens. The archives and library comprise the largest holdings of Staten Island history and science anywhere. Public programs for all ages include weekly "Lunch and Learn" buffets.

nickelsaddup

In 1810 a sixteen-year-old Staten Island farm boy named **Cornelius Vanderbilt** borrowed $100 from his mother to buy a small boat for ferrying passengers and freight across the Narrows to Manhattan. By the time of his death in 1877, "Commodore" Vanderbilt had parlayed that initial investment into a steamship and railroad fortune of $100 million—not bad, even by the standards of twenty-first-century capitalism.

The Staten Island Museum, Staten Island Institute of Arts and Sciences, 75 Stuyvesant Place, Staten Island (718–727–1135; www.statenislandmuseum.org), is open Tuesday through Friday 9:00 A.M. to 5:00 P.M., Saturday 10:00 A.M. to 5:00 P.M., and Sunday noon to 5:00 P.M. Suggested admission is $2.00 for adults and $1.00 for students and senior citizens. Children under 12 are free.

On the south shore of Staten Island is a little-known but historically important community called **Sandy Ground**—the oldest continuously inhabited free black settlement in the nation. It was founded in the early nineteenth century by freed black men from New York who started a farming community; in mid-century they were joined by free black oyster fishermen from Maryland and Delaware.

Descendents of the original settlers still live on Sandy Ground, and the Sandy Ground Historical Society runs a museum and library that examines the life and history of the freed blacks who settled in the area prior to the Civil War. The museum preserves material related to the historic town, which was a way station on the Underground Railroad. Highlights of the collection include letters, photographs, film, art, rare books, quilts, a letter from W.E.B. DuBois, and other artifacts, such as a can of Tettersalve, a beauty product manufactured by Harlem businesswoman Madame C. J. Walker. The Sandy Ground Historical Museum is located at 1538 Woodrow Road, Staten Island (718–317–5796); admission is $6.00. Spring and summer hours are Tuesday through Thursday and Saturday and Sunday from 1:00 to 4:00 P.M.

Clear Comfort, one of the picturesque suburban "cottages" that dotted the shoreline of nineteenth-century Staten Island, was the home of Alice Austen (1866–1952), one of the country's first female photographers. The house was extensively renovated by her father, John, over a period of twenty-five years. By the time he was finished, he had transformed the rundown eighteenth-century Dutch farmhouse into a magnificently landscaped Carpenter Gothic cottage.

Alice lived in the house until illness and financial problems forced her to move in 1945. In the 1960s a group of citizens launched a successful effort to save Clear Comfort, and an exact restoration based on hundreds of Austen's photographs was completed in 1985. The home was designated a New York City Landmark in 1971 and a National Historic Landmark in 1993.

Today the gingerbread-gabled home overlooking the Narrows—the shipping channel for the Port of New York—serves as a gallery for Austen's wonderful photographs documenting life in turn-of-the-twentieth-century America. Changing exhibitions exploring themes inspired by her work and times often use images from the Staten Island Historical Society's Alice Austen Collection of nearly 3,000 negatives. A video narrated by Helen Hayes tells the story of "Alice's World."

The Alice Austen House, 2 Hylan Boulevard, Staten Island (718–816–4506; www.aliceausten.org/museum), is open Thursday through Sunday from noon to 5:00 P.M. and closed major holidays and the months of January and February. There is a suggested donation of $2.00.

Places to Stay in New York City

For the best deals, we suggest the following services and also the Web sites of the hotels listed by www.visit nyc.com. Note that at www.priceline.com, the best hotel deals are available when you "buy" a hotel sight unseen; this isn't as risky as it sounds when you select the neighborhood you prefer and the number of hotel stars you desire.

Often the later you wait to book a New York hotel room—at sites like www.last minutedeals.com—the better the price. However, this requires a taste for risk-taking and probably shouldn't be attempted at peak tourist periods—between Thanksgiving and New Year's, for example—when many hotels sell out completely.

Bed and Breakfast Network of New York
(212) 645–8134 or
(800) 900–8134
www.bedandbreakfast netny.com

Empire State B&B Association
www.esbba.com

Hotel Reservation Network Discount Rates
(800) 964–6835
www.hotels.com

Hotwire
www.hotwire.com

Last-Minute Deals
www.lastminutedeals.com

Priceline
www.priceline.com

Quikbook
(800) 789–9887
www.quikbook.com

Places to Eat in New York City

MANHATTAN
Note: We have added the code letters L and D for restaurants that offer prix-fixe options for lunch or dinner. Some of the D restaurants offer only the pre-theater option, so check before you book. As many places have their menus posted online, check their Web sites in advance to get an idea of dishes being served.

Becco (L, D)
355 West 46th Street
(212) 397–7597
www.becconyc.com

Cascina (L, D)
647 Ninth Avenue
(212) 245–4422
www.cascina.com

Centrico
211 West Broadway
(212) 431–0700
www.myriadrestaurant group.com

Chez Josephine
414 West 42nd Street
(212) 594–1925
www.chezjosephine.com

Gotham Bar and Grill (L)
12 East 12th Street
(212) 620–4020
www.gothambarandgrill.com

L'Ecole (L, D)
French Culinary Institute
462 Broadway
(212) 219–3300
www.frenchculinary.com

Le Pain Quotidien
Many city locations;
check Web site
www.painquotidien.com

Montebello
120 East 56th Street
(212) 753–1447
www.montebellonyc.com

Payard Bistro (D, Saturday)
1032 Lexington Avenue
(212) 717–5252
www.payard.com

Shun Lee Palace (L)
155 East 55th Street
(212) 371–8844
www.shunleepalace.com

New York State Division of Tourism

P.O. Box 2603
Albany, NY 12220-0603
(88) CALL–NYS or (518) 474–4116
www.iloveny.com
Free brochures, maps, free *I Love New York Travel Guide.*

New York State Office of Parks, Recreation, and Historic Preservation

Albany, NY 12238
(518) 474–0456
www.nysparks.state.ny.us

NYC & Company

810 Seventh Avenue
New York, NY 10019
(212) 484–1200
www.nycvisit.com
Formerly the city's convention and visitors' bureau, this is the official tourism organization for New York City. It distributes hundreds of free maps, brochures, and discount coupons for many attractions. The organization offers multilingual guidance and a free copy of the *Official NYC Guide,* which is filled with money-saving coupons for hotels, restaurants, sightseeing, and shopping.

NYC & Company Chinatown Visitors Information Kiosk

Canal and Baxter Streets
(212) 484–1222

NYC & Company and I Love NY Visitors Information Kiosk

City Hall Park
(Barclay Street and Broadway)
(212) 484–1222

NYC & Company Harlem Visitors Center

Adam Clayton Powell State Office Building plaza,
163 West 125th Street
(just east of Adam Clayton Powell Jr. Boulevard/Seventh Avenue)
(212) 484–1222

Times Square Information Center

1560 Seventh Avenue
(between 46th and 47th Streets)
(212) 869–1890
www.timessquarealliance.org

34th Street Partnership Information Booth

231 West 30th Street
(between Eighth and Ninth Avenues)
(212) 868–0521

Bloomingdale's International Visitors Center

Lexington Avenue, 1st floor
(at 59th Street)
(212) 705–2098

Central Park Visitors Center

(at the Dairy)
Central Park West near 65th Street
(212) 794–6564

Fashion Center Information Kiosk

Seventh Avenue
(at 39th Street)
(212) 398–7943
www.fashioncenter.com

Grand Central Partnership

Grand Central Terminal, South Side, Main Concourse
(directly across from Main Information Kiosk)
www.grandcentralpartnership.com

Javits Convention Center
655 West 34th Street, Concierge Desk
Eleventh Avenue (between 35th and
36th Streets)
(212) 216–2100

Lincoln Square (seasonal)
1841 Broadway
(at 60th Street)
(212) 581–3774

Macy's Visitor Information Center
151 West 34th Street
(at Seventh Avenue)
(212) 695–4400

Manhattan Mall
131 West 32nd Street
(212) 946–6100

Saks Fifth Avenue
Ambassador Desk
Fifth Avenue and 50th Street
(212) 940–4686

**United Nations Volunteer Information
Desk**
Secretariat Building at United Nations
First Avenue at 46th Street
(212) 963–7096

Village Alliance Information Booths
(seasonal)
Sixth Avenue and Christopher Street
Astor Place Triangle in the East Village at
Fourth Avenue and Astor Place
(212) 777–2173
www.villagealliance.org

**VISIT Center at Whitehall Ferry
Terminal**
Just south of Battery Park
Staten Island
(718) 447–3329

New York City Parks
www.nycgovparks.org

MTA (New York City subway)
www.mta.nyc.ny.us

Brooklyn Tourism Council
www.visitbrooklyn.org

Bronx Tourism Council
www.ilovethebronx.com

**Staten Island Borough President's
Office**
www.statenislandusa.com

TRANSPORTATION

**Port Authority of New York and New
Jersey**
www.panynj.gov

Amtrak
(800) USA–RAIL
www.amtrak.com

Long Island Rail Road
(718) 217–5477
www.mta.nyc.ny.us/lirr

Metro-North Railroad
(800) METRO–INFO or (212) 532–4900
www.mta.nyc.ny.us/mnr/index.html

New York Waterway
(800) 533–3779
www.nywaterway.com

Staten Island Ferry
(718) 815–BOAT
www.siferry.com

Sylvia's
328 Lenox Avenue
Harlem
(212) 996–0660
www.sylviasoulfood.com

Tavern on the Green (L, D)
Central Park West (between
66th and 67th Streets)
(212) 873–3200
www.tavernonthegreen.com

Terrace in the Sky (L)
400 West 119th Street
(212) 666–9490
www.terraceinthesky.com

Turkish Cuisine
631 Ninth Avenue
(212) 397–9650

BROOKLYN

Convivium Osteria
68 Fifth Avenue
(718) 857–1833
www.convivium-osteria.com

Frankie's 457 Spuntino
457 Court Street
(718) 403–0033
www.frankies457.com

Franny's
295 Flatbush Avenue
(718) 230–0221
www.frannysbrooklyn.com

The Grocery
288 Smith Street
(718) 596–3335

Junior's (cheesecake)
386 Flatbush Avenue
(718) 852–5257

Peter Luger Steakhouse
178 Broadway
(718) 387–7400
www.peterluger.com

Queen
84 Court Street
(718) 596–5955
www.queenrestaurant.com

THE BRONX

Café Sevilla
1209 White Plains Road
(718) 822–9104

Crab Shanty One
361 City Island Avenue
City Island
(718) 885–1810
www.originalcrabshanty.com

Dominick's Restaurant
2335 Arthur Avenue
(718) 733–2807

Jake's Steakhouse
6031 Broadway
(718) 581–0182

Rambling House
4291 Katonah Avenue
(718) 798–4510

Riverdale Garden
4576 Manhattan College
Parkway (242nd Street)
(718) 884–5232
www.riverdalegarden.com

Roberto's
603 Crescent Avenue
(718) 733–9503

QUEENS

Amici Amore1
29–35 Newtown Avenue
(30th Street)
(718) 267–2771
www.amiciamore1.com

Bella Via
4746 Vernon Boulevard
(48th Avenue)
(718) 361–7510
www.bellaviarestaurant.com

Caffé on the Green
201–10 Cross Island
Parkway
(718) 423–7272
www.caffeonthegreen.com

Happy Buddha
135–37 37th Avenue
(718) 358–0079
www.happybuddha.com

Le Sans Souci
44–09 Broadway (between
44th and 45th Streets)
(718) 728–2733
www.lesanssouci.net

Park Side
107–01 Corona Avenue
(51st Avenue)
(718) 271–9321
www.parksiderestaurant.com

Thai Pavilion
37–10 30th Avenue
(37th Street)
(718) 777–5546

STATEN ISLAND

Caffe Bondi
1816 Hylan Boulevard
(718) 668–0100
www.bondiny.com

Fushimi
2110 Richmond Road
(718) 980–5300

Killmeyer's Old Bavaria Inn
4254 Arthur Kill Road
(718) 984–1202
www.killmeyers.com

Parsonage
74 Arthur Kill Road
(718) 351–7979

Yellow Fin
20 Ellis Street
(718) 317–5700

Long Island

Just as New York is simply "The City," Long Island is "The Island," home to hundreds of thousands of commuters at the end of a ride on the bustling LIRR or, worse, the congested LIE. But Long Island is much more than traffic jams and mega-malls. Venture out along Route 25A and enter the Great Gatsby era, when the families of fortune—the Vanderbilts, the Chryslers, the Woolworths, the Phippses, the Guggenheims—built astounding mansions sprawling over hundreds of acres, earning this part of the North Shore the nickname the "Gold Coast."

Further east, of course, the magnificent beaches of the Hamptons beckon. It's funny how summering city folk who want to get away from it all actually seem to bring it all with them. But visit Montauk Point when the weather is blustery, when the wind turns the sea a menacing white-capped green-gray, and feel for the fishermen and farmers who still make a living from this sea and this land. Long Island's natural beauty has also attracted a number of artists—something about the way light reflects off both the sea and the sound gives the eastern reaches of the island a unique glow.

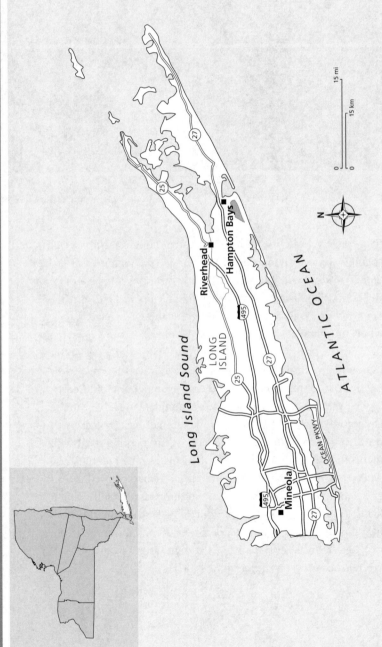

North Shore

Howard Gould, son of the railroad baron Jay Gould, spared no expense when he built the 100,000-square-foot mansion *Castlegould* in 1904 on a prime location overlooking the Long Island Sound. See yet another century represented at the 1912 Tudor-style *Hempstead House,* where second owner Daniel Guggenheim resided. In 1923 his son Harry built *Falaise,* a Norman manor filled with period furnishings. Today all three mansions are part of the 216-acre *Sands Point Preserve.*

Castlegould features large traveling natural-history exhibits that change twice a year, plus interactive exhibits changing on a six-month basis. There are six marked nature trails; two of them are self-guiding and one follows the shoreline. In addition to numerous geological phenomena, such as glacial erratics (large granite boulders dropped from the ice during the last continental glaciation, about 20,000 years ago), there is a wide range of plant and bird life within the preserve. Kids will enjoy following the special Dinosaur Trail, with its replicas of fossilized dinosaur tracks. Pick up trail maps at the visitor center in Castlegould.

Sands Point Preserve is located at 127 Middleneck Road, Sands Point, Long Island (516–571–7900 or 571–7901; www.sandspointpreserve.org). Nature trails are open daily from 10:00 A.M. to 5:00 P.M. A gate fee of $2.00 is collected on weekends. Falaise is open for tours from early May through late October, Wednesday through Sunday hourly between noon and 3:00 P.M., with an additional tour at 3:30 on weekends; tickets are $7.00 for adults and $4.00 for seniors; children under 10 are not permitted. Hempstead House is open

it'sexhausting

More than two million motor vehicles and 80,000 motor boats are registered in Nassau and Suffolk Counties.

weekends from early May through late October, 12:30 to 4:00 P.M.; special natural-history exhibits in Castlegould are $4.00 for adults, $3.00 for children and seniors. Both Falaise and the Hempstead House are closed during the September Medieval Festival.

Planting Fields Arboretum has just the one sixty-five-room Tudor-style mansion, Coe Hall, former home of insurance magnate William Robertson Coe and his wife Mai Rogers Coe, née Standard Oil heiress. The house and the magnificent 409-acre gardens remain much as the wealthy couple enjoyed them in the 1920s, with formal gardens, nature trails, and greenhouses filled with William Coe's pet collections, including imported camellias. Coe also set up a working dairy and kept pigs and chickens, donating much of the milk and produce to the needy during the Great Depression.

But it was trees and shrubs that most commanded Coe's attention, and they were the subject of some of his greatest extravagances. The copper beech on the north lawn, for instance, was moved here from Massachusetts by barge and a team of seventy-two horses when it was already 60 feet high. Working with master landscape gardeners such as A. Robeson Sargent and James Dawson of Olmsted Brothers, Coe created grand *allées* of trees designed to frame the views from the house, and he established rambling azalea walks. As late as the 1950s, in the last years of his life, Coe planted the rhododendron park, which remains one of the outstanding features of Planting Fields.

From April through September (except on Labor Day and July 4), visitors can tour Coe Hall daily noon to 3:30 P.M. The fee is $5.00 for adults and children over 12, $3.50 for seniors, $1.00 for children ages 7 to 12, and free for those under 7. For tour information call (516) 922–8670.

Planting Fields Arboretum, 1395 Planting Fields, **Oyster Bay,** Long Island (516–922–9200; www.plantingfields.org), is open daily 9:00 A.M. to 5:00 P.M. There is a $6.00 entry charge per car daily from May 1 through October and on weekends and holidays the rest of the year. Closed Christmas.

Of course, it's not all champagne and caviar, even on the Gold Coast. The *Holocaust Memorial and Educational Center of Nassau County,* on the 204-acre *Welwyn Preserve,* hopes to "foster a greater understanding of the causes and consequences of one of the darkest periods in world history." The center hosts ongoing exhibits and has a 1,850-volume library. It's at 100 Crescent Beach Road in Glen Cove, Long Island (516–571–8040; www.holocaust-nassau.org), and is open Monday through Friday 9:30 A.M. to 4:30 P.M. and Sunday 11:00 A.M. to 4:00 P.M. Admission is free.

Few people still remember whale-oil lamps or whale-bone corsets, but whaling was once an important industry on Long Island, with ships setting out from Sag Harbor and *Cold Spring Harbor.* Here today the *Whaling Museum*

Whaling Museum

celebrates the skills and adventures of the town's own whalers as well as those of other men who set out to sea in treacherous conditions from colonial times through the nineteenth century.

The Whaling Museum houses a large collection of the implements used in the whale "fishery," as it was known. Here are harpoons, lances, and the tools used in separating blubber from whale carcasses. A permanent exhibit, "Mark Well the Whale," details the history and impact of whaling on the locality. The museum features the state's only fully equipped nineteenth-century whaleboat with original gear; an extensive collection of the whaler's art of scrimshaw; and "The Wonder of Whales" conservation gallery for children.

The Whaling Museum, Main Street, Route 25A, Cold Spring Harbor, Long Island (631–367–3418; www.cshwhalingmuseum.org), is open daily from Memorial Day through Labor Day; closed Monday the rest of the year. Hours are 11:00 A.M. to 5:00 P.M. Admission is $5.00 for adults $4.00 for seniors and students 5 to 18; families (parents and children) $12.00.

The **DNA Learning Center**, the educational arm of Cold Spring Harbor Laboratory, is the world's first biotechnology museum. Two- and three-dimensional displays, computer multimedia, videos, and other elements are utilized to teach visitors about genes in a presentation called "The Genes We Share," free Monday through Friday 10:00 A.M. to 4:00 P.M. and Saturday noon to 4:00 P.M. Other current topics are "Genetic Origins" and "Inside Cancer."

DNA Learning Center, 334 Main Street, Cold Spring Harbor, Long Island (516–367–5170; www.dnalc.org); admission is free.

Be sure to stop by National Landmark **St. James General Store**, 516 Moriches Road, St. James, Long Island (631–854–3740; www.suffolkcounty.gov).

In business since 1857, it's the oldest continuously-operating general store in the country and looks just as it did in 1890. The shelves are stocked with more than 4,000 items, many of which are nineteenth-century reproductions, including handmade quilts, salt-glaze pottery, hand-carved decoys, penny candy, exotic teas, and bonnets. The store is open daily except Monday from 10:00 A.M. to 5:00 P.M.; closed January and February.

The village of **Stony Brook** on Long Island Sound has it all: a scenic location, a fascinating history, great food and lodgings, museums, and terrific shopping. And it owes its present-day success primarily to one man: Ward Melville, whose vision helped the rural village to successfully transform into a suburban center while still retaining its historic integrity. His plan, unveiled to the community in 1939, called for relocating businesses and homes so as to open the view to the harbor. The shops were moved to a "shopping center" at the head of the village green, and today more than forty of the trendiest shops on Long Island are housed at the Stony Brook Village Center. Up the road the Three Village Garden Club Exchange features two floors of antiques and collectibles.

Built in 1751, Stony Brook's **Three Village Inn** was until 1867 the home of Captain Jonas Smith, Long Island's first millionaire sea captain. Today it's a charming inn and restaurant, a winner of the *Wine Spectator* Award of Excellence. It features homemade breads and desserts and house specialties such as cold plum soup, pan-roasted chicken breast stuffed with ham and Monterey Jack cheese, baked lobster pie, and, every Sunday, a "Thanksgiving" turkey dinner with all the trimmings. The Inn is at 150 Main Street, Stony Brook, Long Island; www.three villageinn.com. To make a room or meal reservation (breakfast, lunch, dinner, and Sunday brunch), call (516) 751–0555.

hailsuburbia

Levittown, the country's first instant suburb, was created in 1947 when 17,400 freestanding houses were erected.

Within walking distance of the inn, at 1200 Route 25A, is the **Long Island Museum of American Art, History and Carriages.** This museum complex houses the **Margaret Melville Blackwell History Museum,** featuring American decor in miniature in a gallery of fifteen period rooms and one of the country's finest collections of antique decoys, plus a new exhibition, every two or three months, on a historical theme; the **Dorothy and Ward Melville Carriage House,** with its world-renowned collection of more than ninety horse-drawn carriages; and the **Art Museum,** exhibiting American art from the eighteenth century to the present, as well as collected works of American genre painter William Sidney Mount (1807–68). There are also a 1794 barn, an 1867 carriage shed, an 1875 blacksmith shop, an 1877 one-room schoolhouse, and a colonial burying ground. The museums are open daily in July and August; the rest of the year they're open Wednesday through Saturday 10:00 A.M. to 5:00 P.M. and Sunday noon to 5:00 P.M. Closed Monday (except Monday holidays) and Tuesday. Also closed New Year's, Thanksgiving, Christmas Eve, and Christmas Day. Admission is $7.00 for adults, $6.00 for seniors, $3.00 ages 6 to 17, $3.00 for college students with ID; under 6 free. Admission covers everything on the nine-acre grounds. For information call (631) 751–0066 or go to www.longislandmuseum.org.

islanditems

The largest island adjoining the continental United States, Long Island is approximately 118 miles long and 20 miles at its widest.

Long Island has more than 150 beaches; the largest is 2,400-acre Jones Beach.

King Kullen, the country's first supermarket, opened on Long Island in 1930.

A must-see before leaving town is the working *Gristmill* on Harbor Road, built circa 1751 and renovated through the efforts of Ward Melville in 1947. The mill is open in May and June and September through December on weekends noon to 4:30 P.M.; in July and August it's open Friday, Saturday, and Sunday noon to 4:30 P.M. Admission is $2.00 for adults and $1.00 for children under 12. For information call (631) 751–2244. The Ward Melville Heritage Association, which operates the mill, also offers Discovery Wetlands Cruises; call (631) 751–2244 for information and ticket prices, or reserve online at www.ward melvilleheritage.org.

Central Nassau, the South Shore, Then Heading East

In Nassau County, the city of *Hempstead* is home to the *African American Museum,* founded in 1970 as the Black History Exhibit Center. In addition to local lore and history of slaves and free blacks, who worked at farming, whaling, crafts, and small businesses, the museum includes interpretive exhibits of traditional and contemporary native African culture.

The African American Museum tells the story of Long Island's blacks through displays of photographs, artifacts, lectures, workshops, and performing arts. Local artistic talent is especially promoted. African-oriented exhibits and special programs have included shows devoted to West African crafts, art from Sierra Leone, African toys, and black artistic expression in South Africa.

ANNUAL EVENTS ON LONG ISLAND

JANUARY

Long Island Winterfest
www.liwinterfest.org
(through March)

FEBRUARY

Long Island Boat Show
Uniondale
(631) 691–7050
www.NYMTA.com

MARCH

Hamptons Restaurant Week
www.hamptonsrestaurantweek.com

Saint Patrick's Day Parade
Montauk
(631) 668–1578
www.montaukfriendsoferin.com

Shakespeare Festival
Hofstra University
(516) 463–6644

MAY

Dutch Festival
Hofstra University
(516) 463–6582

Long Island Lighthouse Challenge
Various locations
(631) 207–4331
www.LIlighthouseSociety.org

JUNE

Belmont Stakes
Elmont
(516) 488–6000

JULY

July 4th at Jones Beach
Wantagh
(631) 669–1000

Mercedes-Benz Polo Challenge
Bridgehampton
(212) 421–1367
www.sportpolo.com

AUGUST

Hampton Classic Horse Show
Bridgehampton
(631) 537–3177
www.hamptonclassic.com

Hamptons Wine and Food Festival
East Hampton
(631) 613–3110
www.hamptonswineandfood.com

The African American Museum, 110 North Franklin Street, Hempstead, Long Island (516–572–0730), is open Thursday through Saturday 10:00 A.M. to 5:00 P.M.; Sunday 1:00 to 5:00 P.M. Admission is free.

Another Hempstead attraction is not really in Hempstead but in the south-shore village of *Lawrence,* just across the New York City limits from Far Rockaway, Queens. This is *Rock Hall Museum,* a 1767 mansion built by Tory merchant Josiah Martin.

Rock Hall represents the high-water mark of late Georgian architecture in this part of the country, particularly in its interior detailing. The paneling and

SEPTEMBER

Sag Harborfest
Sag Harbor
(631) 725–1700

Shinnecock Pow-Wow
Shinnecock Reservation
(631) 283–6143
www.shinnecocknation.com

OCTOBER

Hamptons International Film Festival
East Hampton and other locations
(631) 324–4600
www.hamptonsfilmfest.org

Long Island Halloween
Old Bethpage Village
(516) 572–8400
www.oldbethpage.org

The Oyster Festival
Oyster Bay
(516) 628–1625
www.theoysterfestival.org

NOVEMBER

Long Island Festival of Trees
Uniondale
(516) 378–2000
www.ucpn.org

Thanksgiving Antique Show
Old Westbury
(516) 868–2751

Thanksgiving Celebration
Old Bethpage
(516) 572–8400
www.oldbethpage.org

DECEMBER

Charles Dickens Festival
Port Jefferson
(631) 473–5220

Holiday Lights Spectacular
Wantagh
(516) 221–1000

mantels, as well as much of the eighteenth- and early nineteenth-century furniture and the replica of a colonial kitchen (the original kitchen was in an outbuilding), came down virtually unchanged to our own time. Josiah Martin's family, having come through the revolution none the worse for being on the wrong side, lived here until 1823. The following year Thomas Hewlett bought Rock Hall; his family lived in the mansion for more than a century after his death in 1841. In 1948 the Hewletts gave the place to the town of Hempstead—presumably then a larger municipal entity—for use as a museum.

awhaleofadeal

The first pastor of East Hampton's "Old Church," which was built in 1717, received for his salary "forty-five pounds annually, lands rate free, grain to be first ground at the mill every Monday and one-fourth of the whales stranded on the beach."

Rock Hall Museum, 199 Broadway, Lawrence, Long Island (516–239–1157), is open year-round, Wednesday through Saturday 10:00 A.M. to 4:00 P.M. and Sunday noon to 4:00 P.M. Admission is free.

With 8½ miles of waterfront, *Freeport* calls itself "the Boating and Fishing Capital of the East." Woodcleft Avenue, informally known as *Nautical Mile,* is rumored to once have been a haven for bootleggers, pirates, and other scoundrels. Today it is a mecca for sightseers, browsers, and seafood lovers. Restaurants, pubs, fish markets, and gift shops line the avenue, and one of the Island's largest charter/sport fishing fleets sails out of the harbor daily in season.

Though Long Island may be better known for mega-malls, you can still find wonderful independent shops like *Dear Little Dollies.* More than 6,000 dolls fill every nook and cranny of the 5,000-square-foot store. Barbie is here—but so are one-of-a-kind dolls and limited editions by contemporary artists such as Yolanda Bello and Paul Crees; ethnic dolls; and mid-priced dolls from makers including Seymour Mann and Ashton-Drake Galleries. Prices range from $20 to $14,000. Dorothy and Louis Camilleri, owners of Dear Little Dollies, host numerous artist signings in the shop and special shows in the gallery. They also offer a mail-order service; call or check the store's Web site for details.

hopaboard

Two companies offer year-round ferry service across the Long Island Sound to and from Connecticut. Cross Sound Ferry, Inc. (631–323–2525 or 860–443–5281), operates between New London and Orient Point; Bridgeport and Port Jefferson Ferry Co. (631–473–0286 or 888–44–FERRY), runs between Bridgeport and Port Jefferson. Both rides take approximately seventy-five minutes each way.

Dear Little Dollies, 418 Bedford Avenue, *Bellmore,* Long Island (516–679–0164), is open Monday through Saturday 10:00 A.M. to 6:00 P.M. and Sunday from noon until 5:00 P.M.

Not far from Bellmore is the *Bide-a-Wee Pet Cemetery* in *Wantagh,* where Richard Nixon's beloved cocker spaniel, Checkers, rests in peace. Checkers died in 1964 and was buried in plot #5. He is now surrounded by about 50,000 other deceased companion animals. The cemetery is on Beltagh Avenue opposite Wantagh High School.

On Long Island's south shore in **Seaford,** the **Tackapausha Museum and Preserve** is an eighty-acre introduction to the ecology and natural history of the Northeast's coastal woodlands. Tackapausha is named after a *sachem* (chief) of Long Island's Massapequa Indians, who once lived on this land without greatly affecting its wildlife, its plant communities, or the balance of natural forces.

The Tackapausha Museum is a small facility designed to serve as an introduction to the plants and animal life of the preserve itself. Exhibits explain the relationship between habitat groups, the differences between diurnal and nocturnal animals, and the changes in life patterns brought about by the different seasons. There is also a small collection of native animals, housed in as natural a setting as possible. The preserve itself is a lovely piece of land, incorporating a variety of ecosystems. A self-guiding trail takes visitors through the different environments; you can pick up the interpretive map at the museum.

The Tackapausha Museum and Preserve, Washington Avenue, Seaford, Long Island (516–571–7443), is open Tuesday through Saturday 10:00 A.M. to 4:00 P.M. and Sunday 1:00 to 4:00 P.M. Admission is $2.00 for adults, $1.00 for children, and free for those under 4.

From the unspoiled wilderness, step forward to **Old Bethpage Village Restoration,** a re-creation of a Long Island village of the Civil War era, long before there was a Levittown or Long Island Expressway. Starting in the middle 1960s, the officials began moving threatened colonial and early-nineteenth-century structures here. There are now nearly fifty buildings on the site, representing the typical domestic, commercial, and agricultural structures of the time.

Quilting in the Noon Inn, Old Bethpage Village Restoration

Old Bethpage Village has been staffed with historically attired guides and craftspeople plying their ancient trades, including a local militia. Old Bethpage Village Restoration, Round Swamp Road, Old Bethpage (516–572–8400, recorded message, or 572–8401; www.oldbethpage.org), is open Wednesday through Sunday 10:00 A.M. to 5:00 P.M. in summer and early fall. Call for other openings. Closed holidays except Memorial Day, July 4, Labor Day, and Columbus Day, when the restoration is closed the day after each of these days. Admission is $7.00 for adults and $5.00 for children and senior citizens (ticket sales end one hour before closing). Call for information on special presentations and events.

Like Planting Fields in Oyster Bay, the south shore's ***Bayard-Cutting Arboretum State Park*** is another rich man's estate whose gracious gardens and majestic trees can now be enjoyed by all. William Bayard Cutting (1850–1912) was one of New York City's ablest financiers, as well as a lawyer, railroad director and president, insurance executive, and a philanthropist noted for having built the first block of Manhattan tenements to feature indoor plumbing.

In his leisure time (whenever that might have been), Cutting enjoyed improving his scenic Long Island retreat, located right near what is now the state-managed ***Connetquot River State Park Preserve.*** Cutting did not believe in cutting corners, and when he built his sixty-eight-room Tudor mansion in 1886, he had his friend Louis Comfort Tiffany add a few decorative touches. When it came to landscaping, Cutting placed a good deal of trust in another friend, the great Harvard botanist and silviculturist Charles Sprague Sargent. Working with landscape architect Frederick Law Olmsted, who laid out Central Park, Sargent beautified the estate with a variety of trees and flowering plants; azaleas and rhododendrons grow here in profusion. The streams and ponds, with their ducks and geese and graceful little footbridges, are reason enough to spend an afternoon at the park.

The Bayard-Cutting Arboretum State Park, Route 27A, Great River, Long Island (631–581–1002; www.bayardcuttingarboretum.com), is open Tuesday through Sunday 10:00 A.M. to sunset, as well as holiday Mondays between April and October. Admission is $6.00 per car; free from November through March. Admission includes a tour of the first floor of the mansion; from September through May, tours of the newly restored second floor are given on Sunday at 2:00 P.M. for an additional $4.00 charge.

Within a few miles of the Bayard-Cutting Arboretum is the village of West Sayville, with its ***Long Island Maritime Museum.*** The whalers of Cold Spring Harbor were by no means the only brave Long Islanders to go down to the sea to pursue their quarry; here in West Sayville, men went out into dangerous waters to harvest the more prosaic but nonetheless important oyster. The mar-

Travel Light

No cars are allowed on Fire Island. The only way to reach the seventeen communities there is via ferry. Sunken Forest Ferry Service (631–589–0810) departs Sayville for Sunken Forest from May to October; Sayville Ferry Service (631–589–0810) services Fire Island Pines and Cherry Grove, April to November; Davis Ferry Co. (631–475–1665) goes from Patchogue to Davis Park, Watch Hill, and Fire Island Seashore from March to September; Fire Island Ferries (631–665–3600) leaves from Bay Shore for Saltaire, Ocean Beach, Atlantique, Kismet, Dunewood, Fair Harbor, Seaview, and Ocean Bay Park year-round.

itime museum, in fact, includes a restored vintage 1907 oyster house and has among its holdings the largest collection of small craft on Long Island. There is also a restored boat-builder's shop, illustrative of the skill and care that went into the building of these essential commercial vessels. Other exhibits focus on the tools of oystermen over the years.

It isn't all oysters at the Long Island Maritime Museum. Displays of yachting and racing memorabilia, model boats, and artifacts related to the lifesaving service of the nineteenth century round out the museum's collection. Duck and other shorebird decoys, an integral part of American folk art in shoreline communities well into the twentieth century, are also on exhibit. The Bayman's Cottage depicts the style of living at the turn of the twentieth century.

Long Island Maritime Museum, 86 West Avenue (Route 27A), West Sayville, Long Island (631–HIS–TORY; www.limaritime.org), is open Monday through Saturday 10:00 A.M. to 3:00 P.M. and Sunday noon to 4:00 P.M. Admission is $4.00 for adults, $2.00 for seniors and children.

A narrow barrier island off Long Island's southern shore, Fire Island is a popular gay getaway with lots of partying, though plenty of families also summer here far more quietly. *Fire Island National Seashore* stretches for 32 miles from *Robert Moses State Park* in the west to *Smith Point Park* in the east. Though both parks are accessible by car, the towns sandwiched in between can be reached only by boat or on foot. Designated a "forever preserved wilderness area," the seashore is home to a variety of bird and animal life, including herons, wild geese, and deer (be alert for deer ticks, carriers of lyme disease, when you're in high grass). Among the must-see spots here are *Sunken Forest* at Sailors Haven, *Watch Hill,* and *Smith Point.* For information, contact the National Parks Service at (631) 289–4810 or www.nps.gov.

Fire Island Lighthouse, east of Robert Moses State Park (631–661–4876; www.fireislandlighthouse.com), first began guiding ships to New York Harbor in 1826. Today, it's open for tours daily from 9:30 A.M. to 5:00 P.M. in July and August, with limited hours in the off-season. Reservations are recommended. The adjacent museum is open daily when the lighthouse is open. Admission to the museum is free, but the charge to climb the tower is $6.00 for adults, $4.00 for seniors; children must be 42 inches tall to climb.

onbeyond babylon

In 1901 Guglielmo Marconi sent his first radio transmission from Fire Island Avenue in Babylon.

Elsie Collins's *1880 House* is a delightful, antiques-filled bed-and-breakfast just a few blocks from **Westhampton Beach.** There are two large suites in the farmhouse, each with its own adjoining sitting room and private bath, and a third in an adjacent one-hundred-year-old barn. Guests can cool off in the swimming pool after a game of tennis or warm up by the fireplace after a brisk winter's walk on the beach. The B&B, at 2 Seafield Lane, Westhampton Beach, Long Island (631–288–1559 or 800–346–3290), is open year-round. Rates, including breakfast, range from $125 to $150 in winter; $150 to $175 spring and fall; and $175 to $250 Memorial Day through Labor Day. Four- and seven-day rates are available. A two-night minimum (three nights on holiday weekends) applies in summer.

If your poodle has always wanted to sleep in the same bed as Jack Nicholson did, we've got a great place for you: the *Southampton Inn.* (Columbia Films rented the entire inn during the 2003 filming of *Something's Gotta Give.*) This hostelry is truly pet- (and family-) friendly: Fifi can actually have breakfast with you in the library. But the place isn't going completely to the dogs: the ninety-room Tudor-style hotel offers elegant accommodations, fine dining, conference facilities, a heated swimming pool, all-weather tennis, a fitness room, a game room, and beach access. If you're not a pet person, ten Romance Rooms (off-limits to pets, kids, and smoking) have been set aside in a separate building.

The Southampton Inn, 91 Hill Street, Southampton, Long Island (800–832–6500; www.southamptoninn.com), is open year-round. Rates for a double range from $119 to $199 off-season, $149 to $459 from May to October.

In 1954 abstract expressionist painter Jackson Pollock moved with his wife, artist Lee Krasner, to a two-story 1879 shingled house overlooking Accabonac Creek. He lived here until his death in 1956, painting some of his most famous pieces in the studio he converted from a barn.

Today at the *Pollock-Krasner House and Study Center,* visitors can tour the artists' studio and their home, filled with the couple's furniture and belongings, and their library, including Pollock's extensive collection of jazz

Not Where, But When

The streets in the Hamptons may see as much Manolo-shod foot traffic as anyplace on the French Riviera; for travelers seeking the serenity these seaside villages once offered, avoid the summer season. In spring and fall, prices, crowds, and traffic are all far gentler and the weather can be sublime.

albums. Also on view is a documentary photo essay chronicling Pollock's artistic development and detailing his working methods.

The Study Center, established to promote scholarship in twentieth-century American art, houses a growing art reference library built around the personal papers of those who witnessed the birth of abstract expressionism.

The Pollock-Krasner House and Study Center, 830 Fireplace Road, **East Hampton** (631–324–4929), is open June, July, and August 1:00 to 5:00 P.M.; call for appointments the rest of the year. Tours are given every hour on the hour. Admission is $5.00 adults (guided tours $10.00), under 12 free. State and city university students, faculty, and staff are also admitted free.

Who ya gonna call if you come across a stranded sea creature? **Riverhead Foundation for Marine Research and Preservation,** of course. The foundation is in charge of rescuing any whale, porpoise, dolphin, seal, or sea turtle stranded anywhere in New York. Established in 1980, the organization has handled more than 2,000 strandings, including the first and only successful rehabilitation and release of a baby sperm whale.

The Visitor Center briefs people on what to do if they find a stranded creature (don't attempt to push the animal back into the water or obstruct the blowhole; do notify the foundation and keep crowds away). It also has exhibits on sea turtles, harbor seals (when available), and other sea life.

Riverhead Foundation for Marine Research and Preservation's Visitor Center, 467 East Main Street, **Riverhead,** Long Island (631–369–9840), is open from 10:00 A.M. to 5:00 P.M., daily July through Labor Day and weekends only the rest of the year. Admission is $4.00 for adults and $2.00 for children. The twenty-four-hour stranding hotline is (631–369–9829). Visit its Web site at www.riverheadfoundation.org. The foundation also operates seal-watching cruises and seal walks; call for details.

Why is there a giant duck on the side of the road just outside the town of **Flanders?** For the same reason there's a huge elephant on the Jersey Shore: to attract tourists. The 30-foot-long, 20-foot-high white duck was built in 1931 by the proprietor of a local duck farm. Today the **Big Duck** houses a shop run by

Give or Take a Few Decades . . .

Montauk Point Light was erected in 1796 on the recommendation of President George Washington, who calculated that it would stand for 200 years on its location some 300 feet from the sea's edge. Today, the 110½-foot tower—the first in New York State and fourth-oldest in the United States—is only 100 feet from the water, which nibbles steadily at the tip of Long Island. Anti-erosion efforts have been implemented to protect the historic structure, which has already outlasted Washington's estimate.

Friends for Long Island's Heritage and is a great place to stock up on duck collectibles and souvenirs. It's on Route 24, and it's open late May through Labor Day, daily (except Monday) from 10:00 A.M. to 5:00 P.M., with a break for the volunteers to have lunch. For information call (631) 852–8292.

At *Slo Jack's Miniature Golf,* Long Island's oldest, the windmill has been turning since 1960. It's the miniature course of our dreams, complete with a wishing well, paddle wheels, and a 1960s drive-in restaurant (car service no longer offered) that serves up hamburgers, hot dogs, soft-serve ice cream, Mexican food, and local seafood. Official season at Slo Jack's Miniature Golf, 212 West Montauk Highway, *Hampton Bays,* Long Island (631–728–9601), is Memorial Day to Labor Day, but the restaurant is open March through Christmas and unofficially the course is also open during that period. Both are open 9:00 A.M. to 10:00 P.M. There's also a surf shop on the premises.

America's oldest cattle ranch isn't out west—it's on the South Fork of Long Island in *Montauk.* Established in 1658, *Deep Hollow Ranch* puts a different spin on Long Island beach life. Instead of lolling around on the beach at East Hampton, seeing and being seen, try one of Deep Hollow's ninety-minute guided trail rides, which will take you over hill and dale and along a lovely stretch of beach designated for horseback riding. Sprawling across 4,000 acres of land owned by Suffolk County, the ranch offers horses for all levels of riding skill, along with English and western saddle lessons. There are pony rides for the kids, who will also enjoy the petting farm stocked with baby animals. In summer Deep Hollow offers nightly chuck wagon rides and barbecues and a dinner theater. When you hit the trail at Deep Hollow, you'll be following in history's hoofprints: Teddy Roosevelt camped here with his Rough Riders after the Spanish-American War. Call (631) 668–2744 or go to www.deephollow ranch.com for details. Rides are offered year-round.

You might suspect that it's the celebrity clientele such as Billy Joel and Paul Simon that gets the homey *Lobster Roll Restaurant* (631–267–2740) so much ink in major publications like *Gourmet* magazine and the *New York Times*. But this place that many locals simply call "Lunch" (for the sign on the roof) is an institution in these parts and it gets consistently high marks for its fresh seafood, including salmon burgers and, of course, the wonderfully unpretentious sandwich of fresh lobster meat, chopped celery, and mayo served on a hot dog bun. Right on Montauk Highway between **Amagansett** and Montauk, the Lobster Roll serves lunch and dinner daily in summer.

If you're looking for peace and quiet, beautiful beaches, or simply a taste of island life, take a short ferry ride to **Shelter Island,** cradled between the North and South forks of Long Island. The car ferries leave from Greenport on the North Fork and North Haven on the South Shore. The Nature Conservancy owns nearly one-third of the 8,000-acre island, ensuring that this portion, at least, will remain unspoiled.

In 1871 a small group of Methodist clergy and laymen from Brooklyn purchased land on a bluff overlooking Shelter Island Sound. American landscape architect Robert Morris Copeland laid out plans for a camp meeting place. Four years later the Union Church, intended by Copeland to be the camp's visual and social center, was built in a grove, a natural amphitheater that was also the site for an open-air preacher's stand and tents to accommodate the people who attended the early meetings.

Over the years 141 buildings in a variety of styles ranging from steep-gabled, delicately trimmed cottages to larger Stick, Queen Anne, and Colonial Revival homes were built here. The **Shelter Island Heights Historic District** was developed with sensitivity to the nineteenth-century American ideal of respect for the natural landscape. The community embodies this concept and retains its original character.

Location, Location, Location

East Hampton's earliest white settlers were Puritans from Maidstone, Kent, who first landed in Salem, Massachusetts and then went on to found the Long Island town in 1649. In 1660 they acquired from the Montauk Indians "all the neck of land called Montauk, with all and every part and parcel thereof from sea to sea, from the utmost end of the land eastward to the sea-side, unto the other end of the said land westward, adjoining to the bounds of East Hampton . . . with meadow, wood, stone, creeks, ponds, and whatsover doth or may grow upon or issue from the same, with all the profits and commodities, by sea or land, unto the aforesaid inhabitants of East Hampton, their heirs and assigns, forever."

The price: £30 4s. 8d. sterling; in today's currency, approximately $1,000.

There are four trails on the Nature Conservancy's **Mashomack Preserve** for nature study and bird-watching, varying in length from 1½ to 11 miles, and a barrier-free braille trail for the visually impaired. In the village you can rent bicycles at **Piccozzi's Bike Shop** (631–749–0045), grab a bite at **The Dory Restaurant** (631–749–8300), have a lovely meal at the **Victorian Chequit Inn** (631–749–0018), or stop in at one of the other restaurants. By now you'll have fallen in love with the island and vowed never to leave. There are plenty of places that will put you up. The Chequit Inn also has guest rooms, as do a number of other places, including the **Beech Tree House** (631–749–4252), which has suites with full kitchens, and **Shelter Island Resort** (631–749–2001), overlooking Shelter Island Sound. For more information contact the Shelter Island Chamber of Commerce (631–749–0399; www.onisland.com).

Long Island's North Fork is considered by many to be the "undiscovered" fork. Although it's far less crowded than the South Fork, it's quickly becoming a major tourist destination. But hop off the major highway (Route 25) and you'll discover some wonderful off-the-beaten-path surprises.

Cutchogue's Village Green on Route 25 is home to numerous historic buildings, including the beautifully preserved 1649 **Old House,** a National Historic Landmark. Among the outstanding features of this English-style dwelling: the pilastered top chimney and the three-part casement window frames.

Take time to wander through the nearby **Old Burying Ground,** where many of the tombstones date back to the early 1700s and give a fascinating insight into the area's rich history. Among the stones:

REV. THOMAS PAYNE
B. 1723 / D. 10–15–1766
AH CRUEL DEATH WHY DIDST THOU STRIKE SO QUICK
THAT GUIDE THE SOULS AND HEALER OF THE SICK
THEM BY TO PRIZE SUCH USEFUL DEATH DOTH TEACH.

The Old House is owned and maintained by The Old House Society, Inc. and managed by the Cutchogue-New Suffolk Historical Council, P.O. Box 361, Cutchogue 11935 (631–734–6977).

The North Fork is rapidly becoming known for its great wineries including: **Bedell Cellars** (631–734–7537; www.bedellcellars.com) and **Castello di Borghese** (631–734–5111; www.castellodiborghese.com) in Cutchogue; **Jamesport Vineyards** (631–722–5256; www.jamesport-vineyards.com); and **Lenz Winery** in **Peconic** (631–734–6010; www.lenzwine.com). It seems that Long Island has a microclimate quite similar to that of Bordeaux, France and merlot grapes especially seem to thrive here, though you'll also find several other varietals.

OTHER ATTRACTIONS WORTH SEEING ON LONG ISLAND

American Merchant Marine Museum
Steamboat Road
Kings Point
(516) 773–5000

Belmont Park Race Track
Hempstead Turnpike and Cross Island
Parkway
Belmont
(516) 488–6000

Hofstra University Museum
Emily Lowe Gallery
Hempstead Turnpike
Hempstead
(516) 463–5672

Long Island Children's Museum
Garden City
(516) 222–0207

Montauk Point Lighthouse
Montauk Point State Park
Montauk
(631) 668–2544 or (888) MTK–POINT

Nassau County Museum of Art
One Museum Drive
Roslyn Harbor
(516) 484–9338

Old Westbury Gardens
Old Westbury
(516) 333–0048

Sagamore Hill National Historic Site
Cove Neck Road
Oyster Bay
(516) 922–4788

Splish Splash Water Park
Riverhead
(631) 727–3600

Vanderbilt Museum
180 Little Neck Road
Centerport
(631) 854–5555

Walt Whitman Birthplace State Historic Site
246 Old Walt Whitman Road
Huntington Station
(631) 427–5240

If you abhor spitting out a good wine (and would prefer to sip Long Island's splendid wines), safety would dictate that you leave your car at home and travel from vineyard to vineyard on the *North Fork Trolley* (631–369–3031; www.northforktrolley.com), or take advantage of the services of *Vintage Tours.* Proprietor Jo-Ann Perry is a font of knowledge about both wine and local lore. The basic tour begins at 11:30 A.M. (in her air-conditioned van). It costs $45 per person from November until Memorial Day and $55 per person from Memorial Day weekend until the first of December. Tours last from four to five hours. For information call (631) 765–4689 or go to www.northfork.com/tours.

Since 1976, folks have been stopping by the unprepossessing *Hellenic Snack Bar and Restaurant* (631–477–0138; www.thehellenic.com), at 5145

Main Road (Route 25) in ***East Marion*** for some of the best Greek food on Long Island. Among the house specialties: dolmades (stuffed grape leaves), spanakopita (spinach pie), moussaka, and fried calamari. The desserts are all homemade, and fresh lamb, chicken, and pork are prepared on the outdoor rotisserie. The Hellenic is open for three meals daily.

Places to Stay on Long Island

EAST HAMPTON

Huntting Inn
94 Main Street
(631) 324–0410
www.hunttinginn.com

EAST MARION

Arbor View House Bed and Breakfast
8900 Main Road
(800) 963–8777 or (631) 477–8440
www.arborviewhouse.com

MONTAUK

Gurney's Inn Resort and Spa
290 Old Montauk Highway
(631) 668–2345
www.gurneys-inn.com

Montauk Yacht Club and Marina
32 Star Island Road
(631) 668–6181
www.montaukyachtclub.com

QUOGUE

The Inn at Quogue
47–52 Quogue Street
(631) 653–6560
www.innatquogue.com

SHELTER ISLAND

The Pridwin
Crescent Beach
(800) 273–2497
www.pridwin.com

Ram's Head Inn
108 Ram Island Drive
(631) 749–0811
www.shelterislandinns.com

Sunset Beach
35 Shore Road
(631) 749–2001
www.sunsetbeachli.com

SOUTHAMPTON

1708 House
128 Main Street
(631) 287–1708
www.1708house.com

The Southampton Inn
91 Hill Street
(800) 832–6500 or (631) 283–6500
www.southamptoninn.com

WESTHAMPTON BEACH

Inn on Main
191 Main Street
(631) 288–8900
www.theinnonmain.com

Places to Eat on Long Island

BRIDGEHAMPTON

Alison Restaurant
95 School Street
(631) 537–7100

Bobby Van's
2393 Main Street
(631) 537–0590

EASTHAMPTON

The Laundry Restaurant and Bar
341 Pantigo Road
(631) 324–3199

EASTPORT

Trumpets on the Bay
58 South Bay Avenue
(631) 325–2900

MONTAUK

Gosman's Dock
500 West Lake Drive
(631) 668–5330

Harvest on Fort Pond
11 South Emery Street
(631) 668–5574

Surfside Inn
Old Montauk Highway
(631) 668–5958

SAG HARBOR
The American Hotel
49 Main Street
(631) 725–3535

The Paradise Cafe
126 Main Street
(631) 725–6080

SHELTER ISLAND
Ram's Head
108 Ram Island Drive
(631) 749–0811

SOUTHAMPTON
Le Chef
75 Jobs Lane
(631) 283–8581

Southampton Publick House
40 Bowden Street
(631) 283–2800

WESTHAMPTON BEACH
Atlantica
231 Dune Road
(631) 288–6577

Tierra Mar Bath and Tennis Hotel
231 Dune Road
(631) 288–2700

REGIONAL TOURIST INFORMATION— LONG ISLAND

East Hampton Chamber of Commerce
79A Main Street
East Hampton
(631) 324–0362

Greater Westhampton Chamber of Commerce
(631) 473–0340
www.whbcc.org

Long Island Convention and Visitors Bureau
330 Motor Parkway
Hauppauge
(877) FUN–ON–LI or (632) 951–3900
www.discoverlongisland.com or
www.funonli.com

Montauk Chamber of Commerce
742 Montauk Highway
Montauk
(631) 668–2428
www.montaukchamber.com

Sag Harbor Chamber of Commerce
(631) 725–0011
www.sagharborchamber.com

Shelter Island Chamber of Commerce
Shelter Island
(631) 749–0399
www.shelter-island.net

Southampton Chamber of Commerce
76 Main Street
Southampton
(631) 283–0402
www.southamptonchamber.com

NEW YORK REGIONAL TRAVEL INFORMATION

New York State Division of Tourism
P.O. Box 2603
Albany 12220
(800) CALL–NYS
(outside U.S.: 518–474–4116)
www.state.ny.us
www.iloveny.com

New York State Department of Environmental Conservation
Room 679
50 Wolf Road
Albany 12233
General information:
(518) 457–3521
Campground information only:
(518) 457–2500
Camping reservations only:
(800) 456–CAMP
Call or write for free camping brochure.

New York Office of Parks, Recreation, and Historic Preservation
Empire State Plaza
Agency Building 1
Albany 12238
(518) 474–0456
Free guide to state parks and historic sites; brochures on biking, boating, snowmobiling.
(800) 456–CAMP
Camping and cabin reservations for state-operated sites.

New York State Hospitality and Tourism Association
(800) ENJOY–NY
Reservations at member hotels throughout the state.

Empire State Passport
Passport
State Parks
Albany 12238
One-time annual charge allows unlimited vehicle entrance to all state parks.

MAJOR AIRPORTS

Albany International Airport (oldest municipal airport in the country)

Greater Buffalo International Airport

Greater Rochester International Airport

JFK (New York City)

La Guardia (New York City)

Newark (NJ) International

Syracuse-Hancock International Airport

TRAINS

AMTRAK, (800) USA–RAIL

Metro-North, (212) 532–4900;

service between Grand Central Station,

New Haven, Long Island, and the Hudson Valley

BUS

Adirondack Trailways,
(800) 225–6815

Greyhound,
(800) 528–0447

New York Trailways,
(800) 295–5555

FERRIES

New York Waterway-Ferry
and Bus System,
(800) 53–FERRY

Staten Island-Ferry,
(718) 815–2628

TEMPERATURE AVERAGES

Low 26° F, High 77° F

MAJOR NEWSPAPERS

Buffalo News (Buffalo)

Daily News (New York City)

New York Post (New York City)

New York Times (New York City)

Plattsburgh Press Republican (Plattsburgh)

Rochester Democrat and Chronicle (Rochester)

Syracuse Post Standard (morning)/

Herald Journal (evening) (Syracuse)

Times Union (Albany)

POPULATION

19,300,000 (2004 est.)

Indexes

Entries for Museums and Parks and Nature Preserves also appear in special indexes on pages 253–55.

GENERAL INDEX

Wurtsboro, 169
Wurtsboro Airport, 169
Wyoming, 155

Yarborough Square, 57

Ye Jolly Onion Inn, 167–68
Yonkers, 3
Youngstown, 137

Zadock Pratt Museum, 181

MUSEUMS

Adirondack Museum, 48–49
African American Museum, 225–26
Akwesasne Cultural Center, 58
Albany Institute of History and
    Art, 73
Alice T. Miner Museum, 57–58
Alling Coverlet Museum, 119
American Folk Art Museum, 195–96
American Maple Museum and Hall of
    Fame, 64
American Museum of
    Firefighting, 26–27
Antique Boat Museum, 61
Art Museum (Stony Brook), 224
Barn Museum, 174–75
Bronck Museum, 178–79
Bronx Museum of the Arts, 202
Brooklyn Children's Museum, 203
Brooklyn Museum, 204
Buffalo Museum of Science, 142
Burchfield-Penney Art Center, 143
Burroughs Memorial State Historic
    Site, 181
Camp Shanks WWII Museum, 161
Canajoharie Library and Art
    Gallery, 79–81
Case Research Lab Museum, 126
Catskill Fly Fishing Center &
    Museum, 161
Cayuga Museum, 125–26
Children's Museum (Utica), 88–89
Children's Museum of Science and
    Technology (Troy), 29
Coney Island Museum, 206
Crown Point State Historic Site, 47
Delaware and Hudson Canal
    Museum, 173

Dia:Beacon, 14
D.I.R.T. Motorsports Hall of Fame &
    Classic Car Museum, 127
DNA Learning Center, 223
Donald M. Kendall Sculpture
    Gardens, 5–6
Durham Center Museum, 179–80
Elbert Hubbard–Roycroft Museum, 154
Electronic Communication
    Museum, 116–17
El Museo del Barrio, 197–98
Erie Canal Museum, 92–93
Everson Museum of Art, 93
Farmers' Museum, 84–85
Fenimore Art Museum, 84
Fort Klock Historic Restoration, 81
Fountain Elms, 88
Frederic Remington Art
    Museum, 58–59
Fulton County Museum, 79
Ganondagan State Historic Site, 116
Garibaldi-Meucci Museum, 213
Genesee Country Village &
    Museum, 112–13
Glenn H. Curtiss Museum, 106
Granger Homestead and Carriage
    Museum, 117–18
Grant Cottage State Historic Site, 42
Hanford Mills Museum, 182
Harness Racing Museum and Hall of
    Fame, 166
Harriet Tubman Home, 126
Herschell Carrousel Factory
    Museum, 138
Hoffman Clock Museum, 121
Holocaust Memorial and Educational
    Center of Nassau County, 222

PARKS AND NATURE PRESERVES

About the Authors

Bill and Kay Scheller are coauthors of *New Jersey Off the Beaten Path* and contributors to several National Geographic books. They have worked as correspondents for Fodor's and Insight guides, and for *Yankee* magazine's travel publications. They are the authors of *Best Vermont Drives* and *Best New Hampshire Drives*, published by their own Jasper Heights Press.

Some may prefer Paris or Palm Beach, but Lillian Africano and Nina Africano have always divided their time between Manhattan and the Jersey Shore. Lillian Africano has written sixteen books and hundreds of articles in magazines and newspapers. She chairs the Northeastern Chapter of the Society of American Travel Writers and is President of the International Food, Wine & Travel Writers Association. Nina Africano writes about travel, sports, and spas for a number of publications, including www.spareviewmag.com. Together they are the co-authors of Globe Pequot's *Insiders' Guide to the Jersey Shore* and *You Know You're in New Jersey When . . .: 101 Quintessential Places, People, Events, Customs, Lingo, and Eats of the Garden State.*